Mandy Johnson is a former UK dire[...] Flight Centre Limited. After complet[...] [...]he loved the world for three years, before returning to Australia and landing a job as a travel consultant with Flight Centre. She won the company's Million Dollar Consultant and Outstanding Achievement awards; turned around several low-performing retail stores; started up the business's first recruitment and training centre; and eventually worked her way up to jointly start the company's UK operation in 1995, becoming its youngest-ever director at the age of 28.

Mandy now juggles writing and business consulting. She has applied her practical strategies to many other organisations; was the creator and presenter of one of Bond University's most popular executive education programs, 'Winning The War For Talent'; and has been featured in *HR Magazine*, the *Australian Financial Review* and on ABC Radio's *Conversation Hour* for her effective techniques. Mandy currently lives in Currumbin Valley with her husband and two children, and is about to release her second book, *The Recruitment Revolution*.

Katrina Beikoff is a Walkley Award-winning journalist, columnist, media adviser, communications strategy consultant, and author. She won Australia's most prestigious journalism award, the Walkley, as well as the Australian Olympic Writers and Photographers Association Award and the Quill Award, for a world-exclusive doping exposé on US athletes during the Sydney Olympic Games.

For almost a decade, Katrina was a senior writer and investigative reporter for the *Daily Telegraph* in Sydney, during which time she covered major events for News Limited Group mastheads including Melbourne's *Herald Sun* and Brisbane's *Courier-Mail*. She has worked in the UK, Israel and, most recently, in China as a 'foreign expert' adviser at the *Shanghai Daily*. She also spent a year in Canberra as chief media adviser to a federal party leader.

Katrina is now based in Queensland, where she works as a communications consultant and writer. Her first book, *No Chopsticks Required*, about her family's year in Shanghai, was published in 2011. *Family Village Tribe* is her first business book.

See www.familyvillagetribe.com for more information.

FAMILY
VILLAGE
TRIBE

The Evolution of
Flight Centre

Hey Rebecca,

Thank you for all you do. You have a ton of great leadership qualities that you bring to your team everyday and it shows.

"people don't buy what you do, they buy why you do it"

Keep up the great work

Joy

FAMILY VILLAGE TRIBE

The Evolution of Flight Centre

How Stone Age strategies turned a single
store into a billion-dollar business

MANDY JOHNSON
updated by Katrina Beikoff

WILLIAM HEINEMANN: AUSTRALIA

A William Heinemann book
Published by Random House Australia Pty Ltd
Level 3, 100 Pacific Highway, North Sydney NSW 2060
www.randomhouse.com.au

First published by Random House Australia in 2005
This revised edition published by William Heinemann in 2013

National Library of Australia
Cataloguing-in-Publication Entry

Johnson, Mandy.

Family village tribe: the story of Flight Centre Limited

978 085798 149 3

Typeset and internal design by Midland Typesetters, Australia
Printed in Australia by Griffin Press, an accredited ISO AS/NZS 14001:2004
Environmental Management System printer

Random House Australia uses papers that are natural, renewable and recyclable products and made from wood grown in sustainable forests. The logging and manufacturing processes are expected to conform to the environmental regulations of the country of origin.

For John, Jaimie and Callum

CONTENTS

FOREWORD

by Graham Turner, managing director, Flight Centre Limited

It's now March 2013 and I've been looking at the foreword I wrote for the original book in 2005 and thinking about how things have changed. Back then many pundits were predicting the demise of bricks and mortar travel agents with the growing power of the internet. To them it was a no-brainer: How could we survive? Why would customers need us?

Well, we are still here, we are still largely bricks and mortar and we are still getting better and better at what we do. We have record sales and profit most years, and most of this growth is organic – not acquired. In 2005 our sales were about $7 billion, our number of businesses about 1100, our staff numbers were 6500 and our profit was about $110 million. This year (2013), sales will be close to $15 billion, shops and businesses about 2500, employee numbers 16,000 and our profit has nearly tripled to around the $300 million mark. So we are a different company – still largely in travel, but more than double the size. My job is now a different job and that's one thing I like about it – it changes every five years or so as we grow.

In saying this, the last eight years have been tough in some areas. In the 2005 foreword I wrote about learning from the past, simplifying things and not repeating mistakes. Somehow that message was lost in translation. Not only did we repeat errors, we invented new ones – such as a reinvention project called Full Throttle that I now rate as our biggest ever stuff-up. We had boardroom disputes, failed private equity deals and watched as our share price and investor confidence got smashed during the GFC. But we burrowed through all of that, coming out the other side battered and bruised but also stronger and more focused. I guess (I hope) we learnt a lot – yet again – from those turbulent times.

Starting out in travel and setting up Top Deck in 1973 with some friends, Geoff Lomas and Bill James, seems a long time ago – it is! But some things never change. Having fun, great friends, empire building and finding interesting ways of giving customers what they want and need (and still being able to make some money out of it) is still the challenge. Only now, with 15,000 people in eleven countries, size does make a difference.

We are not the largest travel business in the world, but we are certainly up there in size. I do believe we are one of the most success-ful travel businesses, not only in sales and profitability, but also in our culture, our service and product delivery, and our people. With sales of about $15 billion globally, we are not too far behind leading multi-national and predominantly online organisations like Expedia ($34b), Priceline ($28b) and the global corporate travel arm of American Express Travel (about $24b).

One core ethos we have always stuck to is Family, Village, Tribe – our unique company structure based on the arrangement of Stone Age communities over hundreds of thousands of generations. The Family, Village, Tribe model has helped us keep our small business focus and mentality, and has allowed our people to work in the structure that humans innately prefer. No matter how much we have grown, and continue to grow, they still retain autonomy and ownership.

I feel we would have been lost without Family, Village, Tribe – so much so that I am amazed more companies haven't tried to get a good understanding of this basic structural model and adopt it for them-selves. As you'll see in this updated edition, our own understanding of the model has evolved over time. For instance, in the past our villages (three to seven teams or businesses) were not implemented well in many of our tribes (areas of 20 to 30 shops and businesses).

Another major point of difference from eight years ago is our focus and structure being based on brands, rather than just geographical regions or countries. In FCL we have more than 30 different brands, which has helped our growth and success and will be an important part of our longer-term future. Our leadership and operations now deal nationally at a brand level, headed up by a brand leader who is fully responsible for all aspects of the brand in their country. This may just seem like common sense, but we have found we get a much greater level of business and brand success through this singular focus. At the same time, we know it is important in some cases to consolidate or even close brands, as establishing and getting known and respected as a new brand in the twenty-first century is a tough and expensive business.

A big part of our overall success is that Flight Centre Limited is not only a business, not only a livelihood for 15,000 people, but it has its own special life and culture. Not everyone makes a lot of money, but the vast majority, I believe, would say they love working here – whether that's in the front-line businesses, our Australian head office, or in one of the other ten countries around the world where we have 100 per cent equity businesses.

I would like to think that if a young person starts their career with us they will find it a rewarding learning experience, and they will value their start with Flight Centre for the rest of their lives, even if they move on to another company or another career. Talking to our team leaders about this learning experience, I would like to think that they give novices the same working highlights they would expect for their own children in their first job.

My own thinking has evolved as well. Over the last eight years I have become an advocate of Jim Collins' books. They are well researched, well written and easy to understand. His latest book in particular, *Great by Choice*, has some key points about understanding your business. The importance of understanding your actual recipe for success and then sticking to it really rang true for me. Surprising though it may seem, most successful businesses don't change that much over time – or their recipe for success doesn't.

But new CEOs and boards want change even though it is often destructive to their organisation's value. In my view, if you cannot find senior leadership from within your culture and business, then your business model is probably buggered. OK, if your business is really bad then you may well need external help, but I would say this is the only reason to hire from outside.

The challenge FCL faces as part of the future of the travel industry is remaining relevant, not just profitable. I'll let you know how we deal with that when I write the next update to this foreword – a summary of the next eight years of FCL history – in 2020 or so. But enjoy the update to *Family Village Tribe* in the meantime . . .

Foreword, January 2005

It is January 2005 and I've been on long service leave for nearly eight weeks. Flight Centre Limited has just put out a profit warning. In one day our share price fell to $16 (from $19), and so far it has stayed there.

Why have we stuffed things up so soundly? Why do we continue to have to relearn the lessons of the past every so often? The solutions to our problems are somewhere in the pages ahead, I'm sure. It is now up to us to get back to the simplicity of our business model. Reading through Mandy's book, I realise that it has taken us 30 years to identify and develop our fairly unique set of business basics, yet some of these have been undermined or ignored as we have grown. Now we are paying the penalty.

Usually FCL has been a pretty innovative company, not so much in the product or technology sense, but in the way we do things, the way we structure and the way we think. In truth it has just been basic bloody commonsense, of course. But don't we know how short in supply commonsense can be at times?

There is no doubt that size is an issue. Back in 1973–74, when we first started in business with one old double-decker bus and just Spy, Bill and myself at the helm, life was simple. It was about buying an old bus, selling the tours (the more the merrier), throwing a few provisions together from the local wholesale grocery store, doing a basic mechanical checkover and hitting the road. Back then, 'business' meant having fun, making friends and maybe even doing a bit of sightseeing if we were lucky.

Nowadays, with about 8000 people and sales of around AUS$8 billion, things are different. We have serious responsibilities – to our people, our customers and, of course, our shareholders. Many of these people are personal friends and letting them down is not on. It's a challenge, still often fun, but getting the model and operations right has never been more of an urgent priority for us.

Always the empire builder, I do feel a personal obligation to get things right and continue to build a business to last as well as prosper. Inside our company, we talk a lot about 'profitable growth', and that is what FCL is about.

We have built a great company – a *great* company – with teams of people in nine countries, and licensees in many others. I'm truly proud of this. Our Flight Centre brand is now an iconic brand name in several countries and before long, I believe, it will be so in all the countries we operate in. These things don't happen easily or without input from a lot of team players. Our corporate brand FCm Travel Solutions will shortly be a well-recognised global business travel provider operating in more than 40 countries.

I know every company says that its people are its most important asset, but at FCL I feel we generally have lived by this principle. If we haven't at times (and yes, sometimes we do forget), we pay the penalty. We have many people at all levels who have been around for between ten and twenty years, and they are an important part of what makes our company very special. With a back-end restructure ahead of us, I hope we don't forget the people who have made our business so successful.

Every business and every company is different, and I would not suggest for a minute that everyone should operate the same way as us. We have our ways and our culture, and if we stick to it, they work for us. But imposing our ways and our models and structure on a different culture could well end in tears. The ultimate truth about business is that there is no ultimate truth.

It's important that as we grow into the future, we don't forget our history – how we got to where we are, and what made us successful. (And what stuffed us up, too!) Fortunately, none of the current issues we have to come to grips with or fix is really too overwhelming. On the downside, however, they're seriously affecting our profits (or at least our profit *increase*), and our changes will be painful and require a lot of discipline – something we have not been good at.

There's no doubt that if you had a choice, painful changes would be avoided at all cost. Personally, at least, this is a part of the journey I could well do without. Yet as M. Scott Peck wrote in *The Road Less Travelled*, life is never easy: 'It is through the pain of confronting and solving problems that we learn . . . It is for this reason that wise people learn not to dread but actually to *welcome* the pain of problems.' (I've added the emphasis there, please note.) Yeah sure, it's okay for Peck to say this – he's a clinical psychiatrist – but there's a universal truth to his words all the same.

This isn't the first tough time in Flight Centre's history. In fact, as you will discover in the chapters that follow, there have been many over the last 30 years. Looking back, I realise that they're simply blips on the radar. The most memorable ones are now mere anecdotes that we laugh about, shaking our heads at how bloody stupid we were. 'We wouldn't go in that direction again . . . would we?' Too bloody right we will!

Business is hardly war, though. It's interesting, challenging but – except for taxi drivers taking you from foreign airports to city centres – never life threatening. It is fun, and you make many life-long friends and few enemies (I hope). Not everyone working in a business like ours stays forever. For some it's too hard, too challenging, or they're simply not suited to our culture. Many others learn from their experiences with us and go on to be great salespeople, business people and professionals with other companies, or maybe they use their learning from the workplace to be terrific parents and spouses.

On this last score, it's worth pointing out that almost anyone heavily involved in a business small or large can only do it with the help and support of close family. I am no exception. Although sometimes my family has had to come second to FCL – an inevitable part of the realities of modern working life, for all of us, I'm sure – in a general sense our company tries to be a family-friendly operation. It's never a perfect situation for everyone, and at times the right balance was probably not there. Certainly, the support of my wife Jude and our terrific kids, Matthew and Joanna, has made my life in business very satisfying and really quite easy. Whether times are tough, very normal or very good, a great home life evens everything out: work just becomes a challenge or a breeze.

I've been in full-time business for about 32 years now (and I still see it as my own). Failure of any kind – whatever that might mean – is out of the question. I am genuinely looking forward to what the world may bring over the next decade or so. Whether it be technology issues, terror or pestilence, I know it won't all be easy. This is why we must have a positive attitude, but never a blind acceptance of what the future brings our way.

It's a matter of one's approach, and on this subject I often refer our people to a quote by Charles Swindoll on the importance of maintaining a positive attitude. This attribute, he says, is more important than anything else – the past, education, money, failure, success, skill – and has the power to divide or conquer. And amazingly, our attitude is something that we can control; often it's the *only* thing that we do have control over, in fact. The message is simple therefore: we each have a hand in shaping our destiny.

Challenging both conventional ideas and my own views is a key MO in our company. Everyone will tell you how I deny ever thinking up any really bad ideas, but the good ones . . . well, they were mine from inception, of course! Everyone in our senior team understands clearly his or her role in listening to FCL's bullshit detectors – generally the front-line people. Those guys can smell a ratshit idea coming down from head office a mile off.

Succession is one vital ingredient for ongoing profitable growth. I'd like to be here in a full-time key role for at least the next ten to twenty years, but at the same time I recognise that our organisation is just too large and diverse for one person. Shane Flynn's arrival as CEO was the first step in our long-term succession process. In the future we will need to develop other key roles, to help both him and myself fill in the gaps as Flight Centre Limited continues to grow. Flynnie and I see our company's progress as a journey. There is no final destination, just hefty milestones along the way. And really, even after three decades or more, the journey has just begun. We know it won't all be smooth travelling, but we have our vehicle and are packed up, ready to go. The next ten years will really show what we're made of, I guess, and how far we'll travel down that road and what new heights we will reach . . .

Family Village Tribe is a well-written, painstakingly researched history of Flight Centre Limited, and it should give everyone associated with our company a sense of pride and remind them of the lessons of the past. I am confident that Mandy's book will also help company people, new and old, hatch innovative ways to solve the issues we face now and certainly will face at every turn in the future.

For those outside Flight Centre Limited – our shareholders, our clients, our business partners, our competitors and all other interested parties – I trust it gives you more understanding of why we do the things we do, and how we got to where we are.

Enjoy reading our story, and I hope you get some ideas that may help you on your own journey.

PREFACE

In late 2004, Flight Centre Limited embarked on a project that sent tremors through the culture, the people, the very fabric of the company. It was tough. It was upsetting. It left lasting scars, as self-inflicted wounds are prone to do.

It was also the perfect jumping off point from which to launch an update of this unique and rapidly growing international success story. It's often said there's nothing like a good crisis to reveal the character of a person, or, in this instance, a company.

Prior to immersing myself in the company for this book, I had little association with Flight Centre Limited. Of course I'd heard of Flight Centre. I'd even bought shares in the 1995 float. At the time I sold them, a couple of years later, the profit helped me put a deposit on my first house. I was duly chuffed. Then I watched as the share price continued to climb. And climb. And wished I'd never sold.

Having never worked for Flight Centre and approaching the company as an objective outsider, I knew nothing of its character, its characters and its quirks. These things just can't be reflected in stock market performance and can only be superficially covered in the business pages.

Through the bestselling story of Flight Centre's history, maturation and distinct style, told wonderfully by Mandy Johnson in the first edition of *Family Village Tribe*, I did at least come to this book with the knowledge that, in the business world, Flight Centre does things a bit differently. It's unreserved in its commitment to the Flight Centre way, and seems genuinely baffled why more companies around the globe haven't adopted the secrets of its success. I was also sure that investigating what makes this business tick today and how it has grown and changed over the past nine years would be a bucket of fun.

The period since 2004 is illuminating in the overall picture of Flight Centre Limited. It's a time in which the company made huge mistakes, such as the scarring internal overhaul that marks the starting point of this update. It's the period in which the company was tested right to its fundamentals by the meltdown that rocked the financial world. If a global financial crisis wasn't enough, Flight Centre faced it against the chaotic backdrop of having just made its largest ever acquisition in order to break into America. This is the story of how Flight Centre Limited's share price crashed to $3 but has clambered back up to a record high of over $38 at the time of writing. It's a stunning turnaround in an environment where many other global enterprises are still yet to see substantial recovery.

In the same period, Flight Centre has gone from being Australia's largest travel agency to muscling up to the next level and becoming a player in the global business community. It has had to confront a rapidly changing future, with ramifications not only for the travel industry but also for retailers around the world. For business observers, business owners, or those who just love a good yarn, it's a timeframe fertile with anecdotes, experience, pitfalls and tips.

In the process of writing this book, I have been afforded incredible access to people at all levels of the business, and have spoken to many who have previously devoted large sections of their lives to the company. I've been privileged that so many people have been willing to lay bare some of Flight Centre's mistakes, shortcomings and bad decisions. I've also been struck by the pride, ownership and joy people seem to genuinely feel about the company, seeing it as more than just a place of work. I've also experienced a taste of the celebrated culture that is such a feature in any telling of the Flight Centre story. Flight Centre culture is often described, by those within and those no longer with the company, as a cult. As an outsider, I'd have to say it's hard not to think of the company like you would about your home sports team. You barrack for them even if they sometimes don't deserve it. They might break your heart by making mistakes that should have been foreseeable, but they'll always show up ready to play and can reward your loyalty immeasurably.

I have also learned about a cornerstone of the Flight Centre way: evolution and evolutionary psychology. By definition, evolution is on a continuum. Therefore it may have been foolish to think that the philosophy, culture and practices of a company that is a world-leader in adapting evolutionary theories to its business were static. I confess I thought ideas from the Stone Age, once adopted with great success by the company, might be left well enough alone. But even these Stone Age concepts of Family, Village, Tribe are not immune to the company's, and in particular Graham 'Skroo' Turner's, vigorous pursuit of progression. With all this tweaking, trialling, modifying and improving, even on these ancient tribal structures aimed at utilising basic human instinct, I did wonder how anyone could unlock the secrets to the company's success. But of course, as Flight Centre's story shows, the key really is continuous evolution.

Katrina Beikoff
Gold Coast, Queensland,
March 2013

Preface, May 2005

I didn't realise my life had been hijacked until a year after it happened. It was 1992 and I was 24 years old. After three years overseas – travelling overland from Kathmandu to London and then working as a tour leader in Europe, Russia and Egypt for a company called Top Deck – I'd returned to Australia with vague plans for the future. Perhaps I could make documentaries. Maybe I could save enough money for a trip to South America.

Then I received a call from my old boss, Gary 'Boxer' Hogan. (He wasn't a pugilist; his nickname was a legacy from a fight he'd been involved in on his first day at boarding school.) I'd worked with Boxer at Wintergarden Flight Centre while completing the final year of my journalism degree. By now he was the company's Queensland manager, and when he heard I was back, he decided to take me to lunch for old times' sake. Or so he told me. I should have known better.

By the end of the meal I'd agreed to manage the salubrious Redcliffe Flight Centre. This was a retail shop the size of a shoebox, based in what was then 'the sticks' of Brisbane. Its sole distinction was that it was the most unprofitable shop in Flight Centre's Queensland operation at the time, and had been for the past three years. Fortunately, I was 'well qualified' for this challenge: I hadn't worked as a travel agent for three years, I didn't know the slightest thing about managing a business, and I'd never even been to Redcliffe.

So why did I take the job? There were a number of reasons. For one, I'd just started going out with someone and it suited me to stay in Brisbane for a while. (I ended up marrying him.) I'd come home broke, so Flight Centre's attractive pay structure was a powerful incentive. Plus, as a travel junkie, I was excited by the thought of two free overseas managers' conferences a year. And, to be honest, I was flattered by the thought that Boxer had enough faith in me to give me this opportunity.

I started the following Monday. There was no formal training, only Boxer's parting words: 'Just get in there and make it happen.' I didn't hear from him for another month. By the end of the first week I had misquoted three clients, been abused by the existing consultants, who were disgruntled with the change in the status quo, and been fined $1500 by the tax department for not putting in a wage return that I knew nothing about. I rang Boxer to tell him it wasn't working out, but he didn't return my calls.

By the end of the first month, however, my fear had been replaced by determination. It was true we knew nothing about business – our team at this stage consisted of a graphic artist, a secretary and an English teacher, in addition to myself – but we had some goals and everyone was committed to making them happen. I rashly promised the team that by the end of September, a mere two months after I'd come on board, we'd all be on the list to receive prizes at the next monthly awards night. God knows why, but they believed me.

From that moment, we invented some strategies, borrowed others, and celebrated every booking. After work each day we would discuss our progress and ways we could improve. It was amazing the ideas we came up with when fuelled by cheap wine and crackers. Miraculously, or so it seemed to me at the time, we achieved what we set out to do. I had never felt such exhilaration as when every member of our team of 'no-hopers' won a company award that October for their individual sales during the previous month. From then on we made a profit every month, and that year we ended up with two consultants in Flight Centre's High Achievers' Club, and I made it into the Million Dollar Club. (These two 'clubs' are part of the company's annual awards celebration, when particularly successful members are feted and receive plaques for their outstanding retail sales.)

I had one of the best years of my life. I earned $50,000 – which I thought was an astronomical sum at the time. I won awards each month, both for my individual performance and our shop's. I went to Hong Kong and Hawaii for free, partying all night with like-minded people. I made lifelong friendships. I learned more about challenge and motivation in twelve months than in the previous 24 years put together. All in all, I had a ball.

The next six years would destroy any lingering preconceptions I'd had about business. Somewhat inebriated at a function, I told Boxer that the way Flight Centre trained its new recruits was dreadful. Two weeks later I was given an empty shop and told to make it into a training centre.

I had no idea where to start. In the end I recruited two trainers and four trainees, and typed up several hundred training notes from scratch. Then we opened the shop and winged it until we had an idea of what worked and what didn't. After nine months – and another steep learning curve – we had a creditable operation and I'd won the Director's Award for Outstanding Achievement.

With this task accomplished I decided to quit, to fulfil my dream of travelling through South America. Somehow I was instead bamboozled into helping set up Flight Centre in the UK. So off

xxiv FAMILY VILLAGE TRIBE

I went. Starting in April 1995, I fitted out shops, recruited staff, networked computers, negotiated airline deals, organised conferences and ran marketing campaigns. All without any prior knowledge or experience. Eventually I became a director of the operation there.

I left the UK in 1999 with my husband John (who was now also working for Flight Centre) and travelled for nine months. I finally made it to South America after all. On my return to Australia I joined Flight Centre Limited's six-person Australian leadership team, as head of Human Resources, Conferences and Systems. But I found it difficult to settle back in. This role couldn't compete with the trailblazing excitement of running an overseas area, and besides, I was now 32 and there were other paths I wanted to explore. In April 2000 I quit to pursue a full-time writing career.

It was only once I'd left that I recognised how remarkable Flight Centre Limited was. Many things I had taken for granted were quite extraordinary to the outside world. When I did some corporate training to supplement my income, I was besieged with questions about the company. What was the secret of FCL's success? What were they really like to work for? How did they grow so quickly? What was all this 'tribal' stuff about? Was managing director Graham Turner really the maverick that the press made him out to be?

So in 2001 I decided to write this book. I spent the next few years interviewing hundreds of people both inside and outside the company. I travelled to conferences, attended training sessions, organised 'oldies' lunches, surveyed novice consultants, hounded senior people in the travel industry, and continuously picked the brains of every member of the company's executive team. I was fortunate that Graham Turner and the Flight Centre Limited board of directors gave the project their full support, as they saw it as a cultural tool to educate their own people. I therefore had access to the company's confidential files, newsletters, media reports, press releases, financial handbooks and video records.

Family Village Tribe took me three years, two children and several laborious drafts to complete, and in many ways it is quite different from the book I had first thought about writing. People's motivations were often the opposite of what I had imagined. Many of the company's successful strategies had the most unusual origins. And there were far more hurdles to overcome along the way than I had ever realised.

So here's the story of Flight Centre Limited. I hope you enjoy it.

Mandy Johnson
Brisbane, Queensland
May 2005

INTRODUCTION

Flight Centre Limited (FCL) is an anomaly in the business world: a modern-day organisation whose underlying corporate struc- ture comes from the Stone Age; a billion-dollar company started by two 23-year-old veterinarians with no business experience; an inter- national travel agency peopled by train drivers, rugby players, surfers, oil-rig workers, lawyers, teachers, tennis coaches and archaeologists.

Yet the company has achieved phenomenal success. As this book went to press, FCL has a global market capitalisation of (that is, the company is worth) approximately $3 billion.[1] FCL's founding direc- tors,who began with little more than a few thousand dollars each, are together now worth a total of almost $3 billion. FCL's share price, which started at 95 cents, has been on a roller-coaster ride, soaring to a high of over $34, collapsing briefly below $4 during the global economic crisis and resettling at around the $40 mark at the time of writing. Over 100 people working for the company have become millionaires.

On the business front, the FCL juggernaut rolls out one new shop or enterprise globally every 36 hours. It has over 35 different brands (up from sixteen in 2005), employs over 16,000 people worldwide and achieves turnover greater than $13 billion. It has company-owned operations in eleven countries and licensees in another 70. Its net profits eclipsed $200 million for the first time in 2012; five years after its first $100 million and ten years after its first $50 million. It has won Employer of the Year awards in Australia, New Zealand, Canada and the UK, beating mainstays like Wal-Mart and Microsoft. It has generated profit increases in fourteen out of sixteen years since becoming a public company, with a sustained period of average profit increases of 25 per cent per year, and is arguably the fastest growing travel company on the planet.

So why is it so successful? What actually makes FCL tick? From my three years of intensive research, I have identified the following as the fundamental ingredients of FCL's success:

- **The company's underlying premise is 'Let's have fun.'**
- **The company's reward and recognition system motivates people to achieve more than they had ever thought possible.**
- **The company's people physically and emotionally own their own business, within the business.**
- **The company values commonsense over conventional wisdom, hence sees opportunities where others see none.**
- **The company's small-team structure gives its people a continuing sense of personal and social identity that is usually nonexistent in large organisations.**
- **The company's philosophies are inherently just.**

When you read through these points, you may be disappointed. Plenty of companies motivate their people. Many have unconventional ideas. A few have fun. The difference between these businesses and FCL, however, is in the implementation. This makes all the difference.

When the company directors read an article by evolutionary psychologist Nigel Nicholson, which claimed that human beings are more motivated if they're organised into teams that replicate hunter-gatherer groups,[2] they modified FCL into 'families', 'villages' and 'tribes' in accordance with this ideal. Not just the retail area or the management level, but every single department, from Finance through to Technology, from Fit-out through to Marketing.

FCL's implementation of incentives was just as single-minded.

Every person is individually 'incentivised' on the outcome of what they do. From the Branding team member whose pay is based on shop refurbishment, to the in-house financial adviser who is paid on how much he or she increases someone's personal wealth.

In 2003, one FCL national leader earned a whopping $130,000 *in one month* for her turnaround of a struggling overseas area. Conversely, that same year the CEO earned one-sixth of an average Australian CEO's wage as Flight Centre Limited's profit growth plummeted due to the impact of the Iraq War and the SARS epidemic. He didn't mind. He could make it up in one good year.

Underlying all of these concepts is the principle of justice. In his groundbreaking book *A Theory of Justice*, John Rawls, a renowned philosopher and professor emeritus at Harvard University, determined that a just society is one in which people have equal basic liberties, and equal access to offices and positions, and one in which social and economic inequalities are arranged to be of the greatest benefit to the least advantaged.[3] In other words, some can have more if it is acquired in ways that improve the situation of those who have less.

FCL has somehow incorporated all three elements of Rawls's theory into its organisational set-up. For instance, *everyone* wears a uniform, has a bland workstation, shares a hotel room at conferences, and pays for business-class upgrades and car parking from his or her own pocket. Similarly, promotion is merit-based in FCL, with demonstrated achievement being the main criteria. A good consultant today could be a manager in six months, a middle manager in twelve, and run the Marketing department within two years. Crossing boundaries is the norm. That same person could also start up a loyalty program, negotiate advertising deals or open a new business in Chicago.

But perhaps it is Rawls's final point that is the most significant. FCL's salaries are diverse but they do satisfy the professor's criteria because they are outcome-based to benefit people lower in the ranks. For instance, that national leader who earned $130,000 in one month did so by introducing policies that improved each individual's monthly commission figures. Managers of shops get paid more if their consultants produce more (and hence get paid more themselves). By linking paid incentives to outcomes, FCL attempts to usurp the traditional hierarchies and rigid wage structures of more conventional organisations. In the process, a just environment is created.

Of course this is not to say that injustices, unmotivated people and conventional thinking don't exist within FCL. Like most large organisations, the company has its share of imperfections and certainly as it has grown it has struggled to stay faithful to some of its philosophies. Yet the very fact that Flight Centre Limited came up with these ideals in the first place is interesting, and more intriguing is that many occurred without conscious thought. When I asked Graham Turner, FCL's managing director, where the company had received its inspiration from, he told me: 'I really don't know. We didn't sit down at the start and say, for instance, "Let's make a just company." It simply happened.'

This is one of the characteristics of a brilliant business, according to Jim Collins, who spent five years researching what makes a great company and recorded his findings in *Good to Great*. 'There was no single defining action,' he wrote, 'no grand program, no one killer innovation, no solitary lucky break, no wrenching revolution. Good to great comes about by a cumulative process – step by step, action by action, decision by decision, turn by turn of the flywheel – that adds up to sustained and spectacular results.'[4]

FCL matured gradually, turning both good and bad experiences into future strategy. There was no overnight metamorphosis. If you could view the company's life cycle to date, it would look something like the figure on the opposite page.

This book describes each of the events that make up the life cycle and their part in Flight Centre Limited's overall development. It also chronologically portrays the key players and their contributions to the company. Yet the book would not be complete without some additional details on FCL's unconventional managing director, Graham Turner, more commonly known as 'Skroo'. (Like Boxer, his nickname stems from his boarding-school days; it was a play on his surname, after the well-known Turner screwdriver of the time.)

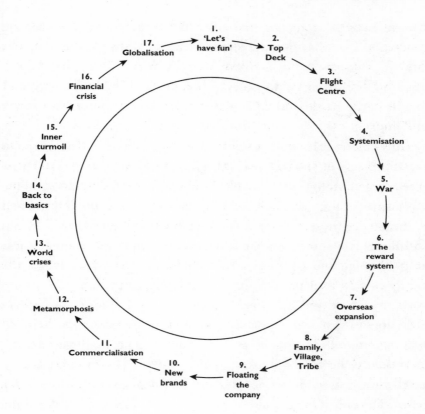

1. 'Let's have fun'
2. Top Deck
3. Flight Centre
4. Systemisation
5. War
6. The reward system
7. Overseas expansion
8. Family, Village, Tribe
9. Floating the company
10. New brands
11. Commercialisation
12. Metamorphosis
13. World crises
14. Back to basics
15. Inner turmoil
16. Financial crisis
17. Globalisation

Many people find Skroo intimidating. A Queenslander by birth, of stocky build, it is his head that immediately captures one's attention. A redoubtable jutting brow gives him an almost Neanderthal profile, while the full force of his deep-set eyes is unsettling, as if the heavy lids mask his intentions. The camouflage is furthered by the brown stubbly beard that shields the lower part of his face.

Turner's behaviour accentuates the uncertainty. He is a paradox: an introvert who loves to share hotel rooms; a multi-million-dollar corporate player whose desk is a cheap workstation in a space crammed with half-a-dozen others; a business icon who hangs his underwear to dry over the office furniture. He's a man of few words, but he makes every one count.

Look for Skroo's influences and it's obvious that genetics comes into play. Turner's mother, Iris, ran a private hospital in Cleveland,

Queensland, prior to her marriage. She turned it into a thriving concern – an unheard-of achievement for a woman of her era. His father, Frank, saw the outbreak of World War II as an opportunity to leave his mundane bank job. He became an RAAF engineer and fought in the Battle of the Coral Sea before notching up 2000 hours of flying.

After the war, Iris and Frank married and moved to Stanthorpe in the south-east of the state, to run an orchard, despite the fact that they knew nothing about apple farming. Skroo's childhood home was a small cottage with galvanised-iron walls, no running water and a bucket tied to a tree for a shower. His best friends were Trump and Blaze, two sturdy draught horses. The only farm equipment was an old plough and a spring cart. It would be several years before the family could afford a second-hand, steel-wheeled tractor.

The orchard was an intensive operation and Skroo's parents had little time to spare, so young Graham and his two sisters, Robyn and Julie, became self-reliant from an early age. When he was three years old, for instance, he taught himself to ride a bike. The nearest place to practise was a steep hill beside his house: he would go to the top and ride down. The only way he could stop was to ride into the wire fence at the bottom of the hill. He'd then pick himself up and march back to the top. It didn't worry him that such a painful buffer awaited him each time he descended – all that mattered was learning how to ride a bike.

The Turners' property was quite isolated, and this reinforced Skroo's independent streak. He had to cycle to the nearest school, Greenlands Primary, which was over six kilometres away. There was only one teacher for the 40 students, of all different grades. However, although Skroo was often left to his own devices, he was an early achiever. 'Graham never had much trouble with schoolwork,' his mother recalls. 'He was always in the top of the class [of four people].'

Skroo's father was a major influence on him. Frank Turner believed that a man could achieve anything if he worked hard enough and believed in what he was doing. He set a good example. Despite his lack of experience, he formed a partnership with a friend to develop new varieties of nectarines and peaches, which they then sold to supermarkets down in Sydney. The orchard was a success, and Frank and Iris were able to 'semi-retire to a few thousand acres of cattle country' 25 years later.

Graham's self-sufficiency made him a natural leader. He was awarded the Queen's Scout badge by the Governor-General – one of only a few Queenslanders to earn the honour at the time. But this same quality also led to some early conflicts with authority. When he started at Stanthorpe High School, a disagreement with his maths teacher saw him refuse to attend that teacher's class. He subsequently taught himself from textbooks and went on to top the class in the exams.

When Graham turned fifteen he became a boarder at Toowoomba Grammar School, and was soon a prefect. This was where he received his nickname. After graduating with As, he went on to study veterinary science at the University of Queensland in Brisbane. His college group was called 'the Block 11 Animals', their main preoccupations being to drink beer, play rugby and row. With his usual single-minded determination, Skroo excelled in all these areas. These distractions aside, he managed to graduate with second-class honours.

As well as individuality, perseverance and his strong dislike of rules for the sake of rules, the young Skroo was blessed with an inordinate amount of luck. A good example of this occurred soon after he'd started his very first job, as a vet in Casterton, western Victoria. He was drinking in the pub one day when a dog was hit by a car outside in the main street. Everyone presumed the animal was dead but the new vet was called in all the same. It turned out that the dog was only stunned and, after Skroo had given it a cortisone injection, it got up and walked away. The townspeople judged it a miracle cure, and soon enough Graham Turner became noted in the area for his veterinary skills.

Skroo would also become renowned for his custom of sprinkling his sentences with F-words in a conversational manner, the way others lace their tea with sugar. These expletives, muttered in his usual laconic drawl, are not aggressive, merely a comfortable habit honed over the years. (For the sake of an accurate portrayal, I have left these expletives in his quotes. I apologise in advance to anyone who finds this word offensive.)

With such distinctive characteristics it should come as no surprise that Graham Turner is not a stereotypical business mogul. He works hard but not obsessively. He exercises daily and takes regular holidays. He is happily married with two children and doesn't aspire to build a family empire. Quite the reverse, in fact. 'Why complicate business by bringing family into it?' he says. 'Kids need to go out in the world and prove themselves to themselves. I would hope my kids want to do their own thing. Mind you, in the longer term it would be great to see the talented kids of our current company people working in the business.'

When it comes to nepotism, he may be uncharacteristic, but he's a classic expansionist. FCL essentially doubles in size every three to four years and, from all accounts, Skroo has been the engine behind much of this growth. Yet as he points out: 'We're into *profitable* growth. One without the other isn't much good.'

Turner is certainly a driving force, but it would be wrong to attribute FCL's success to any single individual. Flight Centre Limited is a team and its achievements have been built on the back of every player. In fact, the easiest way to understand the company's internal workings is to imagine that business is sport and that FCL people are like professional athletes. Their focus is all about improving internal performance. External factors are therefore almost irrelevant. Profit is simply a measurement of how well they play the game.

These are important points as they underlie so much of what perplexes the outside world about FCL. The company is frivolous about things that others take seriously, and it seems almost impervious to disaster. Happiest in the role of underdog, it just keeps winning 'unwinnable' games.

Float the first travel agency on the Australian Stock Exchange? No problem. Replicate the FCL business model in tough overseas markets? Of course they can. Raise $80 million in share capital to buy a corporate travel company during the Iraq War and the SARS crisis? A mere trifle. The striking thing about FCL's culture is that adversity nourishes it and impediments simply spice things up.

But the flip side of FCL's 'have a go' attitude has been some spectacular failures. When I first talked to Skroo about writing this book, he said: 'Mandy, whatever you do, don't write one of those sickly corporate books that glorify the company. We need to have all our fucking mistakes in there – *that's* what has really shaped us.' With the MD's blessing then, I have included the more notable failures, such as the reasons behind the 2005 profit downgrade, as well as Turner's own list of 'FCL fuck-ups', to dispel any myths about Flight Centre's omnipotence.

He also advised me not to get 'bogged down in the technical detail'. To keep things simple, I've referred to the company as 'Top Deck' when talking about the early European operation, and 'Flight Centre' when discussing the retail travel agency, even though it was technically called Top Deck until 1987, and Flight Centres International for some years before the mid 1990s. For the period after the float, I've differentiated between Flight Centre the brand and Flight Centre Limited (FCL), which became the overall parent company. The full evolution is shown in the boxed figure below.

Company evolution

1973–75
ARGUS PERSICUS TRAVEL
UK

1975–87
TOP DECK TRAVEL
UK, Australia, New Zealand, USA

1988–94
FLIGHT CENTRES INTERNATIONAL
Australia, New Zealand

1994–95
FLIGHT CENTRE
Australia, New Zealand, Canada, South Africa, UK

1995–present
FLIGHT CENTRE LIMITED (FCL)
Australia, New Zealand, Canada, South Africa, UK, USA,
China, Hong Kong, India, Singapore, Dubai

The other point Skroo emphasised was that, in line with the company's philosophy that 'Our company is our people', the people who work for FCL should not be referred to as 'employees' or 'staff members'. This required a certain amount of technical manoeuvring on my part, and I hope the result is not too jarring for readers.

His final piece of advice to me was, 'Make it a good story.' So that's what I've done.

Chapter 1

KICKING OFF

The stewardess checking in the London flight looked with disbelief at the two people in their late fifties standing in front of her.

'I'm sorry, these tickets are discount tickets for students only,' she said.

'Oh yes, our son said you'd need to see these,' replied the woman as she placed two newly minted student cards in front of her. The cards stated that Frank and Iris Turner were students at the University of Queensland.

The stewardess issued the boarding passes without further ado. 'Have a lovely trip,' she said.

'Oh, I'm sure we will,' said the woman. 'We're off to visit our son, Graham.'

Story told by Jude Turner, March 2002

The episode described above was by no means the first time that Graham 'Skroo' Turner would break the rules, nor the last. But in 1973, when he landed in London at the start of a working holiday, few people knew of this character trait. To his fellow back-packers, the blond-haired Queenslander with the sun-tanned brow and short scruffy beard was simply a 'hard-drinking, indiscreet, swearing man's man', to use the words of Bill James, another Australian overseas at the time and soon to become Skroo's business partner.[5]

There were a few points that contradicted this first impression, however. His degree in veterinary science was one. Another was the fact that the 23-year-old was an eloquent debater on just about any topic. And after a long session on red wine, if the mood took him, 'he was likely to sprout poetry verbatim from the most obscure of texts', according to Bill James.

After working for several months as a vet locum, Turner joined the annual migration of Australasians to Munich for the Oktoberfest. This two-week celebration was originally intended to honour the wedding of Crown Prince Ludwig to Princess Therese of Saxony-Hildburghausen, on 12 October 1810. But for the 5.5 million festival-goers of 1973, the real attractions were the consumption of vast quantities of beer and the stage-diving shenanigans that went with it.

Skroo and his vet friend Geoff 'Spy' Lomas made a valiant attempt to out-drink the other patrons in the *Hofbrauhaus*. (Geoff's nickname was another to originate from school days: his friends thought he looked like a secret agent when he wore a red-rag hat and dark sunglasses.) As the empty steins piled up, the two University of Queensland graduates reminisced about a poorly run Scandinavian camping trip they'd been on in June. The driver had got lost, the tour leader was totally disorganised, and the tents had been a real hassle to put up. The friends agreed that they could have run it better themselves.

Skroo now broached an idea that had been brewing in his mind. While on a call-out to a sick horse in the northern English county of Yorkshire, he had discovered an old World War II airfield, jam-packed with double-decker buses. One, an ageing Bristol with an AVW engine, had been kitted out as a mobile home, with bunk beds and a kitchen downstairs. It was for sale – the price £650. Skroo suggested that the two of them buy the bus and run their own tours. By taking paying passengers, they could cover their expenses and travel wherever they wanted to go.

Spy was more cautious. His guarded poker player's face gave little away, but the idea certainly appealed to him. Still, it would take many more beers and several days of discussion before Turner and Lomas finally made the historic decision to start up Argus Persicus, a double-decker tour company named after a turkey tick. As they downed their steins in the beer hall, they had no idea that their concept would go on to become a billion-dollar business spawning personal wealth and success beyond their wildest dreams.

On their return from Munich, the new partners went to Yorkshire and bought the double-decker bus, which they christened 'Argus'.

After a few practice runs up and down the street, Skroo drove it back down the M1 to London, and parked it on the footpath outside their flat at 9 Mablethorpe Road in Fulham. They spent the next six weeks before departure modifying the bus's interior to take extra passengers. This made them unpopular with the neighbours (especially when the footpath collapsed under Argus's weight).

To drum up business, Skroo and Spy advertised their six-week tour of Spain, Portugal and Morocco (at £110 per person) in *The Australasian Express*, a local newspaper aimed at travellers from the Antipodes. They also handed out a one-page advertising leaflet in the streets around Australia House and paid their flatmates £10 for every booking they took from these ads. Sales went well and they soon had fourteen passengers.

This was the limit of Skroo and Spy's preparations. When the tour departed on 19 November 1973, they were travelling without insurance, licences, or maps of any kind. They had no spare tyres or a jack, and Spy had never even driven a bus before. Yet despite having to contend with some treacherous black ice in the Atlas Mountains, the bribing of policemen to effect a passenger's release, a bout of food poisoning, and some inadvertent drug purchasing, the group arrived safely back in London a month and a half later.[6]

With the money they'd made from commission on purchases (shop owners paid tour companies a percentage on the goods bought by their passengers), Turner and Lomas had raked in £1500. Bill James, a lanky Australian who had been a passenger on the tour, was flabbergasted by this amount and immediately asked to join the company. 'Even someone with my limited nous could smell a good business venture when he fell over it,' the University of Sydney–educated school teacher admitted.[7] Skroo and Spy agreed to take him on as a partner and he spent his entire savings of £600 buying and fitting out a second double-decker bus.

While James made the modifications to 'Grunt', the Queensland duo headed out on the next tour with 21 passengers. It was easier this time around, as Spy explains: 'At least we knew how far the food-kitty money would go [the £3 a week each passenger paid to cover the cost of meals]. On the first tour our passengers were on starvation rations for the first five-and-a-half weeks, and then we spent the leftover money on high-quality duty-free grog in Calais.' But Lomas would have little use for such knowledge. His mother fell ill shortly after the third trip and he had to return to Australia. Skroo and Bill became 50–50 partners and formed a proper company, Argus Persicus Travel Proprietary Limited.

At this stage Bill was unaware of Turner's grand vision for the future, but he didn't remain in ignorance for long. His partner soon drafted a plan for the rest of 1974 and 1975. 'Skroo let his imagination run wild,' James later wrote. 'He'd drawn up itineraries and departure dates for seven Moroccans [i.e. tours to Morocco], nine Europeans, six Greece/Italy/Yugoslavians, three Russia/Scandinavians (planned as coach-camping tours), as well as shorter trips to the Beerfest, Pamplona, Hogmanay in Scotland, Tulip Time in Amsterdam and T-Day in Venice.'[8]

To accommodate this vision, Skroo and Bill added another bus, 'Tuft', to their stable of double-deckers. (Their bus names were always distinctive and eventually included 'Boogie', 'Chunder', 'Dinga', 'Deep Purple', 'Freckle', 'Knackers', 'Pigpen', 'Scrote' and 'Trouble'.) The partners also persuaded Steve 'Bombardier' Brown, Mark Sullivan, Mark Sims, Greg 'Wombat' Ettridge and 'Sexy' Rex Julian to come on board as new courier–drivers.

It was these new crew-members who convinced the partners that the name 'Argus Persicus' had to go. It may have appealed to Skroo and Spy's sense of humour, but most passengers couldn't even pronounce it. After a brainstorming session in the pub one night, a friend, Di McEwin, came up with the name 'Top Deck Travel', and it was agreed on unanimously.

By March 1975, Top Deck Travel had made £15,000 profit and was running successful tours to many different European locations. But then Kathmandu beckoned. This was the true test as far as Turner was concerned, to reach the isolated capital city high up in the mountain kingdom of Nepal.

To add to the challenge, he decided they should head off before the start of the northern winter so that the Australasian passengers could be home in time for Christmas. Bill James thought he was crazy. No one had attempted an 'overland' trip there at that time of year because of the Arctic-like conditions in much of central Asia and Turkey.

As usual, Skroo won the argument, and they set off on 24 October 1975 with sixteen passengers. This time, for what would end up being a five-month round trip, the Top Deck partners had carried out some meticulous planning. Bill had attended promotional sales evenings given by another operator, Penn Overland, at the Tournament pub on the Old Brompton Road. 'Dick Cijffers, one of their couriers, was the presenter,' he recalls. 'After my sixth film evening Dick must have smelt a rat but never let on. Gracious to the end, he gave me detailed answers to every question I could dream up, and I'm sure he would've been just as obliging if I had come straight out and told him what I was planning.'

Despite this preparation, even today Turner remembers it as an eventful, at times chaotic tour: 'I took a wrong turning out of Damascus and we ended up in the middle of hundreds of armed troops on the Lebanese border.' A few members of the party made the mistake of taking holiday snaps. Machine-gun toting officers and a dozen armoured personnel carriers surrounded the bus and informed the group that they had been taking photos of missile launching sites. Everyone on board was escorted under armed guard to a nearby military compound, where after an hour of lectures on Middle Eastern politics and the confiscation of their used film, they were sent on their way.

An episode in Syria was more serious. In those days it was illegal for anyone who had been to Israel to travel through Syria, its neighbouring country to the north-east. This was generally no problem because the obliging Israelis simply stapled extra pages into each person's passport, stamped them on entry and then ripped them out as the passenger exited the country. Unfortunately, when the group arrived at the Syrian border an Israeli bus ticket, printed in Hebrew, popped out of a passenger's passport. 'Ten hours of not-so-civil questioning followed,' James recounted in *Top Deck Daze*, 'and we seriously feared for our future, before we were eventually set free, and sent on our way again.'[9]

They continued east for the next few weeks through Iran, Afghanistan and Pakistan, and despite a near head-on collision with a bullock cart on the highway during a night drive to Delhi, they arrived safely in Kathmandu some two months after setting out. Skroo flew back to London to take out another tour, while Bill and some of the passengers took turns sitting in the bus in Kathmandu Square, selling tickets back to the UK.

On the return leg, Bill's crew suffered through temperatures of −40 degrees Celsius in eastern Turkey and had to keep the bus running constantly so that it wouldn't seize up. When it finally stopped, due to engine problems, the only way to restart it was to light an oil-rag fire underneath, to unfreeze the engine oil. Despite this, they confounded the critics and made it back to London, just four days before the bus was due to set off on the next trip.

Top Deck's expansion continued at breakneck speed. In April 1976, James returned from an overland tour to discover that Turner had bought four new buses – 'Snort', 'Snot', 'Slug' and 'Belch' – and leased new premises. Another tour company had folded and he'd taken over its offices, at 18 Dawes Road in Fulham. The premises consisted of a retail shop on the ground floor, a two-storey flat upstairs, and a basement. In the spirit of 'If you have it, use it', Skroo put every spare penny into buying another bus and putting on another tour.

Bill was concerned at this frenetic growth. The previous year, he'd got married, to Liz, and his priorities had changed. He'd originally been attracted to the informality of the company, but Top Deck was now a serious player, with 5000 passengers a year and an annual turnover of £5 million.

And there was another reason. 'Skroo was a fantastic partner in the entrepreneurial sense – there was no mountain that couldn't be climbed,' Bill remembers now. 'But he wasn't very *collaborative*.' James felt he was in danger of becoming a glorified bus driver. He toyed with the idea of selling out but couldn't quite bring himself to do it – he had too much respect for Turner's business sense. In the years to come, he would be thankful for having made this decision.

Skroo himself considers this period a very risky one, not to mention a great deal of hard work. Top Deck's biggest problem was that the double-decker buses were old and poorly maintained. Most of them had been public buses and each one had done at least 1,500,000 kilometres by the time Top Deck bought it. Breakdowns were common. One bus, the not inappropriately named 'Bollocks', needed the entire tour group to push it down a hill every morning before the driver could pop the clutch and start it.

Some buses were better than others. Slug, for instance, was actually named because it was one of the fastest in the fleet at the time. 'It had a five-speed gearbox fitted instead of the usual four,' driver Peter Markey recalls fondly. 'This overdrive box gave it a blistering top speed of *45 miles an hour . . .*'

No such fancy transmission on Snort, however, which on one occasion took a full week to make it to Cologne in northern Germany – usually the first night stop on this particular tour. Another bus served as a replacement, but that one soon developed problems of its own. Greg 'Five-Eight' Lloyd was the man unlucky enough to be the tour leader of the trip: 'After sixteen major breakdowns and 72 minor ones (the punters kept tally), we arrived back two weeks overdue and over budget.'

Skroo believed that in comparison to these mechanical failures, all other impediments were easy to overcome. 'We ignored red tape and bureaucracy,' he says by way of example. 'We had no problem getting passengers, and we recruited staff from people we met in the pub who had a bit of nous.' He felt that if they employed people with intelligence, good personalities and enthusiasm, then everything else could be trained or self-taught. Top Deck people came from all walks of life. 'Sexy' Rex Julian was a fitter and turner. Dave Reed worked on oil rigs. Paul 'Toot' Brunton was a train driver. Rod McEwin was a vet.

They also hired one Mick Carroll, a country boy from Leeton in New South Wales. Mick held the record for 103 first cousins, many of whom would end up working for Top Deck. His dapper appearance was in stark contrast to the unkempt look cultivated by the others. An acknowledged 'ladies' man', his hair and moustache were always neatly trimmed. This meticulous attention to detail would be an asset in his future with Top Deck, where he would become a driving force to improve the image of buses, drivers and retail shops.

Carroll arrived in London in 1975 at the age of 26, and became a 'dosser' at Mablethorpe Road. When a courier dropped out of a central European trip that October, he became the last-minute replacement. He had never been a tour leader before but, with the help of an experienced driver and some Michelin guidebooks, he managed to project an aura of professionalism. The tour was a success. After working on the road for the next eighteen months, he became operations manager and would eventually take over the running of the entire UK organisation.

In 1976, Top Deck decided to run six-month London to Sydney tours. No overland company had attempted this before, so the British media picked up the story. Bill James now had the opportunity to return home to coordinate the Asia–Australia leg. He jumped at the chance and sold Mick half of his half-share in Top Deck for £15,000. James and Carroll now owned 25 per cent of Top Deck each, while Turner, with his 50 per cent, became Top Deck's majority shareholder.

When Bill departed for Australia, Skroo and Mick felt that there should be some continuity of management style and decided to appoint another London-based director.[10] Bill Barking (as opposed to 'Bill Speaking'), a canine rescued from the Battersea Dogs Home, became the new recruit. He enjoyed his status and was generally at the centre of every work and social activity. Perhaps his only fault was a tendency to chew up car seat belts when left for long periods of time outside pubs or when the partners went off wind-surfing.

Nineteen seventy-six was also the year that Turner got married, the courtship for which was characterised by his customary determination. Judith Stent had known the then veterinary student briefly in Brisbane before he left for Europe. He had asked her on a date, but she'd knocked him back – 'I couldn't possibly go out with someone with a nickname like *that*,' she remembers now. Jude, as her friends called her, didn't recognise Skroo when, now temporarily resident in London, she bumped into him at the Top Deck office in March 1976. He recognised her, however. Turner convinced her to change her European tour-booking to a Top Deck tour and paid for her cancellation fee.

Jude was also looking for temporary work before her tour left. Not surprisingly something came up at the Top Deck office, so Skroo rang to offer her the job. When Jude set off for Europe in May, she assumed that that would be the last time she'd see Graham 'Skroo' Turner. Not entirely uncoincidentally, her driver got recalled in Athens, and Skroo took his place. Two weeks later, and just three months after they'd bumped into each other back at Dawes Road, Skroo proposed in Dubrovnik, the Adriatic seaport of what was then Yugoslavia. Jude accepted and the pair were married back in Brisbane in December 1976.

While in the Queensland state capital, Skroo set up the company's first Australian retail office, dedicated to selling Top Deck products, at 333 Queen Street. By using his mother's old kitchen cupboards, some seagrass matting, and black, white and yellow curtains from Curtain Wonderland, he kept the fit-out cost down to only $250. Following its success, two more shops were opened – one above a pizza shop at 65 Berry Street in Sydney, and another at 503 Chapel Street in Melbourne.

Bill James became Top Deck's first Australian sales representative. His company car was an old blue Holden utility. It wasn't air-conditioned and the windows wouldn't wind up, so Bill arrived fifteen minutes early for his sales appointments, to allow himself time to dry the sweat off his shirt. He also held film nights at the local RSL Club, where potential clients were treated to wine and cheese while watching Super 8 movies of previous Top Deck tours.

Top Deck was a hard sell in those days as it was regarded as light on quality and heavy on 'piss-ups'. Marketing stickers proclaiming 'I like it better on top' probably didn't help. To make the job easier, Jude and her brother, Mike Stent, put together a 28-page brochure, and used a fair bit of photographic licence while doing so. The beach shots of Casablanca were actually of Mooloolaba on Queensland's Sunshine Coast.

Once the brochure was completed, the new Mr and Mrs Turner returned to London and moved into their first marital home. It wasn't romantic. Skroo didn't believe in hierarchy or privileges so they shared the upstairs flat at Dawes Road with any number of Top Deck crew-members who were between tours. (The record was 28 bodies dossing down in the flat in one night.) The retail office below took the overflow, with people in sleeping bags on the floor. Whoever opened the shop in the morning had to wake everyone up, move them out and throw away the half-eaten kebabs and empty beer bottles that littered the floor.

Mick Carroll based himself in the Dawes Road flat with Jude and Skroo – in fact they all shared the same living quarters for over five years. Bill also stayed with them whenever he was in London. It seems amazing – bearing in mind that by the late 1970s, all of them were nearing the traditionally sobering age of 30 – but by all accounts they didn't fight. 'We didn't need to,' Mick says now. 'We just got on with it.'

In this they were helped by the fact that they weren't always together. James was in Australia a lot, and Skroo and Jude went home every year for six to eight weeks. When they were all in London, they were often working in different areas – Mick might be out at the workshop, say, while Turner held the fort in the retail office.

They were also frantically busy. This kept all parties focused on the task at hand, of course, but, as Mick Carroll recalls, it could also lead to some heart-stopping moments: 'During our peak times we'd have so many tours scheduled that we'd suddenly realise, "Shit, we don't even have a *bus* for that one!" One trip was due to go out in eight days time so we sent one of the guys to Leeds, bought a bus, and then worked day and night to rip out the seats and refit the bus in time for it to depart.'

Everyone pitched in to help. Mick and Skroo would work beside a team of tour leaders and drivers, splashing on the undercoat and hand-painting the outside of the double-deckers, as carpenters like 'Light Blue' built the kitchens and bunks inside. 'Luckily we were young,' Turner admits. 'We worked hard and long (not necessarily that effectively) and played hard – the social life was part of the business.' To reduce the stress, he played rugby with the London New Zealand team and did some jogging, while Carroll was an avid tennis player.

The partners received little monetary recompense at this time. They had no salary and basically lived off the company, which paid for their expenses. Everyone accepted that no one spent much, because there was little cash to spare. Top Deck had a small overdraft facility at the bank but often exceeded its limit. 'When this happened we used to hide out at the workshop because it had no phone,' Mick remembers. 'By the time the bank manager got hold of us to complain, we'd had a few extra days of bookings and had the cash to repay him.'

And they had to contend with other operational difficulties besides financial problems. When sheer demand really stretched their resources, they'd put almost anyone on the road. One new tour leader who took out a five-week European trip was such a dictator that two passengers had left by the time the bus reached Barcelona; another person got off at the French Riviera, and when the tour arrived in Florence, the driver rang to say he was leaving. Carroll had to dismiss the tour leader and scramble around to find an emergency replacement.

Record-keeping was sketchy at best, which often added to these operational difficulties. Top Deck used large red ledger books to register bookings for each tour, but some of the salespeople simply forgot to write up passengers. One tour was so overbooked that the tour leader had to buy a couple of tents so the excess passengers had somewhere to sleep. There was little comeback for these affronted customers. Top Deck's booking condition number 19 stated: 'The company sets its own limits to the numbers of passengers carried on the vehicles but the company is not bound by these numbers under special circumstances as determined by the company.'

To the partners, these were all minor problems. More difficult was dealing with the dangers and hardship that were a reality of life on the road. One of the worst experiences Mick Carroll had was when one of the tour buses was forced off the road in Russia by a truck travelling on the wrong side of the highway. The coach rolled and one of the passengers, a young Australian woman, was thrown through the windscreen and killed. The Australian Embassy in Russia sent word to the police back home to break the news to her parents. Both Skroo and Mick also spoke to them. It was a sad experience for everyone involved, but thankfully it would be Top Deck's only fatality in their many years of operation.

Once on the road, Top Deck crew-members had little back-up and some had to make life-and-death decisions. Darcy O'Donnell was leading an overland tour when word reached them that there had been a revolution in Iran. They decided to go on nonetheless but almost came to regret it. 'In Isfahan, the Revolutionary Guards cut us off and shepherded us off the road at gunpoint,' he recalls. 'We were taken back to their headquarters by the river. It looked like a mediaeval fortress except that it was sandbagged at the top and protected around the perimeter by machinegun-toting guards. After a couple of hours they realised that keeping us was more trouble than it was worth.'

Trevor Carroll (no relation to Mick) had a similar experience. 'We ran into a civil war in Afghanistan and were arrested,' he says now, nonchalantly. 'After a little buggering around we were finally placed under house arrest at a hotel. An early departure to Pakistan worked okay [as a suggested way out of the predicament], but we were fined for having expired visas.' Having dealt with militant political upheaval, it was Mother Nature they had to take on next: 'All went

well until Nepal, when at Pokhara we found that the road had
dropped into the valley. We tried an alternative route. It was a road,
sort of, and we crossed a river by driving the bus onto two large
rowboats joined by planks and forty or so locals paddled us across the
fast-moving river.'

Others were less fortunate. Several crew-members were trapped in
Iran during the revolution in 1979, and another was arrested there
in 1980 for defending the honour of a female passenger and putting
the offending campsite manager in hospital. The gallant lad was jailed
for his troubles and it cost US$1200 in 'fines' to get him out. When
the Russians invaded Afghanistan in December 1979, three busloads
of passengers had to flee the country to avoid the fighting. They
managed to get a flight to Istanbul, leaving their double-deckers aban-
doned in the war-torn country. On another trip a driver had to be
flown out of Pakistan after being struck down with a virus that nearly
killed him.

With conditions like these, Top Deck's people had to be resourceful. When Darcy reached the Pakistani border on one trip, a tour group
immediately ahead of his had just paid a handsome premium for a
quick transit through customs. 'This made things tricky for us', he
admits, knowing as he did that there was no way anyone on board
Grunt could match the bribe. The solution was to hand over his driver
Benny's *Playboy* magazine to the guards – 'so much better than money'.

This wasn't the only eventful tour for Darcy O'Donnell: 'There
was a major fuel shortage in Yugoslavia so we had to make a mad dash
to Italy. The girls made the difference for us here: we put them out the
back of the bus with the jerry cans, and the truckies all stopped and
topped them up for us.'

Visa problems were handled in a corresponding manner. Iraqi visa
applications required a letter from a minister, vouching for the appli-
cant's religious affiliation. Not surprisingly, all Top Deck people were
members of the same 'church': their visa application letters were
signed by the Reverend William Mablethorpe.

Visas took forever to process – certainly far longer than the two
days' notice Top Deck might give its crew. Most drivers would 'lose'

their passport several times a year, so they had three or four to send off to different consulates, as required. For those that didn't, other methods would be called for. In one instance, Top Deck needed a driver for a tour, but the only one in London at the time had no space left in his passport to take the required visa stamp for entrance into Spain. So the tour leader simply cut a page out of a New Zealand passenger's passport (they were getting her a Russian visa at the time) and glued it into the driver's Australian passport. Sure enough, the girl behind the counter at the Spanish Embassy didn't bat an eyelid. They had their visa.

Top Deck's inventiveness was also used for cost-cutting. To avoid paying road tax, drivers cut up Guinness beer mats, which were the same colour as the UK road tax stamps, and put them into their 'tax disc', which sat on the inside of the windscreen. To save the £100 required for the *carnet de passage*, an obligatory permit for the overland trips, the drivers would swap licence plates en route to Kathmandu and simply reuse the same one over and over again.

Passengers, known affectionately as 'punters', were willing accomplices in these cost-saving measures. They never complained when asked to hide upstairs while Top Deck entered venues such as campsites or national parks, where admittance fees were paid by the head. This ploy saved thousands of pounds over the years.

Top Deck's economy applied to salaries as well. Road crew received £27 a week with bonuses of between £3 and £5 per week for good trip reports. But no one seemed to mind the low wages. Most saw working for Top Deck as a lifestyle rather than a job – a way to see the world for free and have the time of their lives in the process.

For the many Australasians, miles away from home, Top Deck became their replacement family. Most of the crew-members had nicknames. There was Hulk, Budgie, Wags, Maggot, Mouse, Bones, Madam Lash, Tom the Pom, Animal, Wombat, Malaria, Dipstick, Chook, Sniffer, Headless, Nancy No Pants, Lucky (who wasn't), Ferret and Dodgy Pete, among others.

Several buses would often meet up in the same campsites, resulting in riotous parties. Trevor Carroll remembers Christmas 1978 in

Kathmandu as a particularly good meet-up, as eight buses all ended up at the Withies Hotel. For many during this period, it was to be the best time of their lives. An ex-driver describes one of his tours as 'an incredible seventy-five days spent with a great bunch of people that I will remember – be *haunted* by – to my dying days'. Even all these years later, people's nostalgia remains strong. An annual Top Deck reunion is held in Australia for all road crew, both new and old, and there's also a reunion website (www.topdeckreunion.com) for people to keep in touch and post their memories. One former courier spoke for many perhaps when he wrote: 'I wish I'd stayed at Top Deck instead of getting a job and a mortgage.'

By 1982, there were more than 220 people working for the company. Top Deck now owned 90 buses and had added to its portfolio Russia–Scandinavia tours (as first proposed by Turner back in '74), ski tours, charter tours, USA tours, and the Deckers' Club. The last of these was a social club for travellers that offered many services, including the organisation of the early concerts for INXS and Australian Crawl in London.

There were now two offices in Earl's Court, replacing the Fulham shop (one in Kenway Road, the other on Earl's Court Road); a three-bedroom house in the west London suburb of Ealing; five Renault cars; and a farm in Woking, Surrey, which was used as a workshop and a base for the buses.

Top Deck began to feel the bite from this rapid expansion. This was of concern to Bill James, who had returned to do another stint in the UK while Skroo headed home to oversee the start-up of the company's new Australian operation. 'Because the bank wouldn't extend our overdraft, we had paid in cash for most of our assets,' James explains. 'This began to put an enormous financial strain on us. We were also absolute novices with regard to management and leadership issues. There were no management accounts. A balance sheet and profit-and-loss account would be drawn up every year for statutory purposes, but by the time it hit our desk it was eighteen months old and of no use whatsoever for management purposes.'

This was to be their downfall. Skroo also admits that the situation had become chaotic: 'When you are running a small business, you have a good feeling for whether you are making money or not. Once we got bigger we didn't have a clue. Even though a lot of money was coming in, no one had any idea where it was going.' Top Deck began to experience cash shortages. Darcy O'Donnell even remembers having to borrow money from a passenger on one of his tours.

The financial problems were compounded by a £40,000 loss from A-Trek, another tour company Top Deck had acquired in 1978. 'We really only bought them as the owner was so desperate,' Turner says. 'It didn't cost us much, but we inherited all their debts and it nearly sent us broke.' Travelglobe, a New Zealand agent who had been selling Top Deck's tours, also went bankrupt, owing them NZ$60,000.

'By December 1982 we were eighty thousand pounds overdrawn,' Bill remembers. 'The bank had already refused to honour the cheques we'd issued the previous week. We'd managed to contain that news, but if word leaked out that we were in a cash crisis, it would spread like wildfire throughout the Australasian community in London and our bookings would dry up overnight.'

He was alone in London at the time because Mick had left on his annual leave and was unaware of the looming crisis. Bill rang Turner in Australia to tell him that the company was going under, and in a big way. Skroo couldn't believe it. How could they be *bankrupt*? Top Deck carried nearly 7000 passengers a year. It had over 200 people working on the road. There had to be some way for them to trade out of their difficulties.

Yet it looked impossible. They'd been struggling for several years to keep the cash flow going, now there was simply no more available money. They could stave off their creditors in the short term, but they had no way of paying them down the track. All the avenues they explored led to dead ends.

When Carroll returned from his holidays, he found his partners despondent. He and James managed to keep the company scraping along for another two months. Then at 3.30 one morning, Bill's phone rang. It was Skroo with a new idea. He had been thinking about why the Top Deck retail offices in Australia were still successful and he'd realised that it was because, unlike the London operation, they all operated as small business units. The managers had shares in the business and were committed to making their shops profitable.

All this meshed with a magazine article Turner had read, about the Australian transport company TNT. As Bill explains: 'It had been a bit like Top Deck – big and unwieldy and in financial difficulties. However, TNT had divided itself into separate logical business units to improve its accountability. As a result of these changes, TNT had managed to transform itself and dramatically improve its profits, almost overnight. Skroo thought that we could apply the same process to Top Deck.'

Bill and Mick thought it was a brilliant idea, but to implement it, they needed time and the help of a good accountant. Their existing company was highly suspect, according to Bill: 'We used a small accounting firm run by two Indian gentlemen, Mr Gupta and Mr Mystry. The firm was aptly named because the accounts they produced were a complete mystery to all of us and to anyone who tried to read them.'[11]

He convinced Peter Barrow, an accountant and one of his old school friends, to fly to London and sort out Top Deck's accounts. Peter's balance sheet, the company's first ever accurate one, revealed a devastating picture. Top Deck was actually £270,000 in debt. The company was insolvent and the partners were legally obliged to close down the business. This was far worse than they'd ever imagined.

James was ready to catch the next flight home to Sydney, but, as Barrow pointed out, the company had probably been trading while insolvent for some time. Since the crime had already been committed, in other words, they might as well hang in there and give their plan a chance to work.

The partners decided to go ahead with the restructure based on the successful Australian model. Peter now had the difficult task of trying to put together an opening balance for each of the divisions, from the almost nonexistent accounts. Only then could they operate as individual units.

In the interim, Skroo, Bill and Mick sold the idea to the people who would become the leaders of Top Deck's nine new divisions. They were as follows: John O'Donnell (for Europe), Steve 'Hulk' Prosser (Asia), Dillon O'Sullivan (America), Chris Greive and Andy Morgan (both handling the Ski division), Murgha Mack (Charters), Graham Sewell (Sales and Marketing), Chris Jacobs (Deckers' Club), Barbara Bates (London Flight Centre) and Dave 'Diesel' Morse (Farm Workshop).

There was little opposition to the concept because each leader was given equity in his or her area. This came from Turner, who had volunteered to give away 50 per cent of his half-share of Top Deck. As he said, 'Better to have twenty-five per cent of something than fifty per cent of nothing.'

The next step was to set the internal charges. The only way each area could run with independent accounts was if it paid a fee to the other units for services rendered. For example, the European operation would pay a weekly bus-hire rate to the Farm Workshop, which covered preparing the double-deckers for departure and the ongoing maintenance required, while the Asia operation would pay Sales and Marketing for advertising.

This caused a lot of conflict. Top Deck had some very strong personalities and the leaders had differing amounts of commercial sense. As these costs affected their bottom line, many were reluctant to give even an inch. Mick, Bill and Skroo were forced to act as referees while the division leaders wrangled over rates. They finally agreed on the charges and the new profit centres began to operate as of 1 May 1983.

The partners now focused on keeping the company afloat long enough for the plan to take effect. They were surprised to discover that some major creditors were prepared to be flexible about repayments. Bill James recalls a meeting with their printers, whom they owed £30,000: 'Bad payers were obviously a regular occurrence for them, but most of their other creditors would try to avoid them at all costs.

We, at least, promised to pay their bill at some time in the future, *and* get them drunk regularly while they were waiting. Which, as far as they were concerned, was a pretty good deal.'

Mick Carroll discovered an inventive way to increase cash flow: 'British Rail was our biggest creditor. I learned that if I wrote a word amount that didn't match the numerical figure on their cheque, it would take them a couple of months to request a new one. This bought us a bit of extra time for payment.' By using these and other techniques, Top Deck managed to limp along through another season.

By November 1983 the situation was starting to improve. Now that each division leader held a personal share in the business, they were incentivised to keep costs down as well as increase profit. The increased accountability also meant that they were now competing with each other to bring in the best results. Some areas began to make, not lose, money. It was still touch and go, but the signs were good.

The momentum continued to grow over the next twelve months. By August 1984, fifteen months after separating into profit centres, the company reported a £300,000 profit – an amazing £570,000 turnaround. 'Outwardly, no one would have recognised the changes,' Bill observes, 'but internally the transformation was like turning night into day.' This experience taught the partners a valuable lesson: Give people responsibility and accountability for their own outcomes, and a share of the profits, and you are guaranteed success. This would underpin much of their future strategy.

Top Deck had fared well compared to the rest of the industry. When it started in the early 1970s, there had been over ten tour companies operating European tours out of London. By the late '80s there were only four – Contiki, Autotours, Tracks and Top Deck – and both Autotours and Tracks would close down a few years later. One of the reasons Top Deck survived was because of its small capital costs. The price of buying and fitting out the double-deckers was very low compared to the price their competitors paid to buy and lease new coaches.

It had been a harrowing few years, however. 'The greatest success of Top Deck was really the growth of buses and passengers,' Turner believes. 'We could never say, "We can relax a bit now" or "We've done pretty well." We had a lot of financial pressure and we were not well organised, so the stress levels were high.'

The near-disaster forced the partners to re-examine their long-term goals. Top Deck was highly work-intensive, had enormous cash requirements and required constant supervision. There were much easier ways to make money. They would eventually sell the business off to the division leaders in 1987. Their future was back in Australia.

Chapter 2

A FINE DISREGARD FOR THE RULES

This stone commemorates the exploit of William Webb Ellis, who with a fine disregard for the rules of football, as played in his time, first took the ball in his arms and ran with it, thus originating the distinctive feature of the rugby game. AD 1823.

Headstone on the grave of William Webb Ellis,
credited with inventing the game of rugby

The first Flight Centre shop opened in Sydney, Australia, in March 1982 and changed the face of the Australian travel industry. Its impact was akin to stirring up a wasps' nest with a stick. It caused disbelief, outrage, hostile retaliation, airline embargoes, government review and even death threats. Within eighteen months the traditional industry rules were in tatters. Yet there was little calculation on Top Deck's part. The company simply saw an opportunity, ran with it, and in so doing changed the rules of the game. They had no grand plan, no organised systems, and hardly any money. What they did have was one very good idea.

Top Deck's inspiration came from its London base. Even though airlines in the UK had to sell airfares at regulated prices, discounting was the norm for travel agents, particularly the 'bucket shop' retailers who specialised in buying and selling airfares at wholesale prices from airlines. Even though these bucket shops were run-down, often in dubious locations and went broke with alarming regularity, they were always inundated with clients because of their cheaper fares.

The Top Deck partners thought this concept of discounting

airfares would work very well in Australia. It was a bold idea considering that discounting was officially illegal. But this was only one of the challenges Flight Centre would have to overcome. To comprehend why the company's notion was so radical, it is necessary to understand the forces operating in the Australian travel industry at the time.

In his book *Australian Travel and Tourism Law*, Anthony J. Cordato has written, 'there was government-sponsored price-fixing in that airfares were set and approved by the government under the Air Navigation Regulations and it was an offence to charge less than the airfares prescribed under those regulations!'[12] In truth though, clandestine activity was rife, as airlines offered travel agents generous incentives and under-the-counter commission deals to boost their sales.

With the introduction of the Trade Practices Act in 1974, the government's position on anti-competitive pricing had become somewhat ambiguous, and by 1980 some of the smaller agents began to tentatively discount. Industry response was immediate and crushing. The International Air Transport Association (IATA) and the Australian Federation of Travel Agents (AFTA) considered it illegal and unethical for travel agents to discount airfares, and were determined to enforce the law. In a statement to the Hobart Magistrate's Court in September 1981, Counsel for the Commonwealth said, 'In response to strong representations made to the Government for action to be taken against illegal discounting practices, steps were taken to strengthen tariff enforcement activities by the Department of Transport.'[13] As a result, two travel agents were successfully prosecuted and fined.

This was a major change in the government's position: it had endorsed price-fixing to the detriment of the consumer. Travel agents were no longer perceived as independent business entities but merely agents of airlines subject to the latter's restrictive rates and conditions. Airlines could now actively prosecute agents who didn't abide by their fares. With this effective ban on discounting, the travelling public were the biggest losers.

This was the state of play when Flight Centre stepped into the game in 1982 and changed all the established conventions. Skroo recalls wryly: 'Discounting airfares was standard practice in the UK and we saw a great opportunity in Australia. The industry rules didn't make sense to us at all, so we didn't take any notice of them.'

The catalyst for Flight Centre's decision was a proposal by an ambitious 24-year-old from South Australia. Dave Tonkin had worked briefly for Top Deck on his arrival in London, and still went jogging regularly with Turner. In 1981 he decided to return to Australia and so he approached Skroo with an idea.

Tonkin had been managing a travel agency for three months in Church Street, Kensington. Owned by two Australians, The Flight Shop was in a good location and had a smart fit-out to match; it was tiny, sold discounted airfares, and had clients queuing to book – a kind of corporatised bucket shop.

Dave thought that this type of upmarket bucket shop would work very well in Australia. But he needed a partner. Despite having a couple of interested parties, he rang Skroo and suggested a jog around London's Hyde Park. By the end of the run, Dave had another offer on the table: set up a Flight Shop–type store in Sydney for Top Deck Travel.

The company already had five retail shops in London and Australia that had been set up to sell Top Deck tours. The partners, however, were very impressed with Tonkin's concept. They now decided to trial the new bucket-shop model in Australia. If it proved successful, then all of their retail shops could borrow its systems. Little did they know that their adoption of Dave's model would eventually spread hundreds of these corporatised bucket shops, and over 2500 other businesses, around the globe.

Turner and Tonkin agreed that Top Deck would put in the $8000 capital required and the two parties would share the profits 50/50. The contract was a one-page document, clause 7 of which stated: 'As a general principle Dave Tonkin is to do all the work and TDT to make heaps of money.'

Because this was the first of an exciting new prototype, they felt the store should have a new name. Skroo thought it should be called International Student Travel. Top Deck had a lucrative deal with a student wholesaler in London that allowed it to issue student cards, and sell discounted student tickets. Top Deck sold these discounted tickets indiscriminately and made a good profit from them. Maybe it could do the same in Australia.

Dave disagreed with the name, however. He thought it was too restrictive. After some discussion, they finally agreed on 'Sydney Flight Centre'. It was simple, and identified them as airfare specialists rather than stock-standard travel agents. With this settled, Tonkin employed three people and leased a 40-square-metre shop in the Carlton Arcade, between Elizabeth and Castlereagh streets, in Sydney's central business district.

With an annual rental cost of $20,800, together with the fact that the venture had minimal funding and owners with little experience in the Australian market, financial analysts would have labelled this store a high-risk venture. Added to this, the very first Flight Centre had a large number of established competitors. In the early '80s there were nearly 3000 travel outlets in Australia, belonging to some 2000 firms, according to statistics released by the Trade Practices Commission. Bank-owned travel agencies and large corporate identities, such as American Express and Thomas Cook, dominated the market and took 75 per cent of all bookings. The airlines and small one-off travel agents fought over the remainder.

Regardless of these poor odds, when Sydney Flight Centre opened on 29 March 1982, its discount tickets sold like hotcakes. For $1600 a Flight Centre client could buy return flights to London that retailed at $2000 in every other agency in Australia; for $800, the same client could travel one-way to London on a ticket that normally retailed for $1200. And the tickets could be on a combination of airlines, with a wide range of stopovers. This type of flexibility and pricing was unheard of. Within a month, Sydney Flight Centre was making up to $60,000 in turnover a week. It made a $100,000 profit in its first year.

The company had obtained its cheap fares from a number of sources, not all of them strictly legal. For a start, it took advantage of the fact that London–Australia return airfares bought in the UK were about $400 cheaper than the Australia–London return airfares set by the Australian government. When a Flight Centre consultant in Australia had a client wishing to travel to London, he or she telexed Top Deck's UK office; the cheaper London–Australia–London ticket was issued and posted back to Australia by registered mail. When it arrived, the consultant then changed the dates on each ticket so that clients could use the sectors in reverse (i.e. Australia–London–Australia). By doing this, Flight Centre came up with an unbeatable fare.

In those days, traditional travel agencies mainly dealt with the well-known, (then) government-owned airlines, such as Qantas or British Airways. Flight Centre didn't care which airlines it dealt with, as long as their fares were cheap. Because it was illegal for airlines to discount to agents, the company did covert deals with carriers such as Philippine Airlines, Garuda, Aeroflot and Pakistan Airlines. A $670 Philippine–Pakistan Airlines fare to London became the standard one-way net. It took at least twelve months for the established agencies to catch on and begin expanding their airline network. By then, many had missed the boat.

For some destinations, like Apia in Western Samoa, there were no special fares, in which case, Flight Centre consultants would give away some of their own commission to discount the customer's airfare. Flight Centre's competitors, who were unaware of its clandestine deals, thought that this was the company's standard modus operandi. In fact it was a rare occurrence.

The success of Sydney Flight Centre was a revelation to the Top Deck partners. The shop had no stock or debtors and required minimal capital input and staff supervision. Naturally, comparisons were soon made with Top Deck's tour business: the entire European division, with 90 buses, 200 people and a lot of blood, sweat and tears, made a maximum of $50,000 profit a year, and sometimes even lost money. Mick Carroll would continue to run this operation for the next five years, but the partners could now see that the Flight Centre concept was their future.

Turner returned to Australia and set up a base in Brisbane. His vision at this point was very simple: 'To have a lot of shops and make a lot of money.' Funding was their biggest obstacle. Top Deck's tour operation was in the midst of its financial crisis and there was no money to spare. 'We decided that the best way to expand was to involve other people,' Skroo says now, 'preferably by them putting in their own money.'

He already had another partner in mind. Geoff Harris, a marketing graduate from Melbourne's Institute of Technology with eight years of sales and advertising experience, seemed an unlikely person to get involved. Appearances were deceiving, however. Geoff was as gung ho about travel as he was about business. He also came from a long line of retailers – his father was a grocer and his grandfather ran a shoe shop. His experience would prove invaluable and he would become a key player in the emerging Flight Centre entity.

Harris had met Mick and Skroo in London in the late '70s. After being offered the job of Top Deck's UK marketing manager, he'd knocked them back but kept in touch. When he returned to Melbourne in 1982, he approached Turner with the idea of setting up an 18–30s travel club in Australia. Skroo had another idea. He suggested that Geoff should open up a Flight Centre in Melbourne.

The 30-year-old Victorian went to check out the Sydney shop first. 'I was impressed,' he remembers, 'and I decided to go ahead with the idea. I approached the State Bank for a loan. I needed three thousand dollars to buy my half-share in the business. They knocked me back. In the end my father loaned me the money.' With an eventual return of several hundred million dollars, it was a prudent investment.

Geoff opened The Flight Shop in Little Bourke Street in Melbourne at the end of April 1982. (It wasn't called 'Flight Centre' because another company had registered this name in Melbourne at the time.) The office was painted white and had red- and blue-striped pillars out the front. It cost $18,000 per annum and, at 28 square metres, was Top Deck's smallest shop at the time. What it lacked in size, it made up for in results, however. It cleared $140,000 profit in its first full financial year, which set a new record for Top Deck's retail shops.

Turner's next investor was his old friend and business partner Geoff 'Spy' Lomas. Spy was now the clinical microbiologist at the Vet School at Sydney University when Skroo rang to see if he'd be interested in setting up a Flight Centre in Brisbane. He agreed and the pair set up a partnership, Lomas taking 25 per cent while Top Deck held the major stake.

In June that year, Spy opened the 30-square-metre Brisbane Flight Centre at 333 Queen Street. It was on the site of an old bank and still had the original vault out the back – which would eventually become Skroo's office. The shop was in the same arcade as Top Deck Travel's retail store, and they soon became each other's biggest competitor. In spite of this, Brisbane Flight Centre also made a profit – of $25,000 – in its first year.

With the addition of more shops, the Flight Centre consultants could now pool their information. So when Philippine Airlines in Brisbane gave the local Flight Centre a very cheap one-way fare to London, the Sydney and Melbourne shops began buying all their one-way tickets via Brisbane. It took some time for the airline to work out why it was selling more Melbourne–London flights out of its Brisbane office than its Melbourne office.

By the end of 1982, the Australian Flight Centre operation had grown to a total of nine retail shops, six of which were start-up businesses. The company had no systems and its people were untrained, with little retail experience. Its shops were poorly branded, in secondary locations. And apart from Dave Tonkin, none of the owner–managers had any experience in running a travel agency. Yet despite these handicaps, the Flight Centre group profit for that financial year was $295,000. Australian travellers simply kept coming back for the discounted airfares.

Flight Centre advertised its cheap airfares in newspapers around Australia, and on windows and sandwich boards out the front of its shops. Although this upfront discounting mentality was totally foreign to the industry at large, the company's timing couldn't have been better. The ideas of American Ralph Nader, one of the first consumer advocates, were beginning to be disseminated in Australia, and there was increasing public debate on issues such as price-fixing and the benefits of competition. Politicians who had once supported travel industry regulation now began to fear the consequences of being seen to be discouraging cheaper airfares.

This worked to Flight Centre's advantage. Rumour has it that the Department of Transport in Canberra did look into prosecuting the company at this stage, but no charges were laid. Even though it was still technically illegal to discount airfares, the government decided to adopt a policy of non-intervention. This was the first step along the road towards industry deregulation.

Flight Centre may have escaped government retaliation but it still faced strong opposition from the rest of the industry. In mid 1982 the airlines, in close association with IATA, had decided to set their own airfares on the UK/Europe route. The *Australian Financial Review* described this new Yield Improvement Programme (YIP) as a gentlemen's agreement to keep fares close to 'legally fixed tariffs'.[14]

To enforce compliance to these YIP fares, IATA decided to police them itself, rather than relying on government prosecution. It set up the Fair Deal Monitoring Programme with the power to levy fines and restrict trade with offenders. Qantas enforced these rules with an iron fist, employing undercover agents to buy 'test' tickets from suspected discounters. This was a direct attack on travel agents, yet few dared challenge their authority, especially as the fine for non-compliance was a hefty $5000.

But Flight Centre's consultants were generally young travellers who had recently returned from overseas. These go-getters weren't weighed down by years of industry convention. One of their number, Lynn Ure (née Stanton), explains: 'We didn't mean to break the rules all the time, but we had to, to get anything done. Skroo told me when I started just to sell, sell, sell, and that if we had to pay for a fine it didn't matter. So that's what I did.'

It wasn't long before she was caught selling a discounted ticket, however. A friend of hers had died a month earlier so Turner asked Lynn if she'd mind using this as an excuse. That was okay by her, so he told IATA that his young employee had been traumatised and didn't know what she was doing. She got off scot-free.

To get around the IATA conventions, Flight Centre consultants came to rely on a network of supporters who admired their drive and enthusiasm. 'When the Qantas agents were on the prowl,' another former consultant remembers, 'one of our wholesale companies would ring us to let us know. Everyone would quote full regulation fares until we knew that the agents were back in their office.'

Flight Centre may have beaten IATA's stringent regulations but this organisation did limit other areas of the business. For instance, the partners knew that under the circumstances it would be almost impossible for Flight Centre to obtain an IATA licence – a necessity if the company wished to issue its own airline tickets. This was no problem with regard to international airfares, as Flight Centre bought its tickets either via the UK or directly from airfare wholesalers, known in the industry as consolidators.

The problem was domestic tickets, however. Flight Centre couldn't ticket these without an IATA licence and the commission paid by consolidators on these fares was so minimal that it wasn't worthwhile for the consultants to sell them. 'In the end we decided to focus on international airfares instead,' Bill James explains. 'We didn't realise it at the time but this was a great way to differentiate ourselves. We didn't end up ticketing domestic flights until 1991.'

AFTA was as outraged as IATA at Flight Centre's lack of convention, but proved just as powerless. Trevor O'Rourke, who was then an AFTA board delegate, admits to having felt more than a little frustrated with the situation: 'At every AFTA meeting the big question was "How are we going to close down these bucket shops?" We came up with numerous ideas, such as boycotting the airlines they were using, but at the end of the day, we were paper tigers. Flight Centre purchased their tickets offshore or via travel industry wholesalers and circumvented our embargoes. There was nothing we could do to stop them.'

The inability of both of these industry bodies to halt Flight Centre's rebel discounting outraged the rest of the travel industry and led to hostile retaliation. Qantas refused to supply the company with its *Fares from Australia* manual, which was the standard airfare tariff required to operate a travel agency in the pre-computer era. Flight Centre consultants had to use all their ingenuity to get hold of a copy, and even the partners weren't above a little skullduggery. Geoff Harris, for instance, confesses to visiting a Qantas office for the specific purpose of slipping one of these highly prized manuals into a manila folder he 'happened' to be carrying at the time.

The airline took great exception to having any of its marketing material on display in Flight Centre shops. One Qantas employee was even instructed by her general manager to go around and scrape off the Qantas stickers on the doors. (In an ironic twist, eight years later this same employee became the airline's personal account manager to the Flight Centre group, by which time Qantas was offering to pay to put its merchandise in the stores.)

Other airlines followed suit. Geoff Harris's girlfriend, Sue, was already working for Cathay Pacific, the Hong Kong carrier, as a supervisor when she applied for the position of state sales manager. Such was Cathay's antagonism towards Flight Centre, however, she was advised that she'd never get a promotion while she was dating Harris. Sue ended up marrying him all the same.

Flight Centre consultants bore the brunt of the bitterness. Some remember being booed off stage and verbally abused at industry functions. There were even threatening notes slipped under shop doors, one of the more sinister being 'Watch your back, you may never make it back to the office tomorrow.' (Dave Churchman, who received that particular note, chose to understand it as a reference to the hangover he'd have after celebrating another great sales success.) A Victorian consultant, Kerri Lester, had been warned off leaving her previous boss's employ at World Travel Headquarters with the stern words: 'This is the worst decision you will ever make in your life.' But it was his company that would close down several years later, not Flight Centre.

The airlines and the industry were unanimous: Flight Centre was a cowboy operation. The company had no respect for the established status quo, no understanding of the time-honoured practices of the travel industry, and its people were untrained and unruly. From their viewpoint, Flight Centre would be lucky to survive twelve months.

They didn't see that Flight Centre was here to stay and would outlast and outperform most of them. This was because the majority of people in the industry never understood Flight Centre itself and weren't privy to Graham Turner's vision of a Flight Centre on every corner. They hated the concept of discounting airfares and couldn't comprehend the company's willingness to source the best fares from anywhere in the world. And Flight Centre's young, irreverent people were a blow to the twin principles of bureaucracy and hierarchy espoused by the rest of the industry at that time.

As a consequence of its isolation within the travel industry, Flight Centre thrived as underdogs. While rivals derided its business ideals and sneered at its strategies, Flight Centre had no serious competition, but it did have a major support group – the public. They loved the cheaper fares and poured through the doors in droves. Shopping around for prices became normal behaviour.

Other travel agents couldn't beat them, so eventually they joined them. The retailers who didn't discount lost a lot of business. 'We closed down four [rival] travel agents in the vicinity of Sydney Flight Centre in our first year of trading,' Dave Tonkin recalls. 'They couldn't compete as they were too scared to discount.' By November 1983, *The Canberra Times* reported a 'wide-scale undercutting' of fares throughout Australia and a corresponding lack of government intervention.[15] Two months later, the trade publication *Travelweek* noted the collapse of the YIP compliance system due to the non-payment of thousands of dollars of fines.[16]

It was obvious to most industry observers that Flight Centre had succeeded in revolutionising the way airfares were sold in Australia, but still IATA was committed to the YIP. In a bid to stamp out discounting in Australia once and for all, the association appealed one last time for government intervention, by applying to the Trade Practices Commission for authorisation of its practices. In the application, IATA claimed that the YIP had brought stability to the market and maintained airline viability. It proposed that set airfares should be enforced with fines for non-compliance of up to US$50,000. This move was supported by most airlines and raised only a few responses from travel agents. Surprisingly, AFTA, whose membership was made up entirely of travel agents, also declined to comment.

The rebuttal from Top Deck Travel, still the owner company of the Flight Centre shops of course, is quoted extensively in the Trade Practices Commission document of 1984:

> As the main aim of YIP was to increase prices, this is exactly what has happened . . . The only way airlines are trying to increase their yields is by increasing fares, not increasing efficiency or loadings . . . Therefore in 18 months we have seen airfare increases of about 50 per cent . . . Whilst consumers are interested in regularity and quality of service, these should be governed purely by competition, not by IATA regulations.[17]

The commission agreed. Its July 1984 ruling reads: 'The Commission does not accept that these tariffs should be enforced to preclude competitive pricing or discounting. The Commission is of the point of view that tariff compliance machinery agreed between airlines does not provide public benefit.' The YIP was formally disbanded in that same month.

Flight Centre's guerilla tactics had worked. Over the next few years, the industry was deregulated and market forces were allowed to prevail. Those who didn't discount disappeared. By the 1990s, bank travel agencies, once so dominant in the market, were nonexistent. Thus Flight Centre had succeeded in changing the rules of play, and a new game had well and truly begun.

Chapter 3

FLIGHT CENTRE – THE EARLY YEARS

We were fairly primitive in the early days. At my first managers' conference we each had a banana on the desk in front of us. We had to stick them in our ears and do pretend phone enquiries.

Dave Churchman, Flight Centre manager

Flight Centre had succeeded in changing the rules of play in Australia based on one very good idea: the concept of discounting airfares. Yet the company was like an adventurous traveller heading off to see the world with an overloaded backpack and only $20 in its pocket. It would take more than this to succeed in the long term. Flight Centre arrived in the early 1980s with few experienced managers, tiny makeshift shops, almost no administrative systems and a chronic shortage of cash. Every spare cent was put into opening new shops, and this frenetic rate of expansion increased the pressure on the growing company.

Despite these drawbacks, by all accounts it was an exhilarating time to work for Flight Centre. The company was made up of intelligent and resourceful people drawn from all walks of life. Together, they formed a close-knit fellowship, thrived on Flight Centre's adventurous approach to business, and became masters of improvisation. This picture is borne out by many first-hand accounts.

'I had an interview on a park bench in the middle of a roundabout with Skroo and Geoff,' Lynaire Monnery (née Harkness)* remembers. 'I got the job and was told I had to paint my own shop. My boyfriend and I contracted ourselves out and charged Flight Centre three hundred dollars for the work.'

Another manager, Jude Evans*, asked her parents to help set up her new shop, in the Auckland suburb of Pakuranga. The store was less than ideal – it had glass walls and was exposed to the sun all day. The start-up allowance didn't include air-conditioning so the consultants wore sunglasses and put their feet in buckets of ice to keep cool. Down in Christchurch, Dave Churchman's* new Riccarton Road store also operated on a shoestring budget: 'We couldn't pay for phones for a few weeks so everyone brought in their home phones. And we had no safe, so we used to keep our banking in the vacuum cleaner.'

On top of these obvious shortcomings, most stores were small, to keep rents down. Kerri Lester's* shop in central Melbourne was so tiny, in fact, that it only had two desks for three people. When a fourth person was hired, they had to move the sink.

Many of the shops were in poor locations. Flight Centre was an unknown to retail landlords, so the company was unable to lease prime sites. In shopping centres, it was only able to rent kiosks set up in the middle of the walkways. There were some serious disadvantages to this. One former kiosk consultant, Mary Vincent*, shared this cramped space with three others. She remembers having to spend most of the day under her desk, in an effort to carry on telephone conversations above the noise around her. Added to these trying conditions, there was no way of locking away their office equipment overnight, so everything had to be packed up and then set up again in the morning.

Even the shops that were in good locations had their share of hassles, as the fit-outs were often pretty rough and ready. In the case of Aileen Bratton's* new store in Toowong, in western Brisbane, the counters were so high that she couldn't even see over them. It was only

---

* Throughout this chapter, an asterisk beside a person's name indicates that he or she was still working for Flight Centre Limited when interviewed by the author.

after Skroo visited two weeks later and asked 'Are you standing in a hole?' that someone came in and shaved them down. The solution wasn't that simple at another Flight Centre, down in Sydney, where Simon Poole's* consultants kept complaining that their chairs were sliding backwards. 'We couldn't figure it out until one day the floor collapsed,' he says.

Physical hardship aside, there were many hurdles for the company's new recruits. Flight Centre's mentality was very much sink or swim – there was little training, and those who started in shops had to rely on their own initiative. For Kerri Lester, 'tuition' consisted solely of picking up her manager's bad habits, which was understandable since managers were often as raw and new to the game as their consultants. Such was the company's rate of expansion throughout most of the 1980s that many consultants became managers by default, as more and more new shops appeared.

What truly amazed a newcomer like Tony Illingworth*, however, was Flight Centre's indifference to conventional business systems. 'On my first day at Flight Centre,' he recalls, 'there was *seventy thousand dollars* overflowing out of a plastic cash-box – no one had done the banking for a week! I was shocked at this casual attitude towards handling money.' It's easy to see why: in his previous career as a bank teller, Tony had been held up at gunpoint three times.

Such oversights weren't that unusual. Flight Centre focused on making money, and administration came a very poor second. Still, it was an accident waiting to happen, as Maxi Quaedvlieg can testify. One of the consultants in her Redcliffe shop had missed the closing time for the bank so hid $15,000 in takings in the bottom of a rubbish bag. When the consultant came in the following morning, she was horrified to see that someone had taken out the garbage overnight; meanwhile, outside in the street, the truck was pulling away . . . Panic set in. 'We bought facemasks and dishwashing gloves, locked up the shop, and headed off in a convoy of cars to the local tip,' Maxi recalls. 'After wading through the rubbish we finally discovered the bag with the fifteen grand still intact inside.' It was a close call.

Some managers were more security-conscious than others. Over in another Brisbane suburb, Indooroopilly, Robyn Blacklock* ordered a safe to store her shop's airline tickets only to find that the delivery guys simply dumped it in the middle of the floor while she was out. 'We couldn't move it so we left it there,' she explains. 'Then we accidentally locked the key in it and couldn't use it anyway.' This was fortunate in a way. Some time afterwards the safe was stolen and later discovered out in the suburbs with the door blown off.

Accounting was treated with the same indifference as banking, it seems. Mary Vincent's question as to the state of her shop's finances was met with a telltale reply from her bookkeeper-cum-musician: 'You're a couple of thousand out – but don't worry about it,' he told her. In Queensland, on the other hand, the shop managers were also the accountants, but this didn't necessarily ensure any greater accuracy and care than the method used at Mary's New South Wales operation. On the rare occasions that their books actually balanced, a reward awaited them in the form of a bottle of port, courtesy of Skroo Turner.

One innovative Queensland manager, Jenny Goldburg, paid her accountant husband Jim $10 an hour to do the books. Other managers followed suit, and soon enough Turner offered him a full-time position as Flight Centre's first in-house accountant. There was one condition: Goldburg had to get all the managers to sign individual letters to say that they were prepared to pay their portion of his costs. Once he'd collected all the signatures, he had the job.

Such centralisation of back-room duties, even on a state level, was a while away yet, however. In the main, managers effectively ran their own businesses with little interference from the partners. This applied to all facets of business operation, from accounting through to creche facilities.

When Robyn Blacklock needed someone to work in her new Brisbane store, she rang up an old friend who'd left Flight Centre some months before to have a baby. 'Robyn asked me to work for her but I couldn't get a childminder,' Grania Fingleton recalls. 'She told me not to worry, just bring her in. My three-month-old baby ended up sharing a playpen out the front of the shop with Robyn's dog Handbrake.'

And just as the question of occupational health and safety was very much at the store managers' discretion, so they had a remarkably free rein financially. Geoff Lomas* invested some of his shop profits on the futures market, for instance. (Spy made a good return on his initial investment, but the stockbroker didn't sell when he was supposed to and the shop came out slightly worse off.)

Such a maverick approach to its retail operation had made the company a whole host of enemies within the industry, of course, but Flight Centre found itself winning a few friends as the decade wore on. One was Brian Egan, of Malaysia Airlines. 'You couldn't say they were organised, well-run shops,' he says. 'One thing they did have going for them, however: I don't ever remember a bounced cheque. They were never dodgy, and we learned to trust them very quickly.' On this score, it is interesting to note that Flight Centre also introduced trust accounts – which separated client's money from the company's general funds – into all its shops by 1987, even though there was no legal requirement for the company to do so.

Jim Goldburg based himself out at the back of George Street Flight Centre, in Brisbane. The store had been converted from a dress shop, and the accountant's office was the old change cubicle. This was typical of the arrangements at the time. Skroo, for instance, was still working in the old bank vault at the back of Spy's shop on Queen Street. He'd set it up with a table and two chairs and used a bedside lamp for illumination. With its steel walls and overall clamminess, the room was like a prison cell. The doorway was so small that people had to turn sideways to enter.

It was in this unprepossessing location that Graham Turner held interviews, did deals and signed shop leases – all in his customary T-shirt and jogging shorts. Every now and then the words 'Fuck, fuck, *fuck!*' would echo out of the vault to startle unsuspecting clients. It was a standard joke among the Queen Street consultants that they'd learned to swear by osmosis.

Turner might've had his own office, but no one could accuse him of being elitist. He was always willing to help out in the shop, no matter what he was (or wasn't) wearing. 'Skroo often jogged in to work from his home in Kenmore,' former consultant Tina Saunders recalls. 'One morning he'd sweated so much that he took off his running gear and dressed in a garbage bag while his clothes dried. He saw no problem in helping serve clients dressed in this attire.'

The other Flight Centre chiefs had their own idiosyncrasies. For Geoff Harris, the Melbourne manager, everything was 'a piece of piss' – there was no obstacle that couldn't be overcome. Not even the fact that he didn't yet have a shop when he began recruiting people for Little Bourke Street. Wayne Ackerfeld* applied for a position after seeing an ad for a 'revolutionary new travel agency': 'We agreed to do the interview at my mother-in-law's house. I remember Geoff turned up and looked like he knew what he was doing. I asked him how many staff he already had, and he replied, "I haven't got any." I took the job anyway because it sounded exciting.'

Harris worked alongside his new charge in this first Victorian shop, both as a consultant and a manager. With almost a decade in sales and marketing behind him, he soon learned to improvise. And never more so than when it came to taking the store's very first booking, only for them to realise that they didn't have a receipt book. 'Wayne kept the client talking,' he recalls, 'while I dashed to the local stationer's, bought a book, and then ripped ten pages out so he wouldn't know he was the only customer we'd ever had.'

Geoff was inspiring to work with, simply because he himself was inspired – or to use his words: 'I never had any doubts at all about the Flight Centre concept. It simply didn't enter into my head.' And unlike Turner and Bill James, he wasn't involved in Top Deck's UK operation so had more time to concentrate on the retail shops. In this he was very successful. 'Geoff was the key retailer,' Skroo confirms. 'And he developed our model in the early to late '80s, making it profitable and replicable. He was definitely more important than Bill, Mick or myself in this area. We all just copied his methods and tried to beat him at his own game.'

This 'development' of the Flight Centre model included an impressive list of innovations: the introduction of the first airfares database; advertising in the Yellow Pages and on day-glo signs on shop windows; daily product and airfare updates for all shops; and initiating monthly dinners with prizes for the sales consultants who sold the most airfares, accommodation and travel insurance. Geoff was also a good recruiter, and many of the people he hired are still with the company today.

After opening and managing six shops in Victoria, Harris set up an old card table at the back of one of his stores and began a full-time role as the so-called 'area leader' of Victoria. His offices quickly became the company's profit leaders. He would prove so successful, in fact, that in 1986 Skroo offered him a share in the business and he became a fourth partner.

In the meantime, Mick Carroll was still holding the fort in the UK. He had little to do with the Australian Flight Centre business, apart from funding some of the early shops with Top Deck's new-found profits. His job was easier following the divisional split in May 1983, as each leader handled his or her own operation and reported to him. As well as helping the division leaders through individual crises, Mick organised many joint marketing events, such as touch-rugby games and concerts, with the popular Australasian magazine *TNT*. With Top Deck supplying the operational expertise and *TNT* providing free advertising, these were a great success and attracted up to 2000 people each time.

Meanwhile, Bill James had returned from his last stint in London to become the leader of what by December 1984 had become six Flight Centre shops in Sydney. 'It was pretty tough,' he admits. 'Unlike the other guys, who built their areas from scratch, I inherited six very independent-minded managers.' Bill wasn't helped by the fact that he disliked conflict – as one consultant, Gavin Durbin*, remembers: 'We called him "Uncle Bill". He was the nice uncle, not the one who smacked you over his knee.'

Bill James was perhaps the only partner who worried about the 'little' things like cash flow and finances. Maybe this was a hangover from Top Deck's troubled times. When Gerrie Larsen* started work as an accountant in Sydney, she asked him about Flight Centre's accounting systems. 'What systems?' came the reply. 'We don't have any . . .'

Despite the rudimentary nature of its business practices and the chaotic working environment on offer, from the start Flight Centre had no difficulty employing people. For their part, job applicants often found themselves accepting positions against the advice of their parents and even their own better judgment, not to mention in the face of almost industry-wide scorn for the company. Lex Noller*, for instance, was a journalist in need of a career change: 'I saw the ad for Flight Centre and applied. The main thing I remember about my interview was that the manager knew less about travel than I did, and I hadn't even started yet.'

Happy to stay true to her area of expertise, however, was Tina Los*, who applied for a role as an accountant. 'The interview was in an old bank vault with this guy called "Skroo",' she laughs. 'I thought, *Oh my God, he's called "Screw"*! He told me he didn't have any accountancy positions but asked if I wanted to be a travel agent. I'd only been from Melbourne to Brisbane, by car. I thought about it for a month, and then I rang him back and told him I'd give it a go.'

Why would someone accept a job that wasn't even the one she'd applied for? In Tina's case, it was the fact that Flight Centre took recruits with no training or prior experience. Travel jobs were in high demand because of the perceived perks of free 'educational' trips and cheap holidays, but many applicants were put off by what they considered an uninspiring career path. In those days you had to complete a travel and tourism course, and then work as a domestic consultant for several years selling bus and train tickets before you could become an international travel consultant.

Flight Centre's fast-track alternative meant that motivated people could break straight into the travel industry. This was a golden opportunity for anyone who was bored in his or her current profession but didn't want to spend several years retraining for another career. If they happened to be ex-travellers also, it was even more appealing, because they could use the knowledge they'd accumulated in their travels to help clients book their holidays. This was a heady combination.

The wage for new consultants in their first three months was 40 per cent of the office commission on everything they sold. For example, if they sold an $1800 airfare to Europe that attracted $200 in office commission, they'd receive $80. After their third month, Flight Centre consultants went on to a salary plus 10 per cent commission, unlike most travel agents, who were paid a flat wage and whose commission was paid to their agency.

This commission-only period was a calculated strategy on Flight Centre's part. If the new recruits were skilled at sales or highly motivated to learn, then they made a lot of money and stayed; those without selling skills, on the other hand, made little money and usually left. The trial system was beneficial to both consultant and employer, therefore, but that didn't stop it from being the subject of parliamentary discussion in New Zealand briefly, after an Invercargill consultant had left in her first month. A Labour MP raised the topic of Flight Centre's 'slave wages', but any controversy ended once the system was explained and it was realised that those who stayed made far more money than their industry counterparts.

Staff turnover after this three-month period was minimal. Even the physical shortcomings were inconsequential to most people, so inspiring, it seems, was the atmosphere during these pioneering early years. Part of this was the fact that, like the Top Deck crew, Flight Centre consultants were kept constantly busy. 'The business just *roared*,' Jenny Goldburg confirms. 'There was never a slow month.'

But a larger part was Flight Centre's complete disregard for the establishment, and the corresponding lack of rules and regulations. This gave people an unprecedented level of independence. For consultants, the lack of restraint translated into exhilarating freedom. People could drink, smoke and swear in their stores, as long as they made money. People sold the airlines and products that they preferred, and competed with each other, and their sister shops, for sales. Two Flight Centre stores on a city street might promote entirely different wholesalers. One shop would be the top seller of, say, Jetset Holidays, while the other only sold Creative Tours products.

It was a combination of this independence, the commission-based wages and the industry opposition that created what Flight Centre called its 'mongrel dog' approach. This was an interesting sales tactic. Like a mongrel dog of uncertain parentage, Flight Centre consultants had little interest in the traditional approach; they used their energy and tenacity to get bookings and outperform their competitors. Shane 'Flynnie' Flynn* sums it up nicely: 'If we were in a scrap we were always going to win it.'

Consultants would do anything and everything to get bookings, adding to their unenviable reputation as they did so. Kim Tomlinson, a Qantas reservations manager at the time, remembers receiving regular irate phone calls from rival travel agents along the lines of: 'Those bloody Flight Centre people have stolen my client. They're making my life *hell*.' Another airline representative recalls how a Flight Centre consultant clinched a deal on a Fiji trip for 100 people by reducing her profit down to $5 a person, much to the disgust of others in the industry who had been competing for the booking. Not only did the consultant get the sale, but she also sold travel insurance and accommodation, and made commission on these products as well.

Some of the 'mongrel dog' stories are almost unbelievable. Robyn Blacklock quoted a client then discovered a cheaper fare after the woman had left the shop. Having failed to get a contact number for the client, Robyn begged the shopping centre manager to let her use the public address system and called out: 'Could Miss Singh going to Hong Kong please return to the Flight Centre. I have found a cheaper fare for you.' The customer came back and Robyn got the booking.

Another consultant advertised a cheap fare in the local newspaper. When he had twenty definite bookings he went to the airline and negotiated a special deal, based on the confirmed seats that he was holding. Fortunately for him, the deal was better than the price he had advertised.

Over the Tasman on New Zealand's South Island, Nelson Flight Centre's Margje de Groot* became an instant legend when she chartered an Aeroflot plane to bring 126 Russian seamen to join a fishing fleet in New Zealand. 'I made a lot of money but it took a lot of effort,' she admits. The plane had to come via Sydney so Australian transit visas were required; the problem was that Margje had no way of obtaining all the passengers' names. The Australian government granted a special dispensation, on the condition that the Russians didn't leave the plane when it landed for refuelling. 'Of course they all poured onto the tarmac,' she continues, 'drinking vodka and smoking cigarettes.' But greater drama was to come: 'On the return journey, New Zealand immigration made me hold on to everyone's passports and boarding passes, to make sure they all returned to Russia. Somewhere between them collecting their documents and boarding the plane, we lost seven of them – they were never found.'

Lynaire Monnery booked everybody she came into contact with. The list is almost frightening: 'My doctor, gynaecologist, dentist, dentist's receptionist, obstetrician, obstetrician's nurse, gastroenterologist, paediatrician, house-washer, gardener, people on planes, people away on holiday at the same destination as me, my husband's work colleagues, my builder, my carpet-layer, my local real estate agents, car salesmen, local bowling club members, my parents' friends, five famous All Blacks, pilots off domestic/international flights, my tennis coach, my pharmacist, my hairdresser, retail shop staff from clothing stores, my brother's boss, my daughter's school teachers . . .' Not surprisingly, Lynnaire became one of the company's top consultants.

The excitement that people felt working for Flight Centre was contagious, cult-like even. Enthusiastic consultants converted their friends and family, and many recruits were ex-clients, who became enthralled with the revolutionary nature of Flight Centre's operation.

Having fun was an integral part of the work environment, and was actively encouraged by the partners. It led to many practical jokes, this one courtesy of Dave Churchman in Christchurch: 'A new consultant in my shop misquoted a client travelling on Air New Zealand. I told her to ring up the airline and say "The eagle has landed", and they would fix it up. She did, and they just said, *"What the hell are you talking about?"'*

Social activities were a good way for people to let off steam, and there were regular organised get-togethers. On Friday evenings it was common to see a client enquiring about fares with a consultant at one end of the counter, while twenty Flight Centre people would be whooping it up on cheap wine and beer at the other end (hopefully not to the annoyance of the customer). For a company that was cash poor, even in these early days Flight Centre invested heavily in such activities. But the amount was repaid in goodwill many times over.

The Flight Centre partners were always involved in these gatherings. Jim Goldburg describes a managers' conference at Olims Hotel in Sydney: 'Skroo got a cheap deal as it was still under construction. We had to climb over scaffolding to get into our rooms, and the ceilings leaked. The first night we had a big party. Someone cut up pieces of soap to look like white chocolate, and we were all so drunk we ate it. Skroo and I had races on room-service trolleys up and down the hallway.'

Almost every Flight Centre person, past and present, has any number of tales of wild times at conferences, award nights and other social get-togethers. The only thing that differentiates them is the level of outrageous behaviour involved. Flight Centre's newsletters provide ample photographic evidence of such exploits and also contain gossip, titbits and many original contributions pertaining to these social events. They make for an interesting read.

For many in the company, there was excitement enough in Flight Centre's rapid expansion, and the sense of being in the right place at the right time. Many new recruits experienced a meteoric rise through the ranks. Not only could they become an instant travel consultant, but within six months they might be manager of their own store. For his part, Wayne Ackerfeld was amazed at the speed of shop openings. 'How can we have two shops in the one city?' he asked his boss when the Little Bourke Street office was joined by another inner Melbourne office. Soon enough, there were four in the Victorian capital.

By all accounts, Graham Turner was the driving force behind this growth. 'Skroo would go out for a few hours and come back with three leases in his pocket,' Jim Goldburg remembers. 'I'd ask when they were opening and he'd say, "Yesterday – and can you pay for them today?"'

Not everyone was happy with this rapid growth, however. Having provided the model for Flight Centre's stores and successfully run the very first shop, in Sydney, Dave Tonkin left early on, in February 1983. He was only 26 at the time and had no desire to build or be part of building an empire. He could see that Skroo was intent on ploughing profits back into the business to open more and more shops. 'My wife and I were more about living for the moment,' he says by way of comparison. 'We preferred to spend the money.' As Sydney Flight Centre was already making in excess of $100,000 per annum and profits were growing rapidly, they saw no need to be part of a larger, more structured organisation.

Dave bought Top Deck's half-share in Sydney Flight Centre for $90,000. This store remained profitable until the 1990s, when he closed it down and set up the high-profile e-commerce company travel.com instead, one of Australia's first online travel companies. Travel.com floated in 1999 but struggled to make profits. The company lost a combined $13.6 million in the 2001/02 and 2002/03 financial years, although Tonkin had resigned by August 2002.

'Travel.com was a little early for its time,' he reflects, 'but it and other online ventures remain the future of travel retailing. Unfortunately the market in Australia is too small for the successes achieved by online travel companies in the USA and Europe. I think travel.com will thrive in the years to come.' (He may be right – travel.com's loss for 2004 was a comparatively low $352,944. The company remains in operation in 2013 and still proclaims to be the company that created travel on the internet.)

While Dave Tonkin went his own way, the Top Deck partners retained the rights to the Flight Centre name and concept to roll out more shops. This was a masterstroke on their part.

Flight Centre realised that for the sake of the future it needed to create a single business entity. The splintered ownership arrangement of the early days was too unwieldy when it came to things such as bank guarantees, shop leases and company returns. This was adding a substantial amount of costs to the bottom line. At the same time, though, the partners wanted to continue to give their managers the ability to invest in their own shops. 'We realised that we needed to own the business outright,' Skroo explains, 'but we didn't want to stifle people's *feeling* of ownership in the business.' The near-bankruptcy of Top Deck had taught the company the importance of this.

After several months of brainstorming, they came up with an idea. Bill James explains: 'Existing managers who had equity in their shops were re-signed onto what was called a "debenture" scheme. This meant the managers still received the same percentage of profit share in their shop, but they no longer held equity.' When someone wanted to leave the company, Flight Centre had a guaranteed payout formula, based on factors such as the increase in shop profits and the number of years the debenture had been held. 'There was no real resistance,' James says, 'as people felt the formula was fair.'

In practice this gave debenture holders more security. Their profit share remained unchanged, and their payout, if they chose to leave the company, was based on a set formula rather than an arbitrary, undetermined figure. It was now easier for them to liquidate their asset if they chose, without involved negotiations. Because Flight Centre was a private company, the loss of equity was inconsequential at this point. There would be a few regrets, however, when the company floated in 1995.

By 1987 it was becoming apparent that the Flight Centre operation was where the Top Deck partners should focus their energies. The business was making a lot of money, but if they were to take it to the next step, they'd need more time and energy. It was now that Skroo, Bill and Mick decided to sell the Top Deck tour operation. None of them wanted to live in London long-term, and with the near-bankruptcy of 1982 still fresh in their minds, they were uncomfortable owning a business that they weren't administering.

After they'd announced their intentions, five of the division managers formed a consortium and decided to buy the business. They paid Turner, James and Carroll £150,000 each for their combined 75 per cent stake (the other quarter-share having been split among the nine division leaders already, of course).

Over the next three-and-a-half years under the guidance of Chris Greive, who became the new MD, the company's value tripled – a result of continuing profit growth and appreciating property assets. By 1990 Murgha Mack bought out the other division leaders for £367,000 each, giving Top Deck a value of £1,835,000. This was a fabulous return, considering that Skroo had given them their original shares for free.

Unfortunately for Mack, that same year saw the start of an economic recession, as a result of which interest rates spiralled out of control. The Gulf War, Chernobyl and a major fire at the farm in Woking, which destroyed the workshop and several buses, followed soon after. In the meantime, the company had centralised administration again. The business eventually went into a decline until 2003 when, 30 years after it began, it was purchased by another consortium. Turner was one of the buyers, and with Chris Greive, Geoff Harris, Peter Barrow and Bill James, currently holds a 20 per cent stake in the company. At the time of writing, Top Deck Travel is running and expanding rapidly under the stewardship of James Nathan, an entrepreneur in tour operations and one of the part-owners. It will be interesting to see what happens next.

Following the sale of Top Deck, Mick Carroll was effectively out of a job, so he returned to Sydney to take up a place within the Flight Centre operation. This marked the beginning of the partners' first major conflict. 'There was no role in Sydney for Mick,' Skroo explains, 'as Bill was already there and wasn't keen to move.'

The partners advised Carroll that he would have to manage a NSW Flight Centre shop until something else came up. It came as something of a rude shock to Mick, who felt that after his years of loyal service running the UK, he couldn't go back to managing a shop, especially when a relative newcomer like Harris was running the whole of Victoria. But Turner was committed to the principle of no jobs for the boys. This was the crux of the dilemma.

The consequence of this unfortunate falling out would become the source of the greatest 'if only' story in Flight Centre's history. After twelve months of heated negotiations, Mick was forced to sell out. 'In hindsight I should've taken the manager's position offered,' he admits today. 'But this was too demeaning for me at the time.' He received $440,000 for his shares, which was a good price in 1988. It would pale into insignificance, however, compared to the $12 million he would've got when Flight Centre floated seven years later. Skroo puts the situation into perspective, though: 'The '80s were a time of high risk for us. We might have gone broke, and then Mick would have been glad to get his $440,000.'

Despite the altercation, Mick remembers his Top Deck days with pleasure, and he, Skroo and Bill still rate each other as friends. 'I had an enjoyable twelve years,' he says, 'with some tough financial stints and long cold winters. But these were outweighed by the business experience I gained, the large number of people I met and the fun I had living and working in different cultures overseas.'

His departure left a gap in Flight Centre's shareholding. Turner, James, Harris and Carroll had owned a quarter of the company each, so 25 per cent was now up for grabs. Jim Goldburg, the company's senior accountant, petitioned Skroo to let him buy in and ended up with 13 per cent, after Turner and Geoff Harris had each taken another 5 per cent. Don McKellow, an ex-pilot and Flight Centre's first 'airfares manager', was offered the remaining 2 per cent share. (He bought in, but the failure of his marriage in 1990 would result in him leaving the company. He would sell 1 per cent each to Bill and Jim.)

Thus the new shareholders became:

- Graham Turner   30 per cent
- Geoff Harris   30 per cent
- Bill James   25 per cent
- Jim Goldburg   13 per cent
- Don McKellow   2 per cent.

Even Geoff Harris questioned his future with Flight Centre. He owned 50 per cent of the Melbourne shops, which by 1987 were making a total of $300,000 profit each year. 'Why share his three hundred thousand with Top Deck?' Bill reasons. 'Why not do as Dave Tonkin had done – split with Top Deck, go it alone and pocket the lot? He would have been set for life.'

But he didn't. After discussing the idea with the other two senior partners, Geoff decided to stay. Bill summed it up: 'I guess Geoff harboured the same gut feeling that I did: with Skroo's foresight, passion and ambition combined with our own joint endeavours, one day the whole might exceed the sum of the individual parts.' They would be thankful for this instinct in the years to come.

Others shared this feeling. Flight Centre was raw and new but there was something special about the company. In Robyn Blacklock's words: 'Flight Centre had this absolute trust and belief in you. Even your own parents don't give you that.'

So even in these early days, many of the ingredients for Flight Centre's future achievements were already in place. Yet the company would need more than this to succeed in the long term. Fun and a spirit of adventure were no substitute for organisational efficiency. Mavericks were good innovators but they were difficult to harness. And all the while, strong-willed managers clashed constantly over the right way forward for the business. For, although most of the shops were going great guns, there were still a number of loss-making stores that threatened to pull the whole company down. This, then, was Flight Centre in 1987. Without some major changes it would be lucky to survive another decade.

Chapter 4

FROM COWBOYS TO CORPORATES

I want our shops to stand out like dogs' balls.

Graham 'Skroo' Turner

B angkok, November 1987. In a room on the ninth floor of the Montien Hotel, 30 Flight Centre managers had gathered together for a conference. Geoff Harris, partner and state leader of Victoria, stood up and addressed the group. 'Could you please take out your business card and place it on the table,' he said. Everyone did. 'What do you see?'

The managers looked around. The cards were every colour of the rainbow. There were aeroplane logos, world globes and even an Australian flag. Some were rectangular and some were square. One was in the shape of a beer coaster. There were matt cards, glossy cards, cards with raised print and cards with rippled edges. What struck home immediately was that no two business cards were alike.

The people who were sitting around that table agree that this was an unheralded turning point in Flight Centre's history, a spectacular wrench of the flywheel. Without this exercise, the managers would never have agreed on the need for a single business model. And without this model, it is doubtful whether Flight Centre would have become the national, let alone global, success it is today.

How did this come about? By 1987 the Flight Centre operation had mushroomed to over 30 stores. And like the wide variety of business card designs, the company's identity was spread across a multitude of shop names: Flight Centre, Top Deck, The Flight Shop, Flight and Travel Centre, Sydney Travel Group and even Bon Voyage Travel. The company was paying a price for this undisciplined growth. As Turner says now: 'Some shops were making big profits, while others struggled with losses. This inconsistency seemed inexplicable.'

The problem perplexed the Flight Centre partners until they each read a book called *The E-Myth*, by Michael Gerber,[18] the chairman of a company that specialised in re-engineering small businesses. His argument was simple: standard best-practice systems rather than entrepreneurial flair were the building blocks of a successful company. This was in complete contrast to the way the Flight Centre partners ran their operation, but it made sense. Now the reason for Flight Centre's unpredictable results became clear.

Gerber used McDonald's as an example. Ray Kroc, the founder of the multi-billion-dollar food franchise, worked on a prototype that documented every facet of the business – from the time the french fries should be left in the warming bin, to the colour of the restaurants, to the way employees should greet customers. In effect he provided the franchisee with an entire system of doing business. A system that would work once it was sold, no matter who bought it. And in doing so he created one of the most successful small businesses in the world.

Michael Gerber believed that other organisations could use Kroc's idea to create their own business model. Or, as he put it, 'create a business whose results are systems-dependent, rather than people dependent'.[19] This was a revelation to the Flight Centre partners. They realised that their shops didn't have *any* standard systems, in any department. They were completely dependent on the whims of the people in charge, a situation that they'd actively encouraged. This was why the shops' results were so varied. If Flight Centre was to keep expanding, then it needed a workable business model, made up of standard best-practice systems that could be copied by anyone, anywhere.

This vision was Flight Centre's first step on the road to professionalism. Yet the path would not be an easy one. The Flight Centre pioneers were like cowboys – tough, independent and scornful of authority – and again, this was something the partners had welcomed at the start, and it had served them very well in most cases. The business card exercise had been an ingenious device to make everyone aware of the need for change. But, as Geoff says, 'The devil was in the detail.'

Everybody thought that their way was the best way. And since the managers were all highly motivated, high-achieving individuals, tempers flared when people found that others didn't necessarily agree with them. 'We had always listened to the people who made the loudest noise,' Skroo recalls, 'even though sometimes they were our poorest performers. After reading *The E-Myth* we realised that our systems should be determined by those who were a proven success within the company.'

As the discussion continued at Bangkok's Montien, managers began to grasp that a standard business model meant they would have to change the way that *they* operated. Many didn't want to do this. One woman was so incensed at the style of uniform chosen, for instance, that she sat down cross-legged in the middle of the floor and said: 'There's no way I'm going to wear that. I'm going to wear what *I* want to wear.'

There was a heated debate about whether the print on the business cards should be raised or non-raised. There were even fights over whether the brochure-holders out the front of the shops should have holes in the bottom to stop people urinating in them.

Colin Schirmer was one manager who didn't want any part of Flight Centre's new direction. He had a shouting match with Harris and reportedly said: 'I've had enough of this bullshit. I'm going to piss off.' So he did. After several months of negotiation he sold his share in Southern Cross Flight Centre and went on to own his own Top Deck Travel business in South Australia and run it *his* way. Schirmer wasn't the company's only commercial casualty. By December 1997 Lew Pulbrook at the Sydney Travel Group/Bon Voyage Travel, Peter Doyle at Top Deck Travel in Queen Street and South Yarra, Melbourne, and John Cook at the Flight and Travel Centre and Westcoast Flight Centre in Perth had also left or been bought out. However, the sheer magnitude of what could be achieved by standardising the Flight

Centre operations under one umbrella was a strong enough incentive for most leaders to stay. After two days of debate in Bangkok they eventually agreed on what were to become the mainstays of Flight Centre's operation.

Their strategy was simple. Rather than competing with the 4000 travel agencies in Australia and fight for 75 per cent of the retail travel market, the company would target the 25 per cent of passengers who still booked directly with airlines. From this point on, they would be 'airfare specialists'.

They needed a name to reflect this, and settled on 'Flight Centres International' (FCI). It was ironic that Flight Centre had no overseas shops at this time, yet in 1994, when the company began a serious attack on the global market, the partners chose to remove the word 'International' from the company title.[20]

The new name was applied to all shops. There would be no more 'Flight Shop's or 'Top Deck's; all stores would become Flight Centres, with their actual name determined by their location. For instance, a shop in the suburb of Clayfield would become 'Clayfield Flight Centre', while the one in George Street in Sydney's city centre would be known as 'George Street Flight Centre'.

Although this was a major change, Flight Centre – that is, Flight Centres International[21] – had much grander plans. Gerber had quoted Tom Watson, the founder of IBM, on his views regarding the computer giant's success: 'I had a very clear picture of what the company would look like when it was finally done . . . I realised that for IBM to become a great company, it had to act like a great company long before it ever became one.'[22] In accordance with this principle, Flight Centre came up with a vision of what the company would look like in the future. Geoff Harris explains: 'Our long-range market strategy was to have a Flight Centre in every major city and suburb that we operated in worldwide. We decided to create a market identity so that people would go to their local Flight Centre, rather than the airline or local travel agent, when they wanted to book a flight.'

Considering that they had 35 shops at the time, this plan was very ambitious. It also required a number of physical changes to transform

it into a reality. In a newsletter distributed after the Bangkok conference, Harris wrote, 'By the end of 1988 all shops will have standard
shopfronts, uniforms, marketing, administration and an office operating manual in place.' This was a substantial undertaking, not to
mention a huge about-turn from the hands-off, 'anything goes'
approach of Top Deck days and Flight Centre's first five years. 'We'd
allowed everyone to operate fairly independently up to this point,'
admits Skroo, 'but we *had* to change our approach. Otherwise we
were never going to have ten, fifty or a hundred shops all operating
well and profitably.'

The first step was to re-brand the stores. Turner wanted them to
'stand out like dog's balls', so they were painted fire-engine red, the
colour of Qantas, which was the dominant airline at the time. The
word 'Flight Centre' in large red letters, with a white or black outline,
was emblazoned across the top of the shop, with the smaller 'Discount
Flight Specialists' underneath. In the window was a large Airfares
board with a horde of destinations and prices, as well as a Discount
Flight Specials board with about six 'special' fares. A crude Concorde-
type aircraft was used as the logo.

Inside the shop, red carpets and curtains, and airline-style counters
with stools completed the new look. The counters were particularly
important because they took up less space than traditional office
furniture, such as tables and chairs. In this way, the company could
lease smaller shops and pay lower rent for the same number of people.
Flight Centre thus had a financial edge over its competitors, allowing
them to genuinely sell cheaper flights. The interiors also appealed to
its clients, who didn't feel like they were paying for fancy overheads.

Oddly enough though, the new shops didn't tempt Flight Centre's
competitors, like Danny Roche. 'We couldn't believe that clients who
were spending $50,000 on their travel would want to sit on a stool for
ten minutes to discuss their holiday,' the rival agency manager says.
'We had big desks with comfortable chairs for the client, and we
would spend four or five hours with each person.'

But it was Flight Centre's new marketing strategies that would
really cement its position at the forefront of the industry. Predictably,

given his background in advertising and marketing, Geoff Harris was the man behind this coup: 'We placed ads in the Airline section of the Yellow Pages under the heading "Reservation Hotline Offering Expert Advice on All Airlines". No other major travel agency group was doing this at the time, so we had no competition.'

Next they decided to advertise on television, the first travel retailer do so. (In fact, in Queensland they were the only travel agents to advertise on television for several years.) Unlike the press ads of the time, they didn't use shots of beaches or pretty scenery to sell tickets. In what would become their standard modus operandi, they focused solely on price. Starting in September 1988, Flight Centre blitzed the market with images of an airline captain offering cheap airfares.

The captain was the subject of much derision. 'Dorky' and 'annoying' were just a few of the words people used to describe his lack of glamour. Still, it was his very ordinariness that worked. 'We proved this a few years later,' Skroo recalls. 'Our marketing guys were always complaining about how awful the captain was so we took him off our ads for a while. Our enquiry level dropped so we brought him back again. The fact that people had a negative reaction to him was actually a positive thing – he made a real impression.'

From this time on, Flight Centre would always feature the pilot character in its advertisements. In 2004 the captain was a real-life airline pilot working for Eva Airways, the Taiwanese airline. Some had been paid actors. (In a strange twist of fate, Tony Gordon, the original captain, died in a plane crash in 2000.)

The bigger splash in the ongoing marketing campaign was due to Flight Centre's adoption of a new slogan, starting in 1988. The need for this came about when Turner went to an advertising agency to organise the TV advertising and was met with the question: 'What's your USP?' He was somewhat taken aback: 'I'd never even heard of this concept before. I thought it was some form of contraception.' He now concentrated on finding a 'unique selling point' that would differentiate Flight Centre from the rest of the marketplace.

At this stage the company's slogan was 'Discount Flight Specialists', but the partners didn't feel this was strong enough to be a USP. There were many travel agents who discounted flights in Australia. Flight Centre only sold international airfares, but there were others doing this as well. So there was nothing unique about either of these aspects of the business.

After much discussion, Turner ended up 'borrowing' a USP from another company. 'Skroo saw an advertisement in the Sydney Yellow Pages for a company called Tymtro Travel,' Bill James remembers. 'It said: "Lowest Airfares Guaranteed". He ripped the ad out, folded it up and said, "All of our ads are going to look like this from now on."'

This hookline would change the whole face of Flight Centre, although its implementation would be far from straightforward. Many consultants hated the concept. Their opposition stemmed from the fact that the only way they could back up the guarantee was to cut their own mark-up price. As each consultant took a percentage of the profits of each booking, this directly affected his or her salary.

The counter-argument was that an effective marketing slogan that was backed up in practice would generate a lot of extra enquiry. This would bring in more money than people would ever have to pay out to stand by the guarantee. Many of the consultants still weren't convinced. Arguments ranged back and forth as people tried to persuade Skroo to can the whole idea.

This conflict was in addition to the many small battles waging around Flight Centre as the ideas of the Bangkok Conference began to take effect. Some managers who had agreed in principle at first were now horrified at the cost of getting their shops re-branded. Others simply disliked the conformity. The uniforms were one thing, of course, another was Turner's insistence that all shops become cigarette-free zones – a decree that outraged the company's many avid smokers. Flight Centre's managers' meetings became battlegrounds as people raged over the new policies, and Skroo's argument for the 'Lowest Airfares Guaranteed' slogan only added more fuel to the fire.

But he wouldn't budge: 'We decided to trial the guarantee on television and in press ads to measure the effect. We found our enquiry level *quadrupled*, virtually overnight.' In addition to this, consultants found that the number of people that they had to pay out was less than one a week. Resistance began to evaporate.

It would take some time to implement it across the board. The Flight Centre partners realised that there was no point paying lip-service to a slogan. If they guaranteed lowest airfares, then they had to offer the lowest airfares to every single customer, and this was hard to police on a day-to-day basis. Some salespeople were still reluctant to beat fares if it meant they lost revenue. They simply said they couldn't beat a rival's fare and turned the customer away.

To maintain credibility, the partners came up with the idea of a price-beating bank account. This gave real teeth to the guarantee. Rather than consultants having to pay to beat a lower quoted fare out of their own commission, they could now claim the difference out of this account. Hence the client got the lowest price and the consultant still made money on the booking. (In one year alone, Flight Centre paid out over $3 million from this account to beat 160,000 cheaper quotes from its competitors.)

'Lowest Airfares Guaranteed' evolved over the years to become a great marketing tool for Flight Centre. This is undisputed in the industry, where it's acknowledged that the company virtually owns this marketing niche. Other variations over time have included 'Cheaper than the Internet' and 'Unbeatable'. Even in the early days, these slogans had a substantial impact. Tom Kenny, who was then Singapore Airlines' Queensland sales representative, recalls: 'We used to get some adverse feedback from time to time from clients about how amateur Flight Centre was. We'd ask, "So why did you book with them?" And they'd go, "The price." Then we'd ask the client if they would use them again, and nine times out of ten they would say, "If the price is right."'

Price was the engine that drove Flight Centre and it led to many innovations. For Flight Centre consultants of the late 1980s to become true airfare specialists they needed more than re-branded shops and effective marketing. As successful and as necessary as these *E-Myth*–inspired measures were, the company needed to change some of its back-end operations as well. For instance, if Flight Centre could find a system to deal with the hundreds of fluctuating airfares in the marketplace, it could jump on specials the moment they came out. This would give the salespeople a distinct advantage over their competitors.

In late 1987 the company decided to employ airfare coordinators in every state. Their role was to become airfare experts, provide cut-throat prices and information to the retail consultants, and build good relations with the airlines. This was a major expense to the developing company, but the investment paid off. As Brian Egan, national manager for Malaysia Airlines, says: 'This gave Flight Centre unprece-dented contact with their local airline representatives. Later on, other travel agents introduced airfare coordinators, but only ever at national level, so they never built up the same relationships.'

The airfare coordinators' job became easier within months of their introduction when Flight Centre became the first major travel agency chain in Australia to introduce a central reservation system (CRS) into all its shops. Many airlines had computerised their reservation systems in the '70s, but travel agents were only just beginning to realise that this was the way to go. 'Computerisation was scary,' Wintergarden consultant Ian Knights admits. 'You made a reservation and then you were terrified as to whether it would generate to the airlines and the passengers would actually get their seats on the plane.'

With the introduction of computers, Flight Centre people could check availability and make bookings on the spot. This gave them a substantial advantage over non-computerised agents, who had to make reservations via time-consuming phone calls to airline offices. And the accidental discovery of another aspect of the computer system would give the company an even greater competitive edge.

Don McKellow, Flight Centre's airfares manager, discovered that the new system had a function to store information, like a notepad. This solved a major problem for him. Up to this point Flight Centre had kept its consultants up to date with photocopied spreadsheets of prices to different destinations. This method was very work-intensive and some prices were obsolete before they were even sent out by courier to the shops.

Don realised he could use the notepad facility in the new CRS system to automate pricing pages. The airfare coordinators now scrapped the old spreadsheet system and loaded all the fares onto the new pricing 'grids', as they became known. Consultants typed in a destination and all the current prices appeared on a single page in front of them. The airlines' rules for each airfare (such as what stopovers a client could take en route) were just a click away. Flight Centre could now quote clients on the spot and in a third of the time. Best of all for the company, it would be at least another five years before the rest of the industry changed over to computerised pricing.

By 1989, Flight Centre consultants were well on the way to becoming airfare specialists. The company had over 1500 pricing grids, with tens of thousands of airfares in the system, and people could quote fares, check availability and book flights with ease. Marg Mulholland, one of Queensland's first owner–managers, remembers this well: 'Our airfare coordinators had became so up to date that they sometimes found themselves in the bizarre position of advising a regional airline office about its own fares when the airline's Sydney head office hadn't told it about the changes.'

There was still one obstacle remaining. At this stage Flight Centre consultants bought their airline tickets from the traditional industry 'consolidators', who acted as middlemen between airlines and retailers. The consultants couldn't negotiate their own deals with airlines based on volume of business and they had no control over the timing or accuracy of airline tickets. This was a real handicap.

Jetset Fares and Ticketing was the dominant consolidator in 1989. This outfit was so important to Flight Centre's operation that the partners had even discussed whether they should become Jetset agents and paint all their shops Jetset blue. There were two reasons why this never happened. One was the very differing cultures of the companies, as Geoff Harris remembers: 'We went for a meeting at Jetset's head office. Not only were we amazed at the opulence of their furnishings, but we were even more astounded when a butler took our coats.'

The second reason was the real catalyst. As Flight Centre grew bigger and sent more ticket requests through, Jetset's service deteriorated. The company simply couldn't handle the extra pressure. Tickets were often late, and when they did arrive, some had the wrong dates, names or destinations on them. Jetset's accounting system was also inadequate to deal with the volume. Flight Centre consultants wasted a lot of time trying to reconcile inaccurate account statements and had to deal with many customer complaints about incorrect tickets.

'We realised that if we wanted to control our own destiny, we would have to start doing our own ticketing,' Skroo says today, before adding that they never actually expected to make any money out of the exercise. They also knew it wouldn't be easy. Flight Centre would need an IATA licence, which was difficult to get, and it would have to negotiate individual deals with each airline. Another necessity would be the invention and adoption of an entirely new business model – one that was very different from its core business of selling flights.

Despite these obstacles, in July 1989, Flight Centre set up its first Ticket Centre in an office above Queen Street Flight Centre in Brisbane. It was a small operation, run by Kelly Marshall, with three others handwriting tickets and couriering them to each shop. This allowed shop managers to focus on selling travel without having to worry about doing their own ticketing.

But the Ticket Centre's biggest handicap was its lack of airline deals. Up until this stage the airfare coordinators had dealt mainly with each airline's administration arm in their bid to get airfares out to the stores quickly and efficiently. With the advent of the Ticket Centre, the company now had to build up contacts with the airline representatives in charge of sales contracts. This was more problematic, and the ticketing operation started with just two carriers on board: United Airlines and British Airways.

The reason for the Ticket Centre's struggles was twofold. Firstly, the established consolidators didn't want to lose the revenue that

Flight Centre gave them, and so used their considerable influence with the airlines to thwart the company's plans. This revenue was substantial and the consolidators were taking all the credit for this business with the airlines.

The other reason was that Flight Centre still suffered from a credibility problem. 'Flight Centre were bucket shops,' Kim Tomlinson of Qantas says, 'and this was the bottom of the food chain as far as most airlines were concerned.' Singapore Airlines' Tom Kenny agrees: 'When I decided to give Flight Centre in Queensland a special fare, I sent a message to my counterparts in Singapore Airlines around Australia to tell them what I was doing, to see if they wanted to match it in their regions. All these anguished messages came back saying, "What are you doing? We don't deal with *bucket shops*."'

This was typical. Those who decided to give Flight Centre a deal were given a very hard time by others in the industry. Garry Court, who was the general manager of Air New Zealand, one of the very last airlines to come around, remembers feeling like he'd 'nearly started World War III' after he finally gave the company a direct deal: 'When I announced it at a meeting with Jetset in Melbourne, the managers were so incensed that I was asked to leave the building and escorted out.'

The Ticket Centre's first few deals gave it more bargaining power with other airlines. Kelly Marshall describes the approach her team took: 'We decided to use the fact that Qantas had vowed not to give us a deal as a positive. We'd say to other airlines, "We're not going to have the Qantas deal so we'll give you all that business as well." Once these airlines could measure the volume of business coming from Flight Centre, their whole attitude changed. Those airlines that had once denigrated Flight Centre as a bucket-shop operator now saw them as a major revenue source.'

Another plus for Flight Centre was that, unlike other agencies, its ticket numbers kept increasing. So, although to some extent Kelly's people would simply make up a figure for the amount of revenue an airline could expect to get from dealing direct, the constant arrival of new Flight Centre shops ensured that they were generally able to deliver. But even as airline opposition started to crumble, the ticketing operation faced another threat, this time from within. For, as airline deals and volumes increased, the Ticket Centre began to be dogged by the same administrative problems as its competitors.

Geoff Lomas took over as manager in 1990. 'The Ticket Centre's first accounting system was one that Skroo had borrowed from a mate,' he explains. 'Its efficiency can be measured by the fact that, in the first year, no one had any idea of what the Ticket Centre's financial position actually was.'[23] The company had bought a computerised ticketing system, but this was also inadequate for high volumes. With no mandate to buy their airfares through the Ticket Centre, dissatisfied Flight Centre consultants now began to defect back to their original consolidators.

This was possible because Flight Centre didn't force its shops to use specific suppliers. It was up to the Ticket Centre people to convince consultants to use them. If they didn't offer the best service and prices, the front-line people could buy their tickets elsewhere. This was an ongoing source of frustration for external suppliers, but the company saw it as the only way to ensure standards of service and delivery.

When Spy took the reins, the Ticket Centre had a lot of ground to recover: 'By this stage there was a real "us and them" attitude. The ticketers, who felt they were doing their best for the consultants under very trying conditions, were handling a lot of complaints.' Over the next few years the Ticket Centre focused on buying new systems that worked, getting more airline deals and rebuilding bridges with Flight Centre's retail staff.

The recovery would be more than the company had ever hoped for. The Ticket Centre became an industry giant, offering exceptional service and 24-hour turnaround on tickets. It also became a prototype for other businesses. Rather than ticketing directly with consolidators, by 2004 such conglomerates as American Express–Travelscene and Jetset–Travelworld businesses had pooled resources and set up their own internal ticketing areas. The golden age of consolidation was over and many companies such as Jetset Fares and Ticketing had gone out of business.

The Ticket Centre's greatest feat, however, was that it became Flight Centre's most profitable business. Considering that the company had no interest in the area of consolidation and was forced to learn by experience, this was quite an accomplishment. By 2004, with Ticket Centres in every global area, the business's annual profit was $28 million, making a mockery of Flight Centre's early belief that it would be a loss-maker.

The success of the Ticket Centre also repaid the airlines that had backed it. Garry Court remembers this with satisfaction: 'In the late '80s, Air New Zealand did four million dollars of business with Flight Centre. By the late '90s it was fifty million. At that stage I felt my original decision to give them a direct deal had been vindicated.' And by ticketing such substantial amounts with airlines, Flight Centre was able to negotiate far better airfare prices for its customers. Thus the Ticket Centre became the driving force behind Flight Centre's 'Lowest Airfares' guarantee.

There was one final piece of strategy required to complete Flight Centre's transformation. This was the need for standard systems within the day-to-day operation. Over time, Flight Centre documented its best practices into a Systems Manual. Each business had a copy outlining the key processes in areas such as sales and service, staffing and training, communication, finance, marketing and technology. This manual was eventually renamed 'the Profit Guide' and became an important reference tool. It gave the operation a consistency that had been lacking in the past.

Flight Centre's belief in standard best-practice systems became a company philosophy:

> In our businesses there is one best way and everybody operates that way. However, by welcoming change, by valuing common sense over conventional wisdom, and through commitment to continuous improvement, we will change to a clearly superior way if it is demon-

strated and proven. We encourage open communication and sharing of power, so that, as individuals, we can make a difference.[24]

This set the framework for constant innovation. Rather than complaining about something, consultants were encouraged to come up with a better idea, prove it, and then it would become standard practice. 'Flight Centre has a lot geared up behind the scenes,' admits Brian Egan from Malaysian. 'It's like that duck on the lake. It looks serene on the surface, but underneath the water its legs are going like the clappers.'

'Flight Centre is so good at change,' enthuses Wayne Ackerfeld, a man who has worked for the company since the start. 'I remember all the things we were never going to change, and then one or two months later they'd be in. For instance, we were only ever going to sell airline tickets and not product; we were never going to sell domestics; we were never going to do our own ticketing; we were never going to buy other businesses; we were never going to be in shopping centres; we were never going to wear uniforms; and we were never going to employ outsiders. Yet when the need is there we just adapt and change.'

None of the changes from the Bangkok conference happened overnight. It took over eighteen months for the existing shops to be remodelled to the new design, rather than the twelve that Geoff Harris had first envisaged. And some employees refused to honour the 'Lowest Airfares Guaranteed' pledge for several years after its introduction. There were even some recalcitrant managers still refusing to wear a uniform well into the 1990s.

The success of Flight Centre's branding exercise was reflected in its increasing profitability – from $1 million in 1987 to over $3.5 million by 1990. And in the long term, the standardised business model was seen as a major triumph. Interbrand, an independent ratings company, continues to list Flight Centre in the top twenty most valuable brands in Australia. An internal survey of clients in the same year showed that nearly half of all the company's enquiries came from shoppers walking past. And ironically, even though Flight Centre's goal was to become 'airfare specialists', by 2003 the company was also the largest retailer of add-on products, such as car hire and accommodation, in Australasia.

Perhaps the biggest lesson Flight Centre learned from *The E-Myth* was that working on the business is as important as working in the business. Without this, it's doubtful that the company would have survived. As Kim Tomlinson points out: 'People's attitude to Flight Centre changed, but that was because they [Flight Centre] changed as well. They turned themselves around and became more professional in their own ranks.'

The cowboys had become corporate players.

Chapter 5

RISKY BUSINESS

I wasn't going to let anything get in the way, not even a war.
Sharyn Bleakley, 1991 Consultant of the Year

On 23 July 1990, Jim Goldburg was tidying his desk before leaving to catch a plane for Hawaii. Flight Centre was holding a managers' conference in Waikiki and the accountant was looking forward to it. As he threw the last file into his drawer, the phone rang. It was a clerk from the Travel Compensation Fund, a government body that licensed every travel agent in Australia. The conversation was brief, but by the time Jim had hung up from the call, Flight Centre had entered the period that Skroo Turner would later refer to as the 'lowest point in our history'.

There were no warning signs. In fact, most people were upbeat about Flight Centre's future, and they had good reason to be. By 1990, 'Flight Centres International' had over 80 shops in Australia and New Zealand, overall profit was approaching the $3.5 million mark, and all stores over ten months old were in the black. The new business model was an undisputed success. So much so that the partners had even set up three stores overseas, in Los Angeles, San Francisco and London.

Flight Centre had also beefed up its management structure. In July 1990 the partners decided that the company needed a dedicated business leader, now that the state-based model was no longer adequate. With little fanfare, Turner became managing director of the whole operation. 'It was obvious that Skroo was the best person for the job,' Geoff Harris says. 'He was far more talented than the rest of us, in the strategic sense.'

This advancement led to a reshuffle and the emergence of some new talent. Gary 'Boxer' Hogan, a science and media studies graduate, took over Turner's now vacant role and continued Queensland's run as profit leader of Flight Centre for the next few years. Chris Greive, a politics and history graduate, and formerly MD of Top Deck in London after its sale in 1987, became the new MD of Flight Centre New Zealand. He would replicate the Flight Centre model throughout that country, growing it from six stores to over 100 profitable offices; in fact, Flight Centre NZ would outperform the high-density New South Wales area in the early to mid 1990s.

Brian Hickey, an accountant whose comprehensive knowledge of business and finance was only matched by his passion for Bundaberg Rum, became state leader of Western Australia, as well as continuing to oversee Flight Centre's head office finances. Queensland-based shop manager Marg Mulholland was now national airfares coordinator, a key role with the advent of the company's ticketing operation. With Geoff Lomas running the Ticket Centre, Jim Goldburg in charge of overall fnances, Geoff Harris overseeing Victoria, South Australia and Tasmania, and Bill James looking after New South Wales and Canberra, Flight Centre had a leader driving every sector of the business.

For Skroo personally, there was a very real change. 'I'd been a kind of de facto leader up to this point,' he says today, 'but now I had to accept total responsibility for the company. This made a big difference.' One of his first meetings as MD with the other partners was to discuss what would become Flight Centre's 'International Strategic Plan for the Next Five Years'. Bill wrote up their ideas, which included discussions about the company's mission statement and marketing position. The document notes:

> We should continue to call ourselves 'Discount Flight Specialists'.
> This is because most of our competitors could not bear the thought
> of labelling themselves as 'bucket shops'. This is too much like

smelly socks and dirty underwear. Fortunately the general public does not have this perception: they don't know what a 'bucket shop' means.

The partners also wrote down their expansion and financial goals. This was a big step – they had never detailed their plans collectively on paper before. Based on shop growth projections, they worked out where the company would be in five years time. The numbers seemed incredible. They were certainly ambitious.

After the meeting, Turner announced them publicly in an interview published by the travel industry magazine *Travelweek*. The reported goals for Flight Centre were to have 150 locations worldwide, $450 million in turnover a year, and an annual profit of $8 million, all by July 1995. 'We were being a bit outrageous,' he admits now, 'but we needed to convince people we were serious, to get better deals.'

The industry responded with scepticism. David Clarke, who was running Jetset at the time, wasn't alone in thinking that Flight Centre was off in 'cloud cuckoo land'.

The behaviour of the company's new managing director hardly reassured people either. Jenny Lourey, British Airways' area general manager for the Asia–Pacific region, recalls a meeting she had with Skroo to negotiate Flight Centre's annual contract: 'Suddenly he started undressing. As he ripped off his shirt to reveal his bare chest, he must have sensed my surprise – he said, "Don't mind me, I'm just going for a jog." Mind you, he did have *some* sensibilities, as he ducked outside to put his jogging shorts on.'

Brian Egan had a similarly memorable experience when he took a group of travel industry leaders on a Malaysia Airlines 'educational' to Kuala Lumpur. 'We were staying at the exclusive Shangri-La Hotel and we met in the lobby bar in the evening for drinks,' Egan remembers. 'Skroo turned up in his running gear, as he'd been for a jog.' This time the change of clothes was at the insistence of another, the hotel's maitre d', and at least it was carried out away from the eyes of his corporate guests. Even so, this just wasn't the way an industry leader behaved, the traditionalists insisted, especially if he planned to be an industry giant within the next few years.

Turner may have retained his laid-back dress sense but there was nothing casual about his attitude towards Flight Centre's finances. The employment of finance man Brian Hickey in early 1988 ushered in a new era of fiscal responsibility, as he and Goldburg spent the next eighteen months standardising systems and educating everyone to their benefits. By July 1990, half of Flight Centre's shops were achieving a zero trust balance – that is, each shop's written-down receipts of income less its recorded expense payouts equalled the money actually present in its bank account, to the exact dollar, each month. This was a result the partners had once thought impossible. Turner was so optimistic, in fact, that he wrote in a Flight Centre newsletter: 'For the first time in recent history we appear to have our accounts under control.'

Little did he know that with the full adoption of licensing and the Travel Compensation Fund (TCF) in Australia, the company's accounts were about to face their toughest test ever. Flight Centre had misjudged both the extent of these new regulations and the corporate compliance required. The result would be a major setback.

Licensing began in Australia in 1986 when the state parliaments of Victoria, New South Wales and South Australia introduced a Travel Agents Act. Tasmania followed in 1987 and Queensland the year after that. According to Anthony Cordato, the Acts had three purposes:

1. To set standards of experience and qualifications for members of the travel industry, in licensing requirements for travel agents and tour operators, and to set professional standards in management and marketing for travel agents.
2. To set continuing financial requirements for travel agents in conducting their business as travel agencies.

3. To protect the public's money by setting up a Travel Compensation Fund to compensate the public where the public's money has
   been lost through the default of a travel agent or tour operator.[25]

To the partners of Flight Centre, however, the licensing campaign
was simply a way of barring new entrants to the industry. They felt
that the other large chains and the banks were pushing licensing in the
hope that it would decrease competition and possibly save them
from extinction. This suspicion was reinforced by the fact that the
Australian Federation of Travel Agents was one of its most fervent
supporters, even though AFTA members would now be subject to
substantial costs and increased regulatory requirements.

In many ways Flight Centre should've been happy with such a
policy of exclusion. The capital required to set up an agency and pay
the annual bonds to the Travel Compensation Fund would be a big
disincentive to possible future competitors. Hickey counters this,
however: 'Our overriding factor was that we hated government intervention. We couldn't understand why "Let the buyer beware" applied
to every other industry except ours. We couldn't help ourselves.'

Flight Centre would be the only major travel agency group that
publicly opposed licensing, while privately, there was no hiding the
contempt the partners felt for the campaign as soon as it was
announced. 'It is very important that we work hard and pay a lot of
money to keep otherwise unemployable people off the dole and in
the public service,' was how their managing director had put it in a
company newsletter at the time. 'This is the only perceivable benefit I
can see in licensing.' A further issue was that even though travel agents
were responsible for funding 90 per cent of the licensing scheme, the
majority of bankruptcies were by wholesalers such as car rental
companies and tour operators.

Flight Centre believed that it would be the consumer who
suffered, because agents would have to pass on the new costs. Turner
felt that if there had to be consumer protection, by far the best way
was compulsory insurance. An insurer could assess a company's financial viability, and that would determine the level of premium the

company had to pay. This would avoid all the bureaucracy and save consumers a substantial amount in public servant wages and government taxes.

In spite of Flight Centre's vocal opposition, licensing and the newly created Travel Compensation Fund were introduced in all states by 1988. Under the new regimen, Flight Centre had to pay an annual levy for each shop to the TCF. It also had to submit its annual accounts so that the TCF could assess the company's financial viability. So when Jim Goldburg sent in Flight Centre's first audited accounts in early 1990, he assumed that with the profits the company was generating, it would just be a formality.

Jim was wrong. What he hadn't realised was that the TCF's statutory requirements differed from commercial requirements. Under the fund's complex point-scoring system, for instance, some of Flight Centre's income was deemed non-eligible. There was also debate over which assets were fixed and which were current.

Flight Centre produced three-monthly and six-monthly accounts to back up its argument. The company also pointed out that it had over 70 shops in Australia and was making $3.5 million in annual profit. But all to no avail. According to the estimates of the TCF, Flight Centre didn't score enough points to meet the re-licensing provision. Unless the company put another $1 million into the accounts, it would lose its travel agent's licence. This was the news that Goldburg received that day in late July 1990.

'We'd completely underestimated the TCF,' he admits. 'We had to come up with one million dollars in three days. It was such a stressful time that even Skroo couldn't sleep.' The problem was that even though they were trading profitably, they didn't have a spare million. Of Flight Centre's annual income, 39 per cent went to pay taxes, 30 per cent was for manager profit-share payments, and most of the rest went to fund expansion. There was simply no spare cash for unexpected contingencies.

To make matters worse, it was a terrible time to be taking out a loan. The '80s bubble had burst and Australia was heading into an economic recession. Interest rates were spiralling wildly and would

soon hit 17 per cent. With this in mind, Flight Centre tried to negotiate with the TCF. The company could hardly expect to find a sympa-
thetic ear there, however, as Brian Hickey explains: 'The fact that
Skroo had been saying in the press that they were a useless organisation, whose sole effect had been to add costs to airline tickets,
probably didn't help our cause. The TCF put up a pretty tough front.'

The partners felt that because of Flight Centre's size and stature in
the industry, it was unlikely that the TCF would close it down. But
the two parties were unable to reach a compromise. In the end, the
Flight Centre partners were forced to remortgage their homes to come
up with the money. After almost seventeen years of trading since
Argus had chugged off from 9 Mablethorpe Road on that first bus
tour, they had to put it all on the line again. 'We'd only just paid off
our house after the sale of Top Deck,' Jude Turner says, unable to hide
her disbelief, 'and now we had *another* mortgage!'

And this wasn't their only debt. To fund the rapid expansion since
1982, the partners had personally guaranteed every shop lease. They
were now, to use Geoff Harris's words, 'in hock up to our eyeballs'.
But at least they'd satisfied the TCF requirements and the license had
been renewed. The partners breathed a collective sigh of relief.

Their respite was short-lived. On 2 August 1990, Iraq invaded
Kuwait, and four months later, on 17 January 1991, the allied Operation Desert Storm began. Australia was officially at war. Bill James
couldn't believe their bad luck: 'The public was blitzed by television
images of fighter planes, missiles and anti-aircraft attacks directly over
the flight path to Europe. This wasn't good for business.' Brian Egan
of Malaysia Airlines puts it a little more dramatically: 'The Gulf War
murdered the travel industry.'

Many people simply stopped booking. Others cancelled the
holidays they'd booked. One client even pulled out of his trip to New
Zealand because he was on a United Airlines flight that went on to
America, and thought the plane might be a target.

This was the first time the Australasian travel industry had seen an
international event impact on its local sales. No one knew what this
meant. Speculation was rife, for example, that businesspeople would

now video-conference rather than fly to overseas conventions. People thought it was the end of travel.

For Graham 'Skroo' Turner, however, it was business as usual. 'So what? There's a fucking war,' he'd tell his consultants. 'Just keep doing what you're doing.' The other partners were of the same mind. They felt that if they took on the belief that the war would kill the business, then it would. There was always going to be a certain amount of business, and it was up to Flight Centre people to stay positive and get as much of this as they could.

In accordance with this philosophy, Flight Centre began advertising more during this period. This had a good effect on sales as most travel agencies had completely stopped advertising. The partners also bombarded consultants with positive messages. One consultant, Nicky Dance, remembers: 'We believed that it was no big deal because that's what we were told.'

Flight Centre was fortunate that many of its clients were backpackers who were still determined to travel to London in spite of the war. But they didn't want to fly over the Middle East, so consultants had to be inventive. They came up with flight routes over the North Pole and via the States or Africa. Some consultants even started selling bus tickets, and in one or two cases made more money than usual, thanks to the generous commission on each ticket.

The company's attitude to domestic airfares also underwent a dramatic reversal. Up to this point, many Flight Centre consultants didn't sell domestic holidays because they felt there was no money in them. It took the same amount of time to make a domestic booking as it did an international one, but there was only 5 per cent commission in it for a consultant, compared to 12–15 per cent for international tickets. In the past therefore, most clients wishing to travel nationally had been turned away.

With the advent of the Gulf War, however, consultants had to make a rapid readjustment. Many of their clients were switching from overseas holidays to safer, at-home locations. It didn't take the salespeople long to work out that 5 per cent commission was better than nothing at all, so they began selling domestic fares with a vengeance.

Unfortunately, Flight Centre's systems weren't geared up to handle the demand for domestic holidays. The consultants had no experience in booking or handwriting domestic tickets, and a lot of costly mistakes resulted. 'We might've made a hundred thousand dollars in actual bookings,' Skroo summarises, 'but the reality was that because of all the fuck-ups, we probably lost two hundred thousand out the back door.'

The partners realised that they needed a Ticket Centre deal with one of Australia's two major domestic carriers to simplify the whole ticketing process and get an improved commission rate. Turner had a meeting on the Gold Coast with Geoff Dixon, Ansett's marketing manager at the time, by the end of which Flight Centre had a deal to book and ticket Ansett domestic flights and holidays. More importantly, there was an override agreement giving Flight Centre a minimum of 10 per cent commission based on the company's volume of business.

This was good for morale, particularly as enquiries were now reaching their lowest ebb. But some shops and consultants were still making money; one of them was Tina Los's – the Melbourne-born girl who'd applied for an accounting job in Brisbane only to find herself accepting a role as a travel consultant. In 1990–91 the shopping centre that housed Tina's office was closed for reconstruction, meaning her team could only take phone enquiries, and it also got flooded and smoked out on separate occasions before the effects of the Gulf War struck. Amazingly though, Brisbane Flight Centre achieved a profit of $100,000 that year.

Enquiries might have been down, but the consultants in this shop were determined that they'd book every single person who rang in, or find out why the caller wasn't booking at that time. They asked for call-back phone numbers and followed people up, sometimes for weeks (to the exasperation of one or two clients no doubt), to see how their travel plans were going.

Aileen Bratton's Toowong store was the only one in the whole brand to make profit in the first month of the Gulf War. 'I just never let the team think it would affect us,' she explains. 'I remember saying,

"I'm not making a loss because of the bloody war."' Similarly, over in Brisbane's George Street Flight Centre, Sharyn Bleakley (née Eckersley) was in the running for Flight Centre's Consultant of the Year award, for making the most sales in one year. She was so focused on this goal that she wasn't going to let anything stand in her way. Sure enough, Sharyn won the award and the car that accompanied it.

But these valiant efforts were never going to be enough to turn the situation around. By Geoff Harris's reckoning, Flight Centre lost around $300,000 in January 1991 and the same again the following month. He and Bill James believed that the UK and US offices should be closed down to concentrate on the Australian and New Zealand operations. 'I really felt we were spread too thin,' Harris says. 'We didn't have the support people to give these shops the back-up they needed, and we were taking resources away from our core business.'

Turner disagreed but, uncharacteristically perhaps, gave in. Still, whether the closure of the UK and US operations was a good decision or a bad one, none of the company's competitors thought it was a big deal at the time. 'There was no conjecture in the industry,' Jetset–Travelworld's Danny Roche confirms. 'After all, Flight Centre only had a couple of overseas shops. We never really thought about it.'

There were losses from the Gulf War and the closure of the overseas shops, of course, but there was little repercussion within the company. Certainly, no one in Australia and New Zealand had to feel that jobs were at stake. This was because, unlike the other major travel agency groups, Flight Centre didn't retrench anybody during this period. 'We will never put off any salespeople during tough times,' Turner states. 'We are helped by the fact that our performance-based wage costs can decrease by up to ten per cent, but the main reason is that we know that enquiry comes back very quickly and then we'll need these people more than ever.'

On 28 February 1991, Iraq was repelled from Kuwait. The war was over. The pent-up demand for travel led to an upsurge in enquiries. Fully staffed and with much of the competition annihilated, Flight Centre was in an excellent position to capitalise on this demand. 'There was an absolute avalanche of bookings and business after the Gulf War,' Wayne Ackerfeld enthuses. 'We were bigger and better than ever.'

Flight Centre finished the year with a profit of $3.6 million, which was a 2 per cent increase over 1990. Considering that the head of AFTA labelled 1991 'the worst year in travel ever', it wasn't a bad result. By Flight Centre standards, however, it was dreadful. Decades later, Skroo still sees this period as the company's darkest hour.

It would take another year of intense effort to get the business back on track, but it wasn't all bad. For one, the enforced compliance to the TCF accounting procedures had a lasting effect on the company's accounting systems. This year was the last one that the directors had to personally guarantee the business to the TCF, and the resultant strong balance sheet was a boon when the company floated four years later. While the Gulf War was the last time that Flight Centre would ever have a trading month in which it lost money.

The new domestic airfare deals also transformed Flight Centre's business model. By 1999 Flight Centre was making so many bookings that its (previously unthinkable) switch to Qantas as its major domestic airline soon resulted in Ansett losing some $150 million worth of revenue.[26] Domestic travel eventually became such a money-spinner that by the end of 2001 it accounted for 40 per cent of Flight Centre's total business – valued at a whopping $1.2 billion in turnover. Many first-time domestic clients became repeat international travellers, adding substantially to this revenue as well.

There was one final, important positive, Turner believes: 'The Gulf War showed us that certain shops and consultants were war- and recession-proof.' No matter what happened, they still made a profit. In contrast, consultants or teams with a negative attitude became self-fulfilling prophecies. Flight Centre incorporated this discovery into its standard philosophies:

We take responsibility for our own success or failure. We do not externalise, rather, if we have success or problems we 'look within' for the reasons. We accept we have total ownership and responsibility but not always total control. It is our own choice whether or not we turn the pressure of work into stress.

It was with philosophies like these that Flight Centre achieved the goals it had laid down in July 1990, as shown in the table below.

	Actual in 1990	Prediction for 1995	Actual in 1995
Locations worldwide	80	150	168
Annual turnover	$120 million	$450 million	$759 million
Annual profit	$3.5 million	$8 million	$13.07 million

WHAT GETS REWARDED GETS DONE

When Terry Patterson's appendix ruptured, he was rushed off in intense pain to the hospital emergency department. As he was hoisted out on a stretcher through the back doors of the ambulance, he managed to shove some of his Flight Centre business cards into the paramedics' hands.

After several days on the critical list and four weeks in hospital recuperating, Terry was released. Not only did he end up booking holidays for the two paramedics, the ambulance driver and many of the patients and employees in the hospital ward, but he was also our most profitable consultant in the following month.

Story told by Gary 'Boxer' Hogan

The kind of dedication described in the above story is typical. The devotion that many Flight Centre consultants exhibit towards the company is almost cult-like, in fact. Take Kathryn McCasker, from the Mary Street Flight Centre in Brisbane, who states: 'It is in all honesty the best company to work for. I sell it to my friends every day. They're sick of hearing from me about it!' Or Sydney's Tina Saunders, who adds: 'It is fun and exciting. You work really hard, but you know you can go a long way so you don't care. There's nothing else like it.' Eulogies like these seem out of place in the business world, and even a bit disturbing. But the evidence cannot be ignored. For people like Terry Patterson, Kathryn and Tina, and thousands of others like them, the company is unique.

Much of their enthusiasm can be attributed to the Flight Centre partners' vision and unconventional ideas about what constitutes 'work'. For his part, Graham Turner believes that most of these policies originated from Top Deck days. 'If you look at how Top Deck started,' he says, 'work and fun were totally intertwined. Everyone drove the buses, and you were just one of the boys. No one was better than anyone else. When we started Flight Centre we just assumed that this was how all businesses operated.' Most other business do *not* operate like this, of course, and that's what contributes to Flight Centre's uniqueness.

Another source of inspiration to the partners in 1989 came from a book by Michael Le Boeuf called *How to Motivate People*.[27] Le Boeuf is a former professor from the University of New Orleans Business School who believes that 'the things that get rewarded get done.' Similarly, he wrote, it is a lack of rewards that is the source of many of society's problems: why employees are demotivated in businesses that pay them by the hour rather than on what they produce or sell; why politicians who are rewarded for simply getting elected oversee huge budget deficits; and why schools that pay a flat wage instead of rewarding on student performance turn out hundreds of illiterate children every year.

His ideas struck a chord with the partners. While the company's pay structure had always been strongly commission-based, Le Boeuf's ideas gave them a rationale behind why such policies had worked in both Top Deck and Flight Centre. With the phrase 'What gets rewarded gets done' a new company philosophy, the partners were now able to identify the attitude and behaviour they wanted within the organisation, that every person should feel as though they were running their own business. In this way, people would have a direct correlation between what they did every day and the rewards they received. This move to making behavioural reward a conscious policy would play an integral role in Flight Centre's progress through the following decade.

Le Boeuf believes that the number one reward for people is money – in his words: 'Companies that give monetary rewards based on performance get performance.'[28] In keeping with this, Flight Centre's basic wages appear quite low. For new consultants, it's approximately $28,000 per year at the time of writing, and even the managing director's is a relatively meagre $80,000. It is only through the performance-related pay structure and other incentives that many Flight Centre consultants earn well over $100,000 a year.

In addition to their base wage, consultants receive a percentage of the income from every single booking they make. For example, if a consultant makes $100 office commission on a client's $2000 airfare to Europe, the consultant might personally receive $10. These percentages are structured upwards in tiers, based on the total office commission each consultant makes per month, which is known as his or her 'commission transfer'. The table below shows the present-day commission structure.

Australian Flight Centre Retail Commission Structure 2004*

Based on individual commission transfer:

• Up to profit-of-seat (POS)**	10 per cent of transfer
• POS to POS + $6000	30 per cent of seat profit
• POS + $6001 and over	35 per cent of seat profit

Example 1: An average consultant who makes $10,000 commission for the month, using the average POS threshold of $7500, would receive an incentive payment of $750 for the first tier and $750 for the second tier – a total of $1500 for the month in addition to their base wage.

Example 2: An excellent consultant who makes $30,000 commission for the month, with a POS threshold of $10,000 to account for their higher costs, would receive an incentive payment of $1000 for the first tier, $1800 for the second tier and $4900 for the third tier – a total of $7700 for the month in addition to their base wage.

* Note that actual figures and percentages vary from country to country.

** Shop expenses are divided by the number of consultants to determine the total cost for one consultant taking up a chair in an office, known as cost-of-seat (COS). The commission that a consultant makes over this amount is profit for the company, so Flight Centre calls it profit-of-seat (POS). In this way, the system motivates people to both increase their commission levels and decrease the business costs in their shops.

Consultants are therefore rewarded for improving their performance to reach the level where they make the most money, which corre-
spondingly makes the most money for the company. (This process
would also be applied to those working in Flight Centre's back-end
operations, such as Finance, Marketing and IT, as discussed in
Chapter 11.)

The incentive scheme is merit-based and egalitarian. But it would
be ineffective without the operational systems that Flight Centre has
set up to allow consultants to control their own business. This is the
real driving force. As Le Boeuf spelled it out: 'Freedom and autonomy
can be very effective rewards . . . In essence you tell people, "Do the
job right and on time, and you can be your own boss."'[29]

Walk into a Flight Centre shop today and one consultant will look
after every aspect of your booking, from the initial enquiry through to
the 'welcome home' phone call. The consultant – let's call her Jaimie –
will determine the price she charges you, the airlines and tour operators she uses and the discounts that you receive on add-ons such as
insurance and car hire. If you're a high-spending client, Jaimie may
even use some of her own commission to buy you a thank-you gift for
the booking, or call a hotel overseas to arrange a bottle of wine
for your arrival. All this without any input or interference from her
manager.

If you return to the same shop to make another booking and
you've been impressed with Jaimie's service, you'll always be referred
back to her as your regular consultant. Hence a good salesperson like
Jaimie builds up a substantial client base of loyal repeat and referral
clients. This works both ways: not only does Jaimie have a guaranteed
income stream but she also gets to know her customers' needs and
preferences, and can offer far better service than in a one-off
encounter.

This is every consultant's goal. Those with big client bases
transfer huge amounts and become the stuff of legends. The highest
commission transfer by an individual in one month is an amazing
$125,000, which equated to an incentive payment of nearly
$38,450 for that achiever. The highest annual individual commis-

sion transfer is $401,963. Victoria's Wayne Ackerfeld, the consultant responsible, entered Flight Centre's Hall of Fame and earned a consulting incentive of around $100,000 for the year, in addition to his base wage.

A rollcall of the top achievers shows that many have no background in sales. Tennis coach, forestry worker and bank teller are a few of the former professions of people who have made the highest annual sales for the company, generating nearly $4 million in total transaction value *each* per year. Sharyn Bleakley is a case in point. Originally a school teacher, she has won Flight Centre's Consultant of the Year award twice (including her Gulf War–defying achievement of 1991, of course) and received four cars as prizes. Flight Centre eventually set up an office for the George Street, Brisbane, consultant in her own home, complete with wall map. In 1996 she gave birth to a baby boy and was also the company's Corporate Consultant of the Year, simply by working with her existing client base.

But commission is only the start of the monetary rewards that the company offers. The incentive scheme escalates when a person becomes a manager. Flight Centre team leaders are pivotal to the success of each business, and they duly receive generous rewards. First, they get an automatic profit share in their shop of 10–13 per cent, in addition to their consulting commission. They can also buy up to 20 per cent more of the profit of their business under a special debenture system called the Business Ownership Scheme (BOS), a form of which was first introduced in 1987. The present-day BOS is illustrated in the table below.

From Flight Centre's perspective, the BOS is the only real way to motivate people to run their shops as their own businesses, as it's the closest thing to equity available. The results bear this out, according to Turner: 'The shops in which a manager has a BOS average 50 per cent more profitability than the company average.' And it's easy to see where this superior performance comes from when one considers that the average annual return on a BOS is over 25 per cent. As generous a yield as this is, it links back to the lessons learned in Top Deck when Skroo gave away half of his shares to the new division leaders: 'Better

---

Flight Centre's Business Ownership Scheme 2005

Under this scheme, managers are able to invest in their shops. Using a set formula based on the shop profit, the manager can buy a percentage of profit share up to the following amounts:

- 1st BOS   maximum 10 per cent of shop profit
- 2nd BOS*   maximum 15 per cent of shop profit
- 3rd BOS or more*   maximum 20 per cent of shop profit

Once a manager has bought a BOS, he or she gets a monthly payment based on the percentage of profit share purchased.

Example 1: An average-earning consultant in his second year manages a shop that averages $8000 profit a month, and owns a 15 per cent BOS.

Base wage	$28,000
Incentive	$20,000
Team leader's incentive	$9,600
BOS	$14,400
Total salary	**$72,000**

Example 2: A high-performing manager in her fourth year holds a 15 per cent BOS in her current shop that averages $25,000 profit a month, and a 10 per cent BOS in her old shop that averages $8000 profit a month.

Base wage	$28,500
Incentive	$57,900
Team leader's incentive	$30,000
BOS in current shop	$45,000
BOS in old shop	$9,600
Total salary	**$171,000**

*   *Each time a manager moves to another shop or business he or she can buy another BOS. These can be redeemed at any time for the face value originally paid for them. Because a shop can only have up to 20 per cent in BOSs at any one time, if a new manager wishes to buy in, then the oldest BOS holder's percentage will be redeemed first.*

---

to have twenty-five per cent of something than fifty per cent of nothing.'

This concept eventually became an official philosophy:

We believe that each individual has the opportunity to own part of their success. This happens through profit-share or our Business

Ownership Scheme (BOS), and ownership means we see the business that we own part of and work in as our business – not just FCL's business.

Monetary rewards are just one of the vital factors that Michael Le Boeuf recognises, but to truly motivate people in the workplace, employers have to go an extra step. 'While money can be a very powerful incentive,' he wrote, 'recognition can be even more powerful . . . It is amazing how hard people will work when the payoff is feeling appreciated and important.'[30] An integral component of Flight Centre's success is a sophisticated system of recognition that honours and praises high-achievers on a regular basis.

This process begins from the moment someone starts with Flight Centre. As part of their induction training, new consultants learn about the many awards they can win for outstanding performance. The categories include: Consultant of the Year, New Consultant of the Year, Most Profitable Business, Most Productive Business, Most Improved Business, Managing Director's Award for Outstanding Achievement, the Achievers' Club (for individuals) and the Profit Club (for businesses). New consultants are taught how to set their own daily, monthly and annual financial goals, based on what they feel they can reasonably achieve. This then determines which award category they will strive for. Flight Centre doesn't set any mandatory targets; the company believes that people develop at different rates, and it's up to the individual and his or her level of motivation as to what targets are set and whether he or she reaches them or not. (And of course, those that don't generally earn little money and leave of their own accord.)

To help achieve their goals, consultants tailor-make a training program to suit their needs. Flight Centre's educational division – once called the Learning Centre and now under the umbrella of HR division, Peopleworks – offers a wide range of courses including technical and sales training, as well as many personal development sessions, some based on the works of internationally renowned motivational trainers such as Stephen Covey and Anthony Robbins.

To track their progress, consultants receive a copy of the Flight Centre Handbook each month. This details every person's individual commission figures and the profits of every shop. The following is an edited sample (for example, the names of the consultants have been removed) from FCL's 2004 handbook:

Flight Centre Chermside monthly commission figures

	Feb	Mar	Apr	May	June	Year total	Average
Consultant 1	18,302	20,090	18,346	16,112	15,681	172,329	14,361
Consultant 2	17,517	13,184	15,429	11,266	17,158	167,922	13,993
Consultant 3	9,691	13,437	14,134	13,491	8,144	124,103	12,410
Consultant 4	12,223	10,198	12,747	8,113	12,762	79,942	9,993
Consultant 5	14,210	15,262	10,105	16,615	27,180	179,484	14,957
Consultant 6	14,305	15,098	11,276	12,081	22,125	170,110	14,176
Consultant 7	–	–	–	–	11,056	11,056	11,056
Total commission	**86,248**	**87,269**	**82,036**	**77,678**	**124,104**	**913,351**	**76,112**
Margin (%)	10.73	9.75	11.14	10.17	10.58	0.31	
Expenses	60,339	62,990	60,642	63,535	79,490	694,165	57,847
Profit	30,478	25,713	23,135	16,177	46,476	258,899	21,575
Turnover (000s)	827	895	737	772	1,171	8,984	749

Also included in the handbook is a table that ranks consultants, novice consultants and shops in order of merit. In this way, all consultants can see exactly how much they've earned and where they stand in regard to everyone else in the company. Those who do well are praised in the monthly newsletter and awarded a prize on stage at the regional Buzz Night – a monthly dinner and information forum for shops in the same area.

But it is Flight Centre's Annual Awards Night, held in July every year, that is the single biggest motivator for most people. As the end of June approaches, consultants' excitement reaches fever pitch. Those in the running for an award know that every dollar counts. Some people even bring sleeping bags to work so they can labour through the night.

Other shop teams, in an effort to keep the overheads down and maximise profit, cancel cleaners and do their own vacuuming.

Holidays are postponed. One consultant who was offered a free ten-day trip to the Maldives turned it down as she was in the lead for Consultant of the Year and couldn't afford to have any time out of the office. Another individual got her mother and husband in after hours to help her process her many bookings.

On the final day of the financial year, consultants ring around from shop to shop comparing their commission figures. In the head office areas, people gather together with glasses of wine to watch the shop results roll in and see how everyone has done. Rumours abound of phenomenal commission transfers. Most are true. When Flight Centre introduced a car as a prize for any consultant who made over $200,000 in individual profit in one year, that profit target had never been reached before. The following year they gave away five cars.

For many people, the impetus for such achievements is the sheer excitement of being applauded on stage at Flight Centre's Awards Nights. These are extravagant events held at five-star venues in such exotic locations as Hong Kong, Singapore, Sydney, Paris, London, Dublin, Barcelona, Pattaya and Las Vegas. The giant room is decorated with elaborate fantasy furnishings and massive video screens. A brand new car – the prize for the year's top consultant – often takes pride of position on stage. The company directors make a spectacular entrance on elephants, camels or even Harley Davidsons. One year in Las Vegas the CEO dressed as Elvis, surrounded by showgirls. Thousand-dollar ball dresses dot the crowd as people wait in anticipation for the presentation of the awards.

These are the main focus of the evening. Exceptional Flight Centre achievers are treated like sporting heroes. Standing ovations and deafening applause greet individuals and business teams as they take to the stage to receive cars, first-class tickets and exclusive holidays. When the Consultant of the Year is announced, balloons and streamers rain down from above. The scene is highly emotional – people cry with joy. The prizes are almost secondary. For most winners, the more powerful motivator is the accolades in front of their peers. It is cult-like, there's no denying it.

When the award presentations end, the party begins. A big part of the suspense of the evening is that the identity of the entertainment is not revealed in advance. In the past, guests have included Christine Anu, Ronan Keating, Mental as Anything, The Village People, The Screaming Jets and Shaggy. Revolving around the event will be guest speakers such as Bob Geldof or dance parties led by DJ Fatboy slim. Not surprisingly, the party continues till dawn.

It is not possible to overstate the importance of this event as a rallying cry to Flight Centre's individuals. Joell Ogilvie, 1990 Consultant of the Year, admits that it was seeing the crowd go wild for the winner the previous year that spurred her on to her achievement – 'That's going to be me next year,' she told herself at the time. And when Flight Centre announced its Las Vegas Awards Night in 2003, team leaders around the world declared that the greatest motivational factor for their people in the 2002/03 financial year was 'the dream of being on stage in Las Vegas' for the upcoming awards. Since then, destinations such as Cancun, Paris and Barcelona have continued the trend.

Personal growth and development are also integral factors in Flight Centre's rewards strategy. With a new shop opening every 36 hours, the company offers people tremendous opportunity. Consultants who demonstrate achievement can be retail managers within twelve months. In fact, in one start-up operation the demand for managers was so great that every person in the first shop became a store manager within six months.

Promotion is merit-based and vacancies are filled predominantly from within the company, apart from positions requiring specialist knowledge. In South Africa a local-born, front-line consultant progressed to become the country's executive general manager in the space of six years. Such spectacular career growth is heady fuel for achievement-oriented individuals. 'I'd been working my guts out for three or four years at my previous job with no recognition,' says

Matthew Fealy from Eagle Street Flight Centre in Brisbane. 'Now, six months after joining Flight Centre, I'm at a future leaders' conference.'

In addition, crossing boundaries is the norm. A good consultant today could be running Flight Centre's Marketing department, negotiating airline deals, or opening new businesses in the USA tomorrow. Within the company's cross-section of multi-million-dollar enterprises, the possibilities are limitless. Among the people who began as travel consultants and worked their way up are FCL's chief executive officer, the CIO, the global leader of Flight Centre's retail businesses, and heads of international operations and wholesale divisions.

Promotion is only one of the ways that Flight Centre develops people. In 1995 the company set up a business called Moneywise, to give everyone free financial-planning advice. With two consultations a year, and advice on call, it has had a profound impact on people's finances. As one person later wrote, 'I now own five houses, thanks to Flight Centre and Moneywise.'

What started as an altruistic gesture had a knock-on effect on company profits, since those who achieved their personal financial goals also made more money for Flight Centre. This positive wasn't lost on Skroo Turner: 'Following the success of Moneywise, we realised that if we helped people grow personally, financially and professionally, we would benefit as a company.'

This ideal generated a new wave of people-focused businesses. As shown in the table overleaf, Flight Centre people now have access to in-house businesses to suit their every need – from health and mental wellbeing to academic qualifications. 'We like to think that people come into Flight Centre as caterpillars and we turn them into butterflies' is how Bill James describes the new life-centric approach.

Flight Centre's annual conferences are another opportunity for personal development. Each area holds two weekend conferences a year, attended by all their people. (Skeleton staff man each shop and then join their workmates in the afternoon or evening – most businesses don't work Sundays.) There are also three conferences a year for team leaders, with two of the three held at overseas venues.

Some of Flight Centre's personal development businesses

- **Healthwise:** Every person in Flight Centre receives free personal fitness evaluations from Healthwise's in-house consultants. They rate themselves against a health and wellbeing index with factors including physical, nutritional and emotional health, and the soundness of their work environment. A Healthwise consultant then helps them to put in place a program to improve their rating. By focusing on people's total wellbeing, the number of sick days has dropped across the company, and productivity and retention have increased.

- **The Guidance Centre:** The centre offers each person four free psycho-logical counselling sessions per year as required, and discounted rates for further sessions. (The service is contracted out to an external group of psychologists.)

- **The William James School of Business:** The school offers bachelor and master degrees in management, and a master's of philosophy in leadership. The degrees are awarded by the US-based Revans University and are inter-nationally recognised.
  The total cost for each management degree is $6500, and the leadership degree is $8750, which can be paid in pre-tax dollars. On successful completion of the degree, Flight Centre reimburses half the cost. Flight Centre had 40 people enrol within the first few months of opening its business school in March 2004.

- **My Career:** This is a career planning system to give people clear direction and improve their job satisfaction and retention.
  Using My Career, people identify the gaps between the skills they currently hold and those they need to achieve future career goals. They can then manage their own career development and progression. Using core compe-tencies, My Career also allows Flight Centre leaders to develop succession plans, target developmental needs and benchmark successful people in differing roles.

- **Flexipositions:** Flexipositions is a free service to help Flight Centre's many mothers return to work following the birth of their children. The service includes a newsletter outlining recruitment options and the development of a flexible hours system to suit their needs. There is also an in-house website link to babysitting, nanny and au pair services, as well as an online register for people to waitlist at their preferred childcare centre. It is also worth noting that Flight Centre offers 52 weeks' unpaid maternity leave.

Conferences have a strong business focus, with sessions from Learning Centre professionals, motivational speakers and industry partners. Flight Centre people look forward to these events as a chance to increase their skills and knowledge. This is not surprising, since improving their ability is directly linked to increasing their earning capacity. The conferences are also a reward in themselves and are eagerly anticipated. People meet old friends, let off steam, party, and have enormous fun. There are talent quests, fancy dress parties, and competitions to spice up the evenings.

Flight Centre's conference expenses are generally subsidised by sponsorships paid by presenters. Airlines, hotels and tour companies also offer the company discounts for these events in recognition of the benefit of having Flight Centre's consultants and leaders experience their products first-hand. These contributions enable Flight Centre to hold its conferences in a variety of locations that would be impossible for a non-travel-related business to afford. In one twelve-month period alone, conferences were held in Zambia, South Africa, Thailand, Mexico, the USA, Canada, Botswana, Tanzania, Bali, Australia and New Zealand. The list of extracurricular activities is equally impressive – ranging from helicopter rides over the legendary Victoria Falls, safaris and game viewing elsewhere in Africa, climbs up the awesome Mount Kilimanjaro, to surf action at Bali and Noosa, and a night out at the Sydney production of *Mamma Mia!*

On the surface, Flight Centre's rewards and recognition policies are not cheap. Combine the costs of incentives, managers' profit share, BOS, Buzz Nights, conferences and various awards nights, and it's clear what a big investment these motivators are for the company. For the Flight Centre partners, however, both back in 1989 and up to the present day, the policies are worth every penny because of the level of ownership they inspire.

To put this in context, take the individual Flight Centre recruits. These people can start immediately, sell products they love, determine their own salary, become a manager within twelve months, earn up to 30 per cent profit-share in several shops, track their ranking within the company, win awards and recognition as high-achieving consultants or business leaders, get free financial and health advice, attain a very cheap MBA, fly to two free overseas conferences a year, make many like-minded friends, and be in the running to open a new business overseas or start up a new venture within the company. This is far more exciting than most career paths available in the retail industry, and in fact in any industry.

More evidence of the strength of Flight Centre's rewards policies – if it's needed – is apparent from the very calibre of the people it attracts. In an internal census conducted in March 2002, Flight Centre recruits were asked to list any achievements they had attained before they started working for the company. The quality of some of these achievements, not to mention the variety, says a lot for the company that managed to secure the respondents' services: 'I won an Emmy Award for my work in a television production'; 'I am an Australian gold-medal holder for swimming – freestyle and butterfly'; 'I was the winner of "Top Sales in the World" for Time-Life, 1999'; 'I represented New Zealand in rugby'; 'I was a member of the world champion Australian rowing team, 1989–92'; 'I won the HAP Walter Humanitarian Award' . . . the list goes on.

Flight Centre eventually formalised its beliefs about work into a company philosophy:

> In our Company we believe that every individual should have equal privileges. We will never have separate offices, receptionists or secretaries. Promotion from within will always be our first choice. We believe that work should be challenging and fun for everyone. Within our company there is no 'them and us'. We are all going forward together.

And it was policies like these that contributed to Flight Centre's swift recovery from the dark hours of 1990–91 and subsequent spectacular growth from 1992 to 1995. With turnover increasing by 25 per cent a year and pre-tax profit growing an annual 40 per cent, by 1993 Flight

Centre was ranked number 29 in the top 500 private companies in Australia. The company also won the Australian Travel Agency Group of the Year award in 1993 and 1994, and Business Queensland's Company of the Year in 1995. Total profits passed the $10 million mark for the first time in June 1995.

In addition, Flight Centre's reward system earned the company a place in Robert Gottliebsen's bestseller *10 Best and 10 Worst Decisions of Australian CEOs*. Fortunately, the renowned business analyst rated it in the 'best' category. He also added an insightful comment: 'these sorts of shops or businesses earn substantially more profits than those with traditional staff arrangements. It is stunning that other major retailers have not followed their lead.'[31]

Chapter 7

'HERE'S YOUR BUS . . . YOU'RE OFF TO KATHMANDU'

They all knew that this was their last resort. If they failed tonight then Flight Centre's Vietnam operation was over.

After ten minutes, the light from a cigar illuminated the darkness. A man emerged from the shadows. He had a massive scar down one side of his face — it was the size and shape of a machete blade and extended from his right eye to below his chin.

He addressed them in broken English: 'You have made a tragic error. You have aligned yourself with the wrong faction.' He explained that to get a Vietnamese foreign trader's licence they needed to pay an incentive to the civil servants involved. As his military division ran all the government departments he could organise this for them.

After months of going through regular channels, they handed over the brown paper bag containing the $5000 'consulting' fees. They had their licence within a week.

Story told by Steve Bowden, inaugural manager of Flight Centre's
Vietnam operation

Aside from the troubles at the start of the decade, the first five years of the 1990s were generally a chance for the Flight Centre partners to explore new ideas without some of the external threats that had dogged them in the late '80s. Like a horse let off a short rein, their boundless enthusiasm and escalating strength made this a very fruitful period. Flight Centres International would experience over 40 per cent growth in annual profits during this time, and start up many new brands and overseas businesses.

The partners had signalled their global intent as far back as 1987, when they set down the goal to have a Flight Centre in every major city and suburb that they operated in worldwide. 'We felt the Flight Centre brand would reach saturation point in Australasia, so this was a logical step,' says Geoff Harris, then state leader for Victoria, South Australia and Tasmania. The closure of the UK and two US shops had been a minor setback, but by 1994, with the continued success in both Australia and New Zealand, the partners felt that it was time to renew their attack on overseas markets.

Their approach was unusual. Most large companies opening in new overseas locations conduct a minimum of a year's research, put in place a $1 million start-up budget, lease a regional head office, and employ a team of experts to begin the operation. But Flight Centre hadn't floated at this stage and the company's resources were still limited. So the partners did what they'd always done. They employed a few people and told them to go and start up Flight Centre operations overseas. As Gary Hogan says: 'It was Top Deck all over again. Skroo was very much a believer in "Here's your bus, here's your keys, you're off to Kathmandu."'

The set-up of the Vietnam operation was a case in point. In 1994 a client contacted Flight Centre about setting up a shop in Ho Chi Minh City. At this stage there were no major travel agencies in Vietnam, but there was a large expatriate community working for the many big corporations based there. Even though the Flight Centre partners had spent a total of 48 hours in Vietnam between them, they decided to open a shop by recruiting a Christchurch manager and her husband to set up the new operation. 'It seemed like a good idea at the time' is Graham Turner's verdict now.

Valerie Bowden and her husband Steve arrived in Vietnam in September 1994. 'We were expecting to start straightaway,' Valerie says. 'We got a bit of a shock when we realised that not only didn't we have a shop, but we still didn't have a licence to operate.' The contract on the store that Flight Centre had leased had fallen through. After another unsuccessful attempt, they finally managed to clinch a deal on premises at 43 Nguyen Hue, the eight-lane main street of Ho Chi Minh.

With the help of a Vietnamese travel agent from Melbourne, the Bowdens managed to get their foreign trader's licence in record time. But there was one last hurdle to overcome: Flight Centre also required a Passenger Servicing Licence (PSL), a new initiative from the Hanoi government, in order to sell airline tickets. Unfortunately the political factions couldn't agree on the actual criteria needed to obtain the licence. Steve flew to Hanoi several times to meet with different army generals, in an effort to fast-track the process. 'Everyone spoke in parables,' he recalls. 'I soon learned that "The river runs slowly in spring" meant "Your licence will take longer to issue."'

Before the New Zealand couple's arrival in South-East Asia, Skroo and Brian Hickey (the last of whom was now Flight Centre's Business Services leader) had travelled to Johannesburg to get a feel for the South African market, following the end of apartheid. They found some distinct business advantages. South Africa didn't have payroll tax or superannuation, for example. This meant that the average wage cost for a business was only 28 per cent of total expenses, compared to Australia's 45–50 per cent. The low wages had a knock-on effect on other expenses, with most of them costing a third of what Flight Centre was used to paying. Best of all, as Turner observed: 'No one was discounting airfares in South Africa. It had a similar feel to Australia twenty years earlier.'

Flight Centre decided to set up a partnership with Penn Travel, a strong local brand with eleven shops in South Africa. Two Flight Centre people, Wayne Hamilton and his wife Treacey Dowd-Hamilton, took Bill James aside and 'locked him in a toilet with a glass of red wine' until he agreed that they could manage the first shop, in the Johannesburg suburb of Eastgate. They flew out in September 1994, the same month that the Bowdens headed to Ho Chi Minh.

Wayne and Treacey soon discovered that there'd been a mix-up with the shopfitter: the store was all set up with counters, brochure racks and brand-new computers, but it had no front doors or signage. A security guard was needed on premises until a new shopfitter could be found to put together a rush frontage.

Their trials weren't over. Penn Travel had been running an advance press campaign with the slogan 'The Aussies are Coming', which had generated a lot of interest. Unfortunately, there was a mistake with the timing, and the advertisement stating 'Opening Today' went into the newspapers before the shop was actually ready for business. Come the supposed first day of business, the shopfitter was the only person there. He made numerous cups of coffee for the disgruntled clients who had lined up along the hallway to buy their cheap tickets.

Despite these hiccups, when Eastgate Flight Centre opened that December it was an almost instant success. It broke even in February 1995, and in the following months it would do so well that it blitzed the existing Penn Travel office results. Wayne Hamilton explains: 'Eighty per cent of what Flight Centre did had never been done in South Africa before. We were the first travel agents ever to discount fares. We even had other travel agents ringing us wanting to buy them from us. In addition, we were the first travel agents to sell the less upmarket airlines. I don't think Penn Travel had ever ticketed a Balkan Air ticket until we came along.'

While business was booming in South Africa, Jim Goldburg, the company's chief finance man, and Turner were looking at setting up another operation, in Canada. A recent skiing holiday in Whistler had impressed them with the possibilities inherent in Vancouver, the major city in British Columbia. This city was the same size as Brisbane but had twice the number of people. It was also English-speaking and had a large travelling population. Vancouver looked promising. On the debit side, however, discounting was standard practice in Canada, so Flight Centre knew it would face some serious local competition.

Simon Canning, a Canadian with many years of experience in the travel industry, heard about Flight Centre's plans via the industry grapevine. He put forward a proposal and the company agreed that he should start up the operation. 'We didn't have any formal agreement,' Canning says. 'In fact, we wrote the financial plan on the back of a napkin. When the fax came through giving the go-ahead I wasn't sure if it was for real, but I quit my job anyway. My friends thought I was mad.'

It was unusual for Flight Centre to appoint someone from outside the company to such a senior position. The challenge for Simon was whether he could implement Flight Centre's distinctive culture with no first-hand experience. To add to the test, there was little practical support from the Australasian operation. As Keith Stanley, Flight Centre's marketing manager at the time, says: 'When I was asked to coordinate the set-up of the new overseas areas, I organised a meeting with the senior managers in Australia. When I asked them what they could provide the new country leaders, they said, "We're not incentivised to do that", and I realised that people like Simon were on their own.' It would be several years before Flight Centre created separate global roles to coordinate and assist these new country leaders.

Once appointed, Canning began recruiting people for Flight Centre's first Canadian shop, situated on Vancouver's main thoroughfare, Robson Street. With a mobile phone as back-up, he conducted interviews in the car park beside the building site. The store opened, with four consultants, in January 1995.

Shortly after this, Jim Goldburg began searching out the biggest shopping centre in the area and found a second site. Burnaby Flight Centre opened in March 1995, and another four new shops would follow in the next twelve months. It was a very stressful time for the Canadian area leader: 'The phones were going nuts and the new recruits were completely inexperienced. We had no IATA licence to ticket our own flights, no licence to sell travel insurance (so we couldn't offer it), no deals to sell any accommodation products, and no payroll system.' To make matters worse, Flight Centre's accounting package didn't allow for the Canadian goods and services tax, and the Vancouver head office kept running out of money . . . With all these trials, it's no surprise that staff turnover at this stage was approximately 30 per cent.

Flight Centre had provided Simon with a copy of its Systems Manual and given him short briefings on different operational areas, but this couldn't compensate for practical experience. For instance, although Canning knew that Flight Centre policy was to employ newcomers to the travel industry, when it came to the actual interview process, he didn't adhere fully to the recruitment criteria. 'I hired lots of the wrong people who were new to the workforce but had no real selling skills,' he admits.

Simon also didn't understand how fundamental in-shop systems were to Flight Centre's business model. Because of this, most Canadian managers made their own decisions on what was appropriate – just like in the bad/good old days in Australasia pre 1988. Consultants in one shop would type up airfare quotes while others would scribble them on the back of business cards. Some consultants wore uniforms and others wore whatever they felt like. Some shops opened on Saturdays, others didn't. And worst of all, the profits remained inconsistent, with some consultants doing well but many others struggling to make money.

Each country had its own set of idiosyncrasies to overcome. While Simon Canning was grappling with standard systems, Flight Centre's biggest hurdle in Vietnam continued to be the pursuit of a Passenger Service Licence. By April 1995 there was still no sign of it. The company decided to open the Ho Chi Minh shop anyway. After almost eight months, the partners felt they needed to get it going. To circumvent the licensing issue, the consultants booked flights in Australia and couriered the tickets up from the Brisbane Ticket Centre. The response was encouraging – the Bowdens' shop took $5000 in its first week of operation.

Flight Centre's euphoria was short-lived, however. Out of the blue, Steve Bowden got a phone call from Hanoi. He flew up as requested, and met with a roomful of military generals. 'They told me they were very sorry but they'd decided to restructure the whole airline industry in Vietnam,' he remembers. 'They anticipated that it would take six to twelve months. In the interim, they wouldn't be giving out any licences.'

Bowden rang Turner and told him the bad news. The company was aware that in Vietnam, six to twelve months could easily be several years, and with Flight Centre about to go public, an ongoing loss with no guarantees was an unattractive prospect. After nine months of effort and $150,000 in outlay, the company decided to throw in the towel.

To Valerie Bowden, they were simply a few years too early. Skroo agrees: 'Someone talked us into it because there was no competition. We soon found out *why* there was no competition.'

The failure of the Vietnam venture didn't quench Flight Centre's thirst for overseas expansion, however. Far from it. The partners began eyeing off another destination.

The United Kingdom, with a population of 58 million people, was on the company's agenda again. Inner London alone, with 7 million people and a population density of nearly 9000 people per square kilometre (compared to Brisbane's 354), was one of the largest cities in the developed world. Flight Centre would need to capture just 1 per cent of the market to be profitable.

But the company knew that even this seemingly simple task wouldn't be easy. In contrast to South Africa, UK travel agencies were well entrenched and highly automated. Thomas Cook, Lunn Poly and Going Places each had over 600 UK stores. Compare this to Flight Centre's 250 Australasian shops at the time, and they were minnows in the market. Discounting was also the norm in the UK. Clients were used to shopping around to find cut-throat deals and there were many competitors for Flight Centre's 'cheapest flights' marketing niche.

A further handicap was the fact that goods in Britain were very expensive. Most costs were nearly double that of Australian stores, particularly with the $2:£1 exchange rate at the time. This would rise to nearly 3:1 in the following years. Wages were also higher, especially as the company had to raise the base salary to cover the greater cost of living in London.

The challenge for Flight Centre, therefore, was whether it could break into this established market and make enough money to cover its overheads. The partners decided to give it a go. In early 1995, Gary 'Boxer' Hogan was appointed to lead Flight Centre's UK operation, and he convinced me to head over and set it up with him. Like our colleagues in South Africa and Canada, we were excited by the thought of creating something new, and hoped to make some serious money out of profit share down the track. But Boxer and I didn't kid ourselves for a moment. We knew we'd be working on a shoestring budget, with little salary, until the operation was in the black.

On arriving in the UK in April 1995, we spent much of the first day debating where to start. With no local partner to help us, there was a lot to do, and it was almost impossible to agree on a course of action. Eventually we decided to dedicate the day to buying a fax machine.

Once this crucial task was completed, we rented a large house in Coulsdon, south London, and began working out of the dining room. 'I met with the American Express sales representative to organise our credit card agreement,' Boxer recalls. 'Not only was the dining room a highly unorthodox venue, but my two-year-old daughter kept coming in to see what was going on. Looking back, I can't believe that people took us seriously.'

Being a travel agent in Britain at that time was on a par with being a toilet cleaner in Australia. Consultants were typically seventeen-year-old school-leavers on subsistence wages. The perception of the role was so bad that one consultant even used to hide under her desk when anyone she knew walked past. She couldn't bear them seeing her working as a travel agent.

But this stigma worked in Flight Centre's favour. The company's policy of employing well-travelled, educated people gave us a real point of difference. One recruitment ad in *The Guardian* brought in so many sackfuls of résumés that the postmen complained about having to cart them all the way up the stairs. After days of sifting through these applications, we'd employed four new recruits, and by August 1995 we were poised to open the first shop, in the south London suburb of Croydon.

Then disaster struck. Boxer remembers it well: 'The day we were meant to sign the lease, the elderly owner didn't turn up. I phoned his solicitor to find out what had happened. Unfortunately the landlord had forgotten all about the appointment. He'd left for a relaxing three-month holiday overseas and was unable to be contacted.'

This put us in a real predicament. We had four fully trained consultants and no shop to put them in. In the end we sent them off to Australia for four weeks while we ran around trying to find another shop. This was easier said than done. Many sites in the UK had been sub-leased up to four times over, and prospective tenants had to get approval from all the landlords and their solicitors before they had a binding contract. This could take up to a year. The process was complicated by the fact that bribes (masquerading as superior landlord payments) were seen as a normal part of the operation.

Boxer eventually leased a site at Putney, and after a quick fit-out the shop opened in December 1995. Due to a merchandising mix-up, however, its window boards were in dollars and all its stationery had Flight Centre's Australian phone numbers on them. And the problems didn't end there, according to Boxer: 'We also had a brand-new computer and back-office system from Australia. The trainer was held up so no one knew how to use it. We just had to muddle through.'

For the new consultants, none of these drawbacks mattered. Flight Centre's recruits were fired up by the excitement of being in on the ground floor of something new and different. 'It was like we were David facing Goliath,' says Chris Galanty, one of the first consultants. 'We were up against hundreds of Lunn Polys and Thomas Cooks, and we were determined to make our mark.'

These feelings were typical of the Flight Centre consultants who worked in the new overseas areas. They were like pioneers opening up new frontiers, faced with few resources but loads of opportunity.

Over in Johannesburg, Shane Flynn was another who relished the challenge of starting up in an unknown territory. 'People could see the company literally growing in front of their eyes every month,' he marvels.

'Flynnie' was to play a major role in South Africa. With the success of the first store, Eastgate Flight Centre, another shop had been proposed, at Westgate. Flynnie had hounded Turner to get the job. 'Eventually he caved in,' he recalls. 'Jim and I worked out the first year's cash flow on the back of a beer coaster, then I had a two-hour meeting with Skroo, got a slap on the back, and it was "See ya later."'

Having taken the earliest flight out of Brisbane, Flynnie soon realised that Flight Centre and Penn Travel were two very different beasts. Penn employed secretaries and juniors and felt that Flight Centre was 'obsessed' with cheap fares. 'For three months I worked closely with Penn Travel and saw how they operated,' he explains. 'I knew we could do it better. Before I'd wondered if we could make it in South Africa. Now my only question was how big and how fast.' By September 1995 the cultural divide between Flight Centre and Penn Travel had become too wide to bridge and the partnership was dissolved.

Soon after this, Shane Flynn became national leader of the company's South African operation, only to face his first serious challenge within hours of taking over. Flight Centre had relied on Penn Travel's licence to sell airline tickets and part of the dissolution agreement had been that Penn would continue ticketing for the company until the end of December. Flynn now discovered that it would take five months to get his own IATA licence. This meant that they wouldn't be able to sell any flights from January to March 1996. The whole operation would have to shut down if a solution wasn't found.

Flynn began a desperate search for an alternative. Part of his problem was that South Africa didn't have consolidators – the middlemen who normally sell tickets to agents – instead, travel agents bought directly off airlines and did their own ticketing. But to do this, one needed an IATA licence. At the eleventh hour, Flynnie managed to convince a tour company to do Flight Centre's ticketing for 1 per cent of the cost. This covered the hiatus until the company arranged its own licence.

Flynn and his team were to face many more challenges. In the early years after apartheid, South Africa was a country in chaos. Electricity supply was intermittent, leading to constant disruptions. Ticket Centre consultants working at night often had to ticket by torchlight.

Telephones and computers were also cut out frequently, because vandals raided the phone lines for their valuable copper-wire wrapping. Even when the lines were intact, the telephone service was often cut off. The phone company simply didn't have enough staff to process the payments it received on time.

Security was another issue. There were, on average, 30 car-jackings a day in downtown Johannesburg. Flight Centre consultants were always having to reissue passports and tickets after they'd been stolen from commandeered courier vans. And occasionally the action got a little too close for comfort, as one manager recalls. While away at a conference, she called up her store and received an unusual response from one of her consultants: 'Hello, Heathway Flight Centre. Sorry we can't help you right now, but the bank next door is getting robbed and there's a shoot-out going on.'

The South African operation certainly couldn't afford to lose any people, through street shoot-outs or otherwise. With clients lining up to do business, Flight Centre couldn't recruit consultants fast enough. Unfortunately, after the years of apartheid, most of their applicants were untrained – even by the company's previous standards.[32] People often listed their travel experience as catching the number 96 bus from Soweto to Johannesburg.

But South Africa did have one distinct advantage over the other start-up areas, and that was that there were only a handful of airlines flying in and out, which meant that new recruits could learn the technical skills of the job in a week. As a result, training could be focused on the areas of sales and service skills far more so than was usual in start-ups, and this had a definite impact on the market. As Wayne Hamilton, who was now manager of Westgate Flight Centre, remembers: 'We just *blew* clients away. They were used to traditional agents who took a week to quote. We gave them a price on the spot and discounted it to boot. They couldn't believe it – and we just kept making money.'

They also set a new record. By June 1997, a little over two years after opening, Flight Centre South Africa broke even. The Flight Centre directors (as the partners had become since the float) flew over to celebrate, so Flynn organised a party at his place. His house was the core of the South African operation. As well as being his residence, it was also used as a hotel by the many Australasian Flight Centre visitors, and as a training centre and lodgings for new recruits on their one-week training course.

Flynnie's hospitality was so good that night that it nearly led to disaster, when Jim Goldburg leaned backwards on the candle-lit bar and accidentally set his shirt alight. Flames suddenly began whooshing over his head. 'Luckily, Wayne threw his merlot over Jim's shirt and put it out,' Flynn remembers. 'From then on we called Jim "the Director Who Came Closest to Death".'

The next day the directors arrived in London and caught the Tube to Putney, on the River Thames, to appraise the new store. They discovered that the opening of this shop had elevated the company's UK operation to a whole new level. There was now an official head office.

Putney Flight Centre had an old, windowless, concrete-lined basement consisting of two small rooms and a foetid-smelling toilet. The area was so small that anyone wishing to do a 'number two' was banished to the McDonald's toilet next door. Apart from suffering from constant colds during the winter months, we (that is, 'the management team') found the impromptu set-up, consisting of large cardboard boxes with timber planks laid across as desks, a big step up from Gary Hogan's dining room.

Still, the inadequacies of the basement were minor compared to the other challenges facing the UK team. The directors soon learned how difficult it was to convince the airlines that Flight Centre was a serious player in the UK. As Boxer puts it, 'We were smaller than a bee's dick.' The sales manager at Garuda Airlines told us that we'd get the fares 'over my dead body'. (Flight Centre didn't have to wait quite that long, but it took several years.) Air India made us pay a bank guarantee, while the representative at United Airlines never even returned our calls.

Finding good shop sites was also a problem. Flight Centre UK now had six shops, but many were over 100 years old and extremely dilapidated. Some flooded after heavy rains. Others were in heritage-listed areas with onerous regulations. And the plans for the Edinburgh shop even had to be signed off by Parliament. Flight Centre had never experienced these kinds of problems in its modern shop sites in Australasia.

But perhaps the biggest obstacle was the sheer volume of people. The shops were always full of clients and the phones never stopped ringing. Where an Australian consultant might take twenty enquiries a day, a UK consultant would take 80, but with nowhere near the support tools that a counterpart in Sydney, Melbourne or Brisbane might have. 'The UK had ten times the number of airfares that Australia had, and Flight Centre's automated fare system couldn't deal with these volumes,' Boxer continues. 'It also had no facility for dealing with charter flights, which accounted for thirty per cent of the British market.'

The difficulties facing us in the UK weren't lost on Skroo and the other visitors. Various strategies were discussed to address these issues before the directors had to head off to another trouble spot.

On arrival at Vancouver, they found Simon Canning attempting to implement Flight Centre's philosophies of incentives into the Canadian operation. Again his inexperience of Flight Centre's culture would work against him, and he ended up overspending in an effort to motivate his consultants. One even remembers that a $25 Virgin voucher was given out for each booking.

Simon was also hampered by the fact that he didn't have any insider knowledge. 'I had a girl from Australia approach me about a position,' he says to illustrate the point. 'I rang her team leader in Australia and he gave her a glowing reference. When she started here she was terrible. I soon discovered that the team leader was highly motivated to get rid of her because of her lack of performance. He would've told me that she walked on water if it guaranteed I took her.'

As for the company's philosophy of autonomy, Canning saw it as 'a lack of support that was almost laughable'. Where Flight Centre believed in standardised branding, he felt 'there was a constant ker-fuffle over shop fit-outs.' He thought the uniforms were 'corny' and blamed the continuing failure of Burnaby Flight Centre on the fact that it was in a poor location rather than, as Flight Centre believed, that it was mismanaged.

In the 1996/97 financial year the area lost $900,000. Consultant commission averaged $3000 per person per month, which was well below expenses. While these results may have looked bad on paper, Simon feels the figures didn't tell the whole story: 'Over a two-year period I found, leased, fitted, staffed, trained, marketed and opened ten shops, including one in Toronto, one Ticket Centre and a national training centre. I won all the early major deals, fulfilled all regulatory requirements and slowed the dollar loss. I did this by myself without any meaningful support from Flight Centre. Hence I thought that this loss wasn't a bad result.'

From the directors' point of view, however, the business would never make a profit without standardised systems in place. In August 1997 Jim Goldburg flew back to Canada and, after a brief meeting, Simon Canning left the company. It hadn't worked out the way either party had planned. 'Flight Centre was exciting, empowering, scary and strange,' Simon says now, in summary. 'A very hard learning curve but one that I'm glad I had. I was lucky to get the chance to do some-thing like that, and relieved when it was over.' He now works as the regional director for the Sabre Travel Network in Vancouver.

Two replacements were chosen, both proven performers and long-standing Flight Centre people. Grahame Hubbard, formerly market-ing manager for New Zealand, had taken over management of the Toronto shop in May 1997, with the task of building a new Flight Centre operation out east in Ontario. Sue Rennick, a Queensland area manager, was now entrusted with the nine shops in 'Western Canada', as the area around Vancouver was called.

It was to be an uphill battle. In truth, just as their predecessor had found, Western Canada paid a price for Flight Centre's lack of attention in the early years. The Burnaby shop, for instance, lost nearly $500,000 in the next two years. Sue focused on implementing Flight Centre's standard philosophies and put more emphasis on training and recruitment, as well as product and airline deals. In addition, she opened more stores in high-street locations.

The new leader was also very clear about only rewarding the behaviour that she wanted. 'Things changed,' one consultant admits. What had once been a $100 spa certificate for a $4000 transfer now became a $25 movie voucher for an $8000 commission transfer. But the curb on over-rewarding the consultants' achievements had the desired effect. By the end of June 1998, the average commission had risen from $3000 to $5500 per person, and one consultant set a record with an $18,000 transfer in the month of July. Two shops, Davie Street and Broadway, broke even, turning around from a $40,000 loss the year before.

While Rennick made headway in Western Canada, Grahame Hubbard was expanding in Ontario. He was fortunate in that his area piggybacked off the Vancouver operation, utilising such facilities as training, recruitment and the Ticket Centre business to speed up growth. By the end of 1998, Ontario had opened six shops.

It also set a Flight Centre record for the smallest loss in a new area in its first financial year. However, this still put pressure on the parent company. The total loss for Canada in 1997/98 was $1.4 million, while the UK recorded a loss of $1.1 million. Only South Africa, with a profit of $795,000, was consistently profitable. Flight Centre's total overseas operation was well and truly in the red.

Back in Brisbane, the mood in the boardroom was subdued. The UK was a particular cause for concern. Only two of its eighteen shops were profitable and, overall, administrative costs had blown out with the large amount of data-inputting required to keep the fares grids up to date. Licensing expenses were another burden, with the UK's travel agent licensing authority requiring $1 million in guarantees a year for the company to keep trading.

But we – the executive team – felt that the worst was over. We knew we had a winning business model, one that was very different from our competitors'. The consultants were smart and industrious, and Gary Hogan and I were constantly refining the systems. Even though we still had no empirical proof, we felt that there was no reason why the operation shouldn't work.

One night Boxer sat down and analysed all the figures. He discovered two things: 'I worked out that all the consultants who had been with the company for longer than twelve months were profitable. As the business was expanding so rapidly this was only twenty-five per cent of the company. I also realised that we needed to get to a pivotal number of shops to be able to absorb the larger support costs of areas such as airfare coordination. I figured that once we had about thirty shops, both these conditions would be met, and we would be consistently profitable.'

With this in mind, the team focused on opening more shops and getting more airline deals. By the end of 1998 we had nearly 90 per cent of the airlines signed up, and had all fares, to all destinations, programmed into the grids, with a guaranteed 24-hour service on all tickets. Consultants could therefore quote clients on the spot in half the time as before. Uncompetitive pricing, misquoting and minimal commission were relegated to the past.

The company now observed a strange phenomenon. The average UK consultant's monthly commission of £4000 hadn't changed in twelve months. Despite all the improvements, consultants still maintained that this was the most money they could physically make in a shop. Flight Centre realised that the final hurdle it had to overcome concerned people's belief in their own ability.

Boxer convinced a high-performing consultant from Australia to come and work for us. In her first month she transferred £8000 in commission. The following month, at least five UK consultants also transferred £8000. 'We just needed someone to raise the bar and show everyone that it could be done,' he explains. 'Once they realised this, the sky was the limit.'

With the turnaround in the UK, the company's overseas strategy was beginning to bear fruit. The same factors that had worked for Flight Centre in Australia and New Zealand were now starting to pay off in the new operations.

For the 1998/99 financial year, Shane Flynn and his team set themselves a growth target of 50 per cent in South Africa. This meant they had to make a profit of R6 million and finish the year with 32 shops. Flynnie had a T-shirt printed with 'Name: Shane Flynn, Goal: 6 million' and wore it to every conference. But even he was surprised by the results. 'We thought we'd been pretty ambitious,' he admits, 'but by our January managers' conference we'd already made the six million rand, and we still had five months to go. I remember I took off my T-shirt and we got a felt pen, crossed out the six and changed it to a nine – which is what we ended up making.'

That same year, 1999, the UK and South African managers held a joint conference in Vienna. Mike Palmer, the UK director of global management consultants Priority Management, presented one of the sessions. He'd sent out questionnaires to all attendees to complete before their arrival – the object of the exercise being to analyse Flight Centre's culture in both South Africa and the UK, and compare it to benchmarks calculated from a database of thousands of respondents from businesses in North America, Europe, Asia and Australasia.

Palmer was amazed by the results. This conference was the first time Flight Centre's managers from the UK and South Africa had ever got together, yet their graphs were identical. Despite the differences in geography, society, recruitment and leadership, the Flight Centre business model had been replicated in exactly the same way in both countries.

Even more surprising was the strength of people's belief in the company. As the management consultant says: 'Flight Centre was the first company we had ever tested in which its people rated the company's performance higher than their own.'

This was high praise indeed when one considers the achievements of some of the people in the two overseas areas. An example of such a high achiever is Sue Garrett, who in July 1997 had the gall to announce that her team's goal was to be Flight Centre's number one shop globally for the year. Such pluck would normally be applauded in the company – expected even – but the reality was that Sue was a brand-new manager in a brand-new shop in a relatively new country, South Africa. 'I suggested that she might want to lower her sights a bit, so the team wouldn't be disappointed,' Shane Flynn remembers. 'Perhaps they should target number one shop in South Africa instead.' Naturally, her people were less than impressed with the national leader's advice. But if his words had any effect on them, it was to spur them on to great heights. At the company's 1998 Annual Awards Night, their store was Flight Centre's Most Profitable Business Worldwide, and a South African consultant won the New Consultant of the Year award globally. Sue Garrett would eventually replace Flynnie as national leader of South Africa when he returned to Australia in 2002.

The 1998/99 financial year saw Ontario open seven stores and make CAN$102,000 profit – a record for a new area in its second year. Western Canada also broke even for the first time. And after three-and-a-half years, the UK achieved a profit turnaround of over £500,000 to £154,019. It had 26 shops at the time.

But this was only the beginning. The following year *every* area made a profit. The UK also set a record for the highest average commission for new consultants, and – bearing in mind that this was an area that almost didn't make it – nothing was more amazing than when Steve Williamson from the UK won Flight Centre's Consultant of the Year Worldwide award for the 2000/01 financial year. As a *Sunday Times* correspondent noted in 2003, 'the only negative aspect of Flight Centre UK's operation is that everyone ends up speaking with a slight Australian twang.'[33]

By the end of June 2004 the total combined profit of the over-seas areas was approximately $36 million, over 30 per cent of the company's total. These regions also took out many of Flight Centre's awards that year, including Corporate Consultant of the Year, Ticket Centre Consultant of the Year, Most Profitable Student Flights Team, Most Profitable Corporate Team, and Most Profitable Ticket Centre. In addition, four out of the top ten New Consultants of the Year Worldwide came from these areas.

Yet for many, the real satisfaction lay in the fact that they had achieved the goals they'd set out at the beginning. Each overseas area now had over 100 shops and other businesses. As Chris Galanty, who became the UK country leader, says today: 'We're no longer David. Walk through central London these days and we now have over thirty shops. This is amazing when you think of where we came from.'

For others it was the opportunity of working and learning in an overseas company that had the greatest impact. The experience they gained would prove invaluable in their future roles. Sue Rennick went on to become the global leader of Flight Centre's retail shops, Flynnie became CEO, and Boxer took on the role of chief information officer.

Overall, Flight Centre's global strategy had paid off: three successes and only one failure. And in a final postscript to the Vietnam venture, a friend of Steve Bowden's went past the old shop in Ho Chi Minh City some years ago. 'Inside there were people eating bowls of noodles at Flight Centre's bright red counters,' he remembers. The shop with its faded red and white signage had remained there since May 1995, a sad reminder of the failed enterprise. And, not surpris-ingly, at the time of writing there are still no major travel agencies in Vietnam.

Chapter 8

FAMILY, VILLAGE, TRIBE

'Neanderthal' Turner out of touch with modern thinking.
Headline for letter to *Travelweek*, September 1989

Thirty-five thousand feet above sea level, Graham Turner sipped on a glass of shiraz and flicked through the magazine he'd bought to entertain himself on the flight from Brisbane to Launceston. Always a reader with eclectic tastes, ranging from astrophysics to natural history, he skimmed over a number of stories until his attention was caught by one about hunter-gatherer tribes, written by a Professor Nigel Nicholson.[34] For the next ten minutes, Skroo was riveted, his red wine forgotten.

Just as the works of Gerber and Le Boeuf had done years before, this piece heralded the beginning of another major transformation in Flight Centre's organisational structure. It would become the most significant crossroad in the company's evolution; the foundation to its future success. It provided a framework for Flight Centre to make the transition from small company to big corporation without imploding, and it helped the company set a benchmark in corporate excellence. It would prove to be a radical business process that universities and other businesses around the world would analyse, study and attempt to replicate. And all this change revolved around one simple fact: that for 99.9 per cent of human history, man has been a hunter-gatherer.

In his articles and subsequent book *Executive Instinct*,[35] Nicholson explained that hunter-gatherers have existed for 4 million years, farmers for a mere 10,000. He argued that this has had a major effect on humankind. Even though people today like to pride themselves on their modern rationality, their natural inclinations actually duplicate those of their prehistoric ancestors:

> Until recently, the conventional wisdom was that humans differed from other animals in possessing minds like blank slates, on which learning and culture could write the story of human nature. It told us that every newborn baby has her psychology inscribed by how she is raised. We now know that this is profoundly wrong. Far from being a general-purpose computer, the brain is a heavily hard-wired library of programs that shape our identity.[36]

Using Darwin's theory of survival of the fittest, Nicholson argued that this genetic programming has been passed down from our hunter-gatherer ancestors via natural selection and reproduction. Thus we have inherited many of the traits that were necessary for survival in prehistoric times: we still fight furiously when threatened, use emotion rather than reason, and seek status and adornment to increase our chances to reproduce. Although many of these behaviours serve no practical purpose in our modern-day society, they are effectively 'hard-wired' into our mentality. Or, as the LBS professor put it, 'You can take the person out of the Stone Age . . . but you can't take the Stone Age out of the person.'[37]

Nicholson went on to describe the significance 'evolutionary psychology' has on the modern corporation. He believes that there's a limit to how much a company can change a person's evolved nature – skills can be taught and behaviours can be shaped, but the intrinsic, hard-wired traits are ineradicable. So rather than trying to force people to fit the company's mould, businesses should structure themselves to suit the way people prefer to work. That is, go with the grain rather than against it.

Skroo found this whole concept intriguing, not least because, as Le Boeuf's *How to Motivate People* had done with Top Deck's success, the hunter-gatherer theory reflected much of the practices that Flight Centre already had in place. Egalitarianism, autonomy and sharing were all typical of hunter-gatherer communities, for instance, and were equally characteristic of Flight Centre.

The words of Robert L. Kelly, another academic in this field of study, strike particular parallels between the company's philosophies and early human civilisation. 'Many hunter-gatherer peoples emphasise autonomy in their everyday lives,' the anthropologist has written, with each person being 'headman over himself'.[38] And on the subject of sharing, Kelly noted, it is only the amounts that differ: in the Mamainde tribe of Brazil, meat is distributed equally among the families in a band; Yora hunters of Peru keep about 40 per cent of the game they acquire; and Australian hunters from the Gunwinggu tribe keep a third. Like Flight Centre, all members of the community get to share in what is produced by the group.

Flight Centre had also unconsciously emulated hunter-gatherer tribes when it came to leadership. Turner has been accused of being Neanderthal, and in the true definition of the word, this is not an inaccurate description – even if the comparison was intended to be unflattering at the time.[39] For according to Nigel Nicholson, prehistoric leaders were not necessarily the best hunters; rather, they were the hunters who shared the meat among their people (stewardship), who chose good sites to hunt and camp (strategic decision-making), and who could control the aggressive males and put to use the energies of the dominant women. Anyone who knows Skroo Turner would agree that he excels in all three areas.

What caught the managing director's attention during that flight in 1995, however, was the way the hunter-gatherer idea could be applied to corporate structure. When he discussed the theory with the other partners, they all realised that, according to Nicholson, the bigger Flight Centre grew, the less it would resemble a hunter-gatherer community. People would become more and more disconnected from the way they inherently preferred to work. If Flight Centre didn't make some changes to the structure now therefore, it was likely that in ten years time the whole business would suffer.

The partners could see that wherever Flight Centre had emulated the structural organisation of hunter-gatherer groups, it had been successful. Small retail shops with six or seven team members worked very well. There was a lot of individual autonomy – consultants set their own goals and targets, had their own clients, did their own local marketing, paid their own bills and received a share of the takings. But like tribes of old, these teams also had to work together to survive. The shop responsibilities were divided equally into what Flight Centre called 'directorships', and each team tracked its own performance through daily and weekly meetings and analysis of the office's monthly profit-and-loss statement.

In contrast, the company had experienced less success when it tried to set up larger groups. A perfect example of this was the Elizabeth Street Flight Shop in Melbourne, which opened in 1986 with seven people, grew to eleven in its second year and was up to sixteen in its third. The results of this upstaffing had surprised everyone. 'The first year we made a profit of two hundred thousand dollars,' the manager at the time, Wayne Ackerfeld, remembers. 'The second year we also made this, but by the third year, when we'd doubled the staff, we effectively halved our profits to a hundred and twenty thousand.' It appeared that when Flight Centre increased team size over a certain number, productivity went down and profit suffered.

The company's state results demonstrated the same anomaly. Queensland had been Flight Centre's leader in profit growth throughout the first half of the 1990s. By 1995, however, with 50 shops reporting to a state leader, Queensland was still making profits but its annual growth was starting to fall. Flight Centre's back-end areas also lost efficiency as they added team members.

It was obvious that group size was important. But if Flight Centre wanted to make organisational change, it needed to know exactly how a hunter-gatherer community was structured. This was a difficult question. Much of the debate was conjecture, as these people had left little trace, and any modern-day examples hardly welcomed the intrusion of anthropological research teams. Nicholson, for his part, argued that our ancestral environment consisted of small family-sized teams in loose-knit tribal networks.

His theory was supported by the results of neurological experiments. Apparently decision-making performance falls off rapidly as the group size grows beyond seven. The human brain simply cannot simultaneously retain and process more than seven 'information chunks' at once. Telephone numbers were even originally set at seven digits because of this principle. A conclusion could therefore be drawn that family-sized groups of a maximum of seven people form the most efficient work teams.

But there were some activities that were too big for single families, Nicholson realised. Large game drives – which required a number of beaters to move the animals along, as well as hunters up ahead to kill prey – required families to work together. Tribal networks were also necessary for intermarriage and religious ceremony. So a new question asserted itself: how big were these hunter-gatherer tribes?

The answer came from another British-based academic, Robin Dunbar, professor of psychology at the University of Liverpool, who demonstrated a connection between brain size and tribe size in a series of experiments. Nicholson would summarise the point in *Executive Instinct*: 'Sure enough, there is a remarkably strong and clear correlation, from the smallish packs of the not-so-bright monkeys to the large troupes of very smart baboons.'[40] Using this correlation, Dunbar worked out that the 'natural' size of the human community was about 150 members. This was the limit of the social network that the human brain could contain and navigate.

The Flight Centre partners decided to use the same figures to transform their organisational structure. In this way they hoped that as the company got bigger, it could remain adaptable and egalitarian. The partners called this operation 'Family, Village, Tribe', and from mid 1995 began restructuring the company into units as follows:

- **Families** – teams consisting of a minimum of three and a maximum of seven people
- **Villages** – three to five geographical teams that support each other
- **Tribes** – a maximum of around 25 teams with a single tribal identity that come together for celebration and interaction.

Their first step was to make small 'families' a physical reality. This was easy to do in the retail shops, where most teams were already this size. The company had learned from its experience with Elizabeth Street Flight Centre that setting up a second retail outlet nearby to deal with over-enquiry was more successful than opening a giant shop or call centre. The small-team effect and its corresponding increase in profits outweighed the economies of scale experienced in the larger, more traditional outlets.

The company's back-end businesses required more reorganisation. Most had grown through need rather than planning and many had mushroomed well beyond the ideal family size of seven. Finance alone had 40 people, which meant that the manager had little time for emotional support and nurturing. Communication was difficult. Accountability was limited. The sense of identity of each group had become blurred and indistinct.

The partners now applied the 'family' concept to these back-end areas. Where before they had one large finance team, now they had ten teams of four people. The training area was segmented into communities of Novice Induction, Ongoing Training and a Team Leader Training Centre. Marketing, Property, Fit-out, and Technology soon followed suit. As well as improving communication and purpose, people also had more opportunity to become leaders following the change.

The physical reorganisation of these work areas involved some cost, but this was offset by the productivity gains from the more-motivated teams. There were also some logistical challenges. For example, Flight Centre hired a person in New South Wales to do its property leasing. Originally this person reported to a property leader based in Brisbane and was part of the 'family' there, but the geographic separation proved impossible when it came to emotional support, and the role was subject to high staff turnover. Skroo labelled this the 'shag on a rock' syndrome. 'We have clearly demonstrated that, unless people sit in families or teams together, they never work out,' he said at the time. 'We have to find a team for these people or we will be guaranteed constant failure.'

Villages were easier for Flight Centre to introduce because most didn't require any physical restructuring. The three to five geographical families in each village operated a 'buddy' system and conducted joint activities such as training sessions, celebration dinners and film nights. In emergencies, the teams helped each other out by sharing people and supplies. The villages also acted as an informal emotional network. People could air their grievances and brainstorm solutions about the similar problems they faced on a day-to-day basis.

Families and villages were important, but it was the largest groups, the tribes, that would have the biggest impact on the company. Up to this point, Flight Centre had state leaders and country leaders who were overseeing an ever-growing number of shops. This system had worked well until the middle part of the 1990s but was now proving unmanageable. If Professor Nicholson's theory was right, it was really just a question of size.

Flight Centre broke the old geographic areas up into distinct tribes of a maximum of 25 teams each, which equated to approximately 150 people. Flight Centre Queensland, for instance, was now split up into four areas: one in the far north, two in Brisbane and one on the Gold Coast. New South Wales was split into four, Victoria into three, New Zealand into two, and so on.

A tribal or 'area' leader, as the state leader job title became known, was appointed to head each tribe. These area leaders effectively became the owner–operators of these businesses and were remunerated on the profit growth of their area. They could also buy into their business through the BOS system. The significance Flight Centre placed on this role is illustrated by its description in the company's systems manual, the Profit Guide:

The Role of an Area Leader

In a nutshell, you are the 'entrepreneur' who takes your FCL Business or Service Area and makes it successful. Quantitatively, you must grow your area in numbers of businesses, sales, margins and profits. Most importantly you must employ, develop and inspire the people in your area to be successful business and seat owners. Ultimately you must create the business that people never want to leave.

Ask yourself every day…
'Is what I did today, this week, this month, contributing to profitability of my business and the development of my people?'
You need to:
- Give focus/vision/direction with 100% buy-in
- Develop brightness of future for your people and a sense of community spirit
- Be motivated and be a motivator
- Have self-confidence/high self-esteem
- Lead by example
- Be a good communicator
- Be an astute business person/strict disciplinarian
- Be honest
- Have 100% ownership of your area.

How to Use Your Time
Spend 20% of your time on perspiration-type activities and 80% of your time on inspirational activities. SWOT [the global executive team] suggest the following activities should take up most of your time:
- Recruiting and retaining the right people is the number one activity
- Inspiring/motivating your people and total information-sharing with your people
- Taking care of the customer at every opportunity – use your area's six-monthly customer survey as a tool
- Communication of new company initiatives, new focuses.

Expected Outcomes
As an Area Leader, you are expected to: increase profits between 20–50% each year, increase sales between 20–100%, increase margins to 9–10%, increase staffing numbers by 15–20%, and increase business numbers between 15 and 50%, depending on how established your area is.

The new area leaders revitalised Flight Centre's community life. With the help of their own family – which included an accountant, a marketer, a recruiter and a trainer – they created elaborate tribal identities. Examples of Flight Centre tribes included SEXtraordinaires, Gladiators, Urban Legends, Euphoria, Surf 'n' Turf, Ab Fab Triad, Generation Next, Bottoms Up, Simpletons, The Grizzlies, Magic Kingdom, and The Far Side. Each tribe had its own catchphrase, such as 'Right here, right now', 'No limits, no barriers' or 'Ain't no mountain high enough'.

Like contestants on the reality TV show *Survivor*, tribes compete fiercely with each other for results and recognition. This internal competition has been found to be good for productivity. 'When people feel comfortable and not at risk they tend to be compliant,' is Turner's rationale. 'Hence you get a soft, fat company and no one does much.' The tribes are driven by their desire to outperform each other, regardless of what's happening outside the company.

Many tribes excel in ingenuity. After tiring of their treatment as a continual underdog to the Australian operation, the two areas that constituted Flight Centre New Zealand, for instance, spelled 'New Zealand is Number One' with their bodies and filmed it from a helicopter to play at an Australian managers' conference. A NSW tribe wore white linen suits and blue gollywog wigs to let everyone know it had arrived at the 2002 International Awards in Singapore. As a way of demonstrating their distinctiveness, the women from the Flight Centre Shockwave tribe even pulled a 37-tonne Qantas 737-300 aircraft 100 metres along the runway, thus making national news and the Guinness Book of Records until a minor technicality saw them excluded.

Initiatives like these enable Flight Centre people to live and participate in a system attuned to their ancient heritage. They have lots of fun and, like their hunter-gatherer ancestors, blur the boundaries between work and non-work. Instead of having to play in a band at night to alleviate the boredom of their day-to-day life, Flight Centre people can play in their own band at Buzz Nights. Or they can run in the London Marathon with their tribal colleagues – or hot-air balloon, white-water raft, dance the flamenco or act in a play at their tribal conferences.

The tribes are also a way for Flight Centre people to get involved in their local community. Most Flight Centre shops give a substantial donation each year to the charity of their tribe's choice. Consultants from the Toronto tribe, for instance, collected all the courtesy toiletries from the hotels they stayed in for a year and gave them to an abused women's shelter. The Shockwave tribe built a children's playground locally in Berhampore in Wellington.

By 1999, it was apparent that the Family, Village, Tribe system was working well. In Queensland, profits increased as area leaders with a vested interest in their tribes reinvigorated the small communities. Flight Centre experienced similar results across the company.

Such a result is hardly surprising – and again it pays to turn to anthropological research for the reason. This is how the Kalahari hunter-gatherers known as the San people were described by Professor Richard B. Lee some 30 years ago: 'these people still retain something that may ultimately prove to be far more valuable than physical amenities in this . . . world: *a continuing, functional community and family organization and a continuing sense of personal and social identity.*'[41] Sound familiar?

Flight Centre's Family, Village, Tribe structure gave its people this constant framework. Even though the company was doubling in size every three years at this point, within the family cells there was a rhythm and regularity to each person's life. No matter where they worked or in what capacity, there was a sense of belonging that made people feel part of something greater than themselves.

The structure also made Flight Centre more adaptable. When demand in a shop or business increased, the partners simply started a new business. Similarly, when a tribe grew greater than 150 people, it was split into two. The system was self-replicating. The partners didn't have to keep readdressing their corporate structure, and they could make big changes rapidly, without affecting their culture.

Family, Village, Tribe also aligned with Flight Centre's preference for a flat management structure. Area leaders reported to national leaders, who reported to the global executive team. There was no need for an elaborate hierarchy. 'Hierarchies didn't exist in hunter-gatherer tribes as they weren't big enough to need them,' Skroo reasons. 'They only developed following the discovery of agriculture ten thousand years ago, when people began to congregate in cities and needed to be organised. They are a necessary evil for large companies, but it's important to remember that they aren't natural to humans and they are a cost to the business. It's the front-line salespeople who make the money.'

As a result of the company's adoption of hunter-gatherer princi- ples, the organisation is a more expensive corporate structure than traditional business set-ups. Where most companies would have one area leader, Flight Centre has five. Where competitors would have one megastore, Flight Centre has three individual shops. Traditional accountants often question the commercial sense of these decisions; they see the increased costs, but fail to consider the growth in produc- tivity that accompanies a corporate structure aligned with human nature. Yet this has been a key factor in the company's success.

In the last decade Flight Centre has doubled every three or four years. Without the Family, Village, Tribe concept, this level of growth would've been impossible to sustain. At the same time though, the rate of expansion has also led to some erosion of the hunter-gatherer prin- ciples, particularly in the non-retail units. 'The village system is not working well in some areas,' Skroo Turner admitted early in 2005. 'We are looking at standardising it to make it more effective. Also, in certain back-end finance, businesses and IT areas, sometimes we haven't been faithful to our philosophy in terms of numbers. We know that whenever that happens, our productivity drops.'

Flight Centre is not the only corporation to implement the princi- ples of evolutionary psychology. Ricardo Semler, CEO of Brazilian company Semco, also went back to the drawing board in an attempt to find a 'natural' style of management, which turned out to be, in Nigel Nicholson's words, a 'highly successful self-organizing communitarian system built around small sub-units'.[42] Similarly, Virgin and Gore-tex, British and US companies respectively, achieved phenomenal success by breaking down the size of their internal communities.

But these other three companies were unaware of the evolutionary psychological perspective of what they were doing, according to the London Business School professor. They applied their policies through instinct rather than rational deliberation. Therefore, Flight Centre's Family, Village, Tribe restructure was not just the successful implementation of an abstract idea, but also a management first in corporate practice. As Nicholson told me in 2001: 'Flight Centre is the only company I know of that has *consciously* applied these types of strategies to business.'

Chapter 9

THE MILLIONAIRE FACTORY

29 July 1995. Planes had been landing on the tarmac every half-hour. Buses transferred the passengers from the airport to their hotels. Valets sprinted along corridors with hairdryers and ironing boards. By 7 pm, two thousand people from all ends of the earth were assembled in the convention centre overlooking Sydney Harbour. It was Flight Centre's Annual Awards Night, and they stared in anticipation at the large screens that had been set up around the room to magnify the events on stage. Skroo took the floor. The audience hushed.

'We stand on the threshold of a new era for Flight Centre. We are about to float the company on the Australian Stock Exchange.' The crowd broke into spontaneous cheering. He waited for the noise to die down. 'Now, this isn't insider trading...' He paused and the big screens showed a slow-breaking grin lighten his features. 'I'm just giving you a bit of a tip. You should buy every Flight Centre share you can. Mortgage your dog, your husband, your wife, anything you have to. Now, I can't guarantee it but I believe anyone who buys fifty thousand dollars worth of Flight Centre shares will be a millionaire in ten years time.'

He was five years out.

Story told by Keith Stanley, Flight Centre's marketing manager

The float was the high tide of Flight Centre dreams. It made multi-millionaires of the founders and catapulted them into Australia's 'richest' lists. It made millionaires of over 100 Flight Centre people. It feathered hundreds of nests, in fact, and put the company squarely on the corporate map. But it almost didn't happen. 'We definitely weren't interested in floating the company,' Bill James insists. 'We didn't need to raise capital, the process was hellishly expensive, and we had seen several companies who went public go back to private.'

The question came up in mid 1994 because the company was searching for a way to involve more people in equity. Flight Centre also wanted to create an exit strategy for the existing partners. At that stage the only way for any of them to realise their investment was to sell the company, and the only travel entities large enough to buy Flight Centre were airlines. This was a far from attractive prospect, according to Jim Goldburg: 'We all knew they'd fuck the business up.'

The partners looked at private shareholder schemes, but they all had drawbacks. 'Because they weren't market-related,' Turner explains, 'many of these schemes involved complex formulas to work out the value of the shares. As most of the people that would be putting money in were small investors the rules re prospectuses, etc., were almost as onerous as those that applied to a public listing.'

Still, the public option of floating the company seemed like an unnecessary complication. After all, Flight Centre had no debt, nearly every office it opened made a profit, and the business was generating more money than it could spend. There didn't seem to be any reason to float.

It was at this point that Chris Greive, the company's New Zealand MD, read the book *Sam Walton: Made in America*, written by the founder of the legendary Wal-Mart empire.[43] Chris was so impressed by what he read that not only did he buy a copy for every Flight Centre person in New Zealand, but he also did the same for everyone on the executive team. This was to have a big impact on Flight Centre's future direction.

In his book, Walton described the company's float and how Wal-Mart's credibility had soared to new heights. He explained how it had put the company in a new league of players. But Walton's most potent argument for Flight Centre was that the only genuine measurement of a company's success was a publicly listed share. After reading his book, the partners back-pedalled. At a breakfast meeting at Auckland's

Sheraton Hotel in November 1994, they agreed to float 21 per cent of the company.

It sounded easy. After all, it was the height of the technology boom and even 'mums and dads' were buying shares. Also, Flight Centre's performance record was very impressive, as the following tables demonstrate.

Number of Flight Centre consultants with sales in excess of $1 million			
	$1m+	$1.5m+	$2m+
1992	22	0	0
1993	39	0	0
1994	86	3	0
1995	181	6	1

Number of Flight Centre shops earning profit in excess of $100,000			
	$100k+	$150k+	$200k+
1992	27	1	0
1993	22	4	0
1994	28	6	1
1995	34	14	7

In reality, the partners would need great reserves of determination and tenacity. Flight Centre was the first travel agent to be listed on the Australian Stock Exchange and it had to combat a lot of cynicism. An example of this is provided by Steve Wilson, whose company Wilson HTM was appointed as the joint underwriters of the float (with ABN Amro Morgans): 'I personally spoke to one director of Qantas who I knew well and asked him what he thought of Flight Centre, to which his reply was, "I wouldn't touch it with a barge pole." He said Qantas considered the fees paid to agents were a margin that they could capture, and they had a deliberate plan to in-source distribution at the expense of the agencies. Furthermore, he said the travel industry was a business dominated by mum and dad operators who just wanted to have a job and an annual holiday in some exotic place and the odd cheap trip within Australia. It could not have been a more damning assessment.'

This viewpoint was echoed by a number of prominent members of Wilson's own firm, who were opposed to the issue but, as underwriters, were committed to buying any shares that were unsold. Their fears were aggravated by the fact that in 1994 Flight Centre was very much an unknown in business circles. And what was known was not reassuring: the company was run by mavericks with unconventional ideas, and it wasn't even a member of AFTA, the main travel industry body.

But Wilson himself found that the closer he looked at Flight Centre and its results, the more encouraged he became: 'We had quite a surprise when we first saw the numbers for Flight Centre. They were outstanding and suggested there was something pretty special here. The company was achieving fantastic growth but was run by a team who were extraordinarily down to earth. The whole thing smelt of cost-consciousness, and this gave us a lot of comfort.'

To gain credibility, the partners realised that Flight Centre needed a chairman with clout in the business world, and conversation soon turned to Norm 'the Moon' Fussell, an institution in Australian business. (His nickname stemmed from his apparent habit of circumnavigating the globe every 28 days.) Fussell's imposing corporate résumé included fifteen years at MIM, five of them as CEO, and he also knew just about everyone in business, particularly in the airline industry. More impressive to Jim Goldburg was the fact that Norm had actually met Sam Walton.

But how were they to attract such a big fish to their small pond? To their surprise, he agreed to a meeting. And despite Jim and Skroo feeling the need to apologise for the lack of 'fancy offices or boardrooms', there was an instant rapport between both parties. 'I became a believer very quickly,' Fussell says. 'Flight Centre had a very clear vision of the market and said "To hell with the competition".' He was also impressed by the way Graham Turner empowered people around him. 'There's no use having a dog if you do all the barking,' he adds.

Norm Fussell agreed to become chairman of 'Flight Centre Limited', a name that reflected Flight Centre's status as a public company. The next step was another prerequisite of a listed company – choosing the directors. Geoff Harris, Bill James and Goldburg became executive directors, as did Turner, who also traded his previous job title for 'chief executive officer' honours. Chris Greive was offered a position on the board, as he had transferred his shares of Flight Centre New Zealand into a sizeable chunk of the new company stock. He declined the offer, however, because of the distance involved in flying from Auckland to attend board meetings in Brisbane. (Greive eventually became a director on 1 August 2001 but resigned the position on 29 January 2004, when he left the company to pursue his own interests.)

With females accounting for over 80 per cent of the company, it was only natural that Flight Centre would want at least one woman on its board of directors. Marg Mulholland, who had taken over Boxer's job as Queensland state leader knew the company inside out and was therefore the obvious choice. She became an alternate director.

Two directors were chosen at the non-executive level: Howard Stack, a lawyer, and Peter Barrow, Top Deck's original accountant. For the position of company secretary, Brian Hickey's name was put forward. 'Skroo told Norm that I had held this role in a previous job,' the then business services manager says. 'This wasn't strictly true, of course. I had to rush out and research what a company secretary actually did.'

With the board of directors appointed, the joint underwriters guided Flight Centre through the rest of the process. This included setting the float date and price, putting together the prospectus to be approved by the Australian Stock Exchange, and conducting the 'due diligence' check to ensure that Flight Centre had all the necessary information to satisfy the stock exchange regulations, in both the financial and legal sense.

So as not to impinge on the usual Christmas festivities, it was decided that the float date should be 1 December 1995. The pricing of the shares was more difficult to determine, however. The board agreed that a key goal was that as many Flight Centre people as possible should buy in and (hopefully) see a good return on their money. For, as Geoff Harris explains, 'If we'd overpriced the shares, it would've been terribly morale-sapping.' They eventually set the price at 85 cents for Flight Centre people and 95 cents for the public.

While these questions were being discussed, the due diligence process was under way. Part of this focused on understanding what drove Flight Centre's phenomenal success, with much of the work by Wilson HTM going towards determining whether there was any likelihood of success 'spoiling' the organisation. This is called the 'Merc in the garage' syndrome, whereby many companies driven by a strong entrepreneur slow down after the success of a share-market listing, which crystallises the value of their investments. In Flight Centre's case, the underwriters found the reverse was true – the company had genuine and achievable ambitions far beyond its current scale.

But Flight Centre still had to overcome investors' objections. Some people saw the company's lack of tangible assets as a serious risk, for example, as Brian Hickey recalls: 'We'd meet with fund managers and say, "We've got cash, people, systems and retail presence." They'd say, "What else have you got?"'

And then there were the usual petty judgments of the traditionalists to consider. One institutional adviser took Steve Wilson solemnly aside to tell him he was concerned about the way the float would go in the institutional market because of the way Skroo and his team dressed and behaved. Apparently the Flight Centre CEO was not regarded as 'professional' because of his use of matey nicknames, his 'common' swearing, and his short-sleeve shirts, unruly hair and generally casual manner.

Both of these objections would fizzle to nothing as investor confidence grew, but, perhaps sensing the impossibility of change in this second area, the underwriters focused on selling the positives. 'The company really was a breath of fresh air,' Wilson says by way of example, before adding a possible tagline: 'Down-to-earth people running things in a friendly but driven and goal-oriented way.' Flight Centre's cost-consciousness was also a selling point. The fact that the boardroom at head office had no outside windows and was just three or four laminex tables pushed together was frequently used as an example.

Then, at the eleventh hour, the whole float exercise nearly fell over. Four days before the prospectus was lodged, the Australian Securities and Investments Commission decided that it had an issue with Flight Centre's Business Ownership Scheme. Flight Centre had to rapidly compile a submission and redraft some of the prospectus wording before ASIC agreed to a solution. It would take until 2001, and several changes to the Corporations Act, before ASIC would give the company unequivocal approval for this scheme.

Once the prospectus was sent out on 11 October 1995 (at which point public and Flight Centre people alike could begin buying shares), the board members set off on a road-show around Australia and New Zealand to explain the process to their people. Many of these individuals knew nothing about shares so Skroo explained how it worked and why they should buy in. He was very convincing.

Jackie Sommers, one of Flight Centre's area leaders, was impressed enough to tell her father about the float, even though he'd never bought a share in his life. Born in 1945, James Sommers was from the hide-your-money-in-the-mattress school. Jackie nearly had a heart attack therefore when he bought 50,000 Flight Centre shares. 'If Jackie hadn't worked there, I probably wouldn't have done it,' he admits. Scott Kyle-Little, an electrician who was working as Flight Centre's fit-out manager, was another early convert. Despite being turned down by his bank and advised against overcommitting by the company's in-house financial advisers, he took up 80,000 shares.

Still, overall there were few purchases by Flight Centre people in the first three weeks. The directors were on tenterhooks, not least because they'd insisted on having 5 per cent of the float set aside for in-house purchase, much to the brokers' disapproval. The company waited. And waited . . . Eventually, because there appeared to be so little demand, the brokers began selling off some of the in-house allocation to external investors.

Then in the last week before the float date, the underwriters were suddenly swamped with demand. Gerrie Larsen, an accountant with

Flight Centre in Brisbane, was one of these last-minute buyers. She had some encouragement: 'Skroo walked into our office and said, "Are you guys buying any *fucking shares*? You'd better go and borrow as much money as you can and buy some."' Gerrie didn't feel comfortable borrowing, but she did clean out her savings account.

In the end, the offer was so oversubscribed that there were heated arguments over who should have to scale back. Brian Hickey recalls being told that he could only buy 50,000 in the 85-cent Employee Scheme, so he bought another 50,000 in the general float. This was not unusual. Flight Centre people purchased over 25 per cent of the shares available. Their overwhelming faith in the company set a new Australian record for take-up by in-house people.

When Friday, 1 December arrived, there were many anxious investors. It was a big risk, buying shares in the first-ever travel agency float in the history of the Australian Stock Exchange. Outside of Flight Centre circles, however, it was a day of no real note. *Time* magazine was more interested in so-called 'monster mice' – 'Scientists breed ferocious rodents that rape and kill', a subtitle claimed – while *The Australian* headlined with 'Abalone diver bashed shark with stone to survive attack'.

Unaware of such momentous events, most of the board members gathered in a meeting room on the sixth floor of the Australian Stock Exchange in Brisbane. They filled in time by making bets on where FCL's share price (share code 'FLT') would be at day's end. Turner's prediction would be closest – not an unusual situation, apparently.

A sudden, thunderous roar from the street below interrupted the directors' conversation. They looked out the window and saw a volcano of popping champagne corks, as more joyous cheering erupted from a small crowd gathered in front of the electronic share-price billboard, outside on Eagle Street. The stock exchange employees were bewildered. They'd never witnessed anything like this before.

'Don't worry,' FCL's chief executive officer told them. 'It's just some of our people making that racket. They bought their shares at 85 cents each and they've just listed for $1.14. They're pretty happy.'

And they weren't the only ones. The original partners were now very wealthy men. Bill James was in Sydney on the day of the float, having pre-committed to a managers' lunch. 'I remember I got a call saying the first sale was $1.14,' he recalls. 'By the end of the day, the shares were worth $1.23 and I was thoroughly pissed. I remember walking along Oxford Street at 2 am eating a hamburger and thinking, *My God, I'm worth seventeen million dollars overnight*. It was like winning the lottery – absolutely mind-boggling.'

Geoff Harris agrees that the opening day went better than they'd ever dreamed it could. Meanwhile, Jude Turner celebrated the family's $20 million windfall with a few glasses of champagne. 'I don't remember much of that day,' she says now. 'Apart from the fact that when I went to the ATM machine to withdraw some money, the machine advised that I had insufficient funds. I had to borrow some money off someone to pay for my drinks.'

For Jude's husband, the period immediately before and after the float of the company was the highlight of his career. Jim Goldburg's comments on this provide an insight into what makes such high-achieving individuals tick: 'To be honest, I think Skroo was a bit bored before the float came along. Flight Centre was growing at over twenty per cent a year and was just like a sausage machine – it was a bit ho hum.'

The float revolutionised Flight Centre's standing in the corporate world. Brand awareness skyrocketed. New business clients besieged FCL's corporate outlets. The company began to be featured regularly in the press, and its executives were inundated with requests for press interviews and investor meetings. Perhaps more importantly for Graham Turner, Flight Centre Limited now had the cash to acquire other companies, and this opened up a whole new set of challenges.

The fundamentals of the company remained unchanged, however. Its goal to be the world's most successful travel provider still existed. Its front-line operations remained untouched. Its business models were unaffected. Apart from the extra compliance requirements in areas such as finance, the company's culture was almost identical.

Identical, that is, except for one small factor: the new in-house investors became even *more* profit-focused than ever. A big part of their motivation was the fact that share options were soon added to FCL's wages system, with people being allocated options based on the nature of their role. In effect this meant that if the company's people achieved their targets by the end of the financial year, they could purchase their pre-set amount of shares (options) based on the share price at the start of the financial year. And if the price had increased during the year, as FCL's did during this period, each person could then sell his or her stock and enjoy a substantial windfall. 'People's focus on company targets was *thirty per cent higher* than in the pre-option era,' Skroo stresses.

Shares soon became the all-consuming topic of conversation within the company. For many of those who had bought in, the dilemma was when to sell. The share price hovered around $2 for the first couple of years, and a number of people sold out at this stage, as Scott Kyle-Little recalls: 'One of the guys I worked with bought fifty thousand shares at 85 cents and sold out at $1.20. He boasted about his profit and told us what suckers we were for not selling ours. Funnily enough, once the shares passed the $2 mark, the subject never came up again.'

Geoff Tyerman, working in the Brisbane IT department, had an equally sceptical parent. 'My one and only piece of stockbroking advice for my dad was to buy FCL shares when they were around the $3 mark,' he says. 'Right after he bought them, they dipped down again and stayed at $2 for a while. He kept hassling me, saying, "These shares are no good." He finally sold out at $7 and made a great profit.'

The main reason why the share price didn't move much initially, of course, was that the market was waiting to see if Flight Centre Limited could deliver on its projected goals. There were other issues as well, the principal one being the company's poor liquidity – that is, the number of shares available to be traded on any given day. Because five main players held 80 per cent of the company's shares (they being Turner,

James, Harris, Goldburg and Greive), there weren't enough in the market to keep up with demand. This meant that even small sales of FCL's stock had a substantial effect on its share price. It also meant that the Australian Stock Exchange couldn't include the company in any of its investor indexes, such as the highly influential S&P/ASX 200. FCL's exclusion from the latter really affected the company's early progress post-float, since the Standard and Poor is Australia's institutional benchmark index, measuring the performance of the most liquid stock in the nation's equity market and driving hundreds of financial decisions every day. With a market capitalisation of close to $1 billion at the time, Flight Centre Limited was one of the largest listed companies in Australia not to be included on these indices.

Added to this disadvantage, FCL was the first travel agency to float, so no one quite knew which category the shares belonged in. Originally the company was put in with other Miscellaneous companies, then transferred into the Tourism/Leisure category, which lumped it in with theme parks and casinos; two years later it was moved into Transport, along with the airlines. For his part, Turner believes that this is still the wrong place for FCL and questions how a retailer can be compared with aviation companies such as Qantas or Virgin Blue.

With little comparative measurement therefore, many fund managers sold their FCL shares in 1997 at $3, as they thought they were over-priced. And they weren't alone in this belief. It would take several years for the market to believe that FCL would deliver what it said it would. From late 1998, however, the company's continual delivery of growth and profits won over even the most hardened sceptics. And as shown in the table on the following page, the result was that the share price began to skyrocket.

By the year 2000, the FCL Millionaires' Club numbered over 100 people as the share price hit the $20 mark for the first time. The few stockbrokers who had supported Flight Centre were now deemed to have the Midas touch, but it was many of FCL's people who would collect this gold. Those with share options priced at $7.66 at the start of the 1999/2000 financial year couldn't believe their good fortune

FCL share price performance 1995–2004	
Float	$0.95
1995/96	$1.95
1996/97	$3.65
1997/98	$2.90
1998/99	$7.30
1999/00	$19.10
2000/01	$28.00
2001/02	$27.25
2002/03	$22.00
2003/04	$19.11

when by year's end the shares were valued at $18, giving a $10 profit per share. Every shop manager that year had 2000 options, so by the end of May it became obvious that they were looking at a bonus of $20,000 if targets were met. Not surprisingly, there was a flurry of activity in June that year, with record profits in many areas.

For the next twelve months, the share price ranged from $17 to $22 before reaching an all-time high of $28 in June 2001. Underwriter Steve Wilson was amazed: 'As big a bull as I am, never in my wildest dreams did I imagine that Flight Centre shares would hit $28 some six years on from listing.' One of the earliest to jump on the investment bandwagon, Scott Kyle-Little retired at this point, with his shares worth $2.2 million.

Not everyone was happy, though. FCL's float remains one of the greatest 'if only' corporate stories in Australia. One of the company's managers (who refused to be named) missed out on millions when her husband talked her out of buying $50,000 worth of shares after they'd already spent three times that on an extension to their house. 'I kick myself now,' she says. 'I can't even talk about it because I get so cranky.'

When Bill gave a presentation at his son's school in 2002 he started out by saying, 'If you had bought twenty-five thousand FCL shares at $1 in 1995, imagine what they would be worth today.' As he went about explaining his point, the whole class broke into an uproar. It turned out that their teacher had told the class before-hand that he'd almost bought shares, but hadn't, and was still ruing his decision.

From the high of $28 in 2001, the shares would fluctuate over the next few years, down to a low of $16 following a profit downgrade in January 2005. Yet for Bill James and his fellow directors, whose original shares were valued at 95 cents, the float brought unimagined wealth. With the new-found millions, their futures were boundless. Bill, Geoff and Jim eventually relinquished their formal positions within the company while retaining their shares. They now had the freedom to pursue other dreams. And having picked up shares at 85 cents as well as the standard price, company secretary Brian Hickey had also scored big before opting to retire in December 2000. 'I always said I was going to retire when the shares hit $20, and I did,' he says.

Geoff Harris would step down in 1998. He became a director of Boost Juice and the Reach Foundation (the children's charity), as well as sitting on the board of the AFL Hawthorn Football Club. Jim Goldburg would be next, in 1999. He took on a directorship at Cellnet, and founded CKG Properties with Grant Kenny, the former Australian Ironman and Olympian. Jim was also a founding commit-tee member of the Mater Medical Research Group.

Bill James took a different path. 'I've been poor much longer than I've been rich,' he explains. 'I've found that money doesn't buy happi-ness but it does buy you time – quality time. I made a conscious decision to simplify my life and focus on building relationships with the people I care for, rather than networking.' After stepping down from his duties as an executive director within a year of the float, Bill acted as a cultural ambassador for FCL, flying up to speak to new recruits at its twice-monthly induction.

The float also increased the directors' profiles, which for James and Harris has been a definite downside. Bill likens the situation to being a beautiful woman – never knowing whether others like you for who you are or for what they perceive they can get from you. 'I get lots more requests for loans now,' the former school teacher says, 'and I'm never sure of people's motives.' Geoff agrees with him: 'Because our shares are in the public domain, we get more exposure in magazines like *Business Review Weekly*.[44] Bill and I have had to get silent numbers, and my kids got hassled more at school.'

For Skroo, though, the float made 'no great changes'. He does cede that he finds himself getting hounded more by 'suspect charities' and that people recognise him now due to the media exposure – 'but that's part of the job.'

It may've been business as usual for Skroo Turner, but for many others, FCL's float had been the vehicle to their financial independence. The company that had started as a ramshackle tour operator had made them their fortune. And for those 'wannabe' entrepreneurs wishing to replicate the success, his advice is simple: 'Start with a lucky break. Then have a clear dream . . . and stay focused and passionate about achieving your dream. Accept that it is mainly about having the right attitude and working with the right people; the business or field is unimportant.'

Chapter 10

SEEMED LIKE A GOOD
IDEA AT THE TIME

*When asked why Flight Centre Limited started up a particular brand or
acquired a specific business, Graham 'Skroo' Turner's tongue-in-cheek
reply is always: 'It seemed like a good idea at the time.'*

P eter 'Skinny' Forsyth's joint venture with Flight Centre certainly
seemed like a good idea at the time. But in 1995 with the
business going downhill he decided to quit. Skroo offered him
shares in the upcoming float as a payout. 'You can stick your shares up
your bum,' he told Flight Centre's then MD. 'I'll take the money.' As
he admits, these would prove to be the worst twelve words of his life.

Turner and Forsyth had cooked up Flight Centre's second wholesale brand (the Ticket Centre was the first) over a Chinese meal.
Skinny had been running Infinity, a successful wholesale business with
Continental Airlines, until September 1993, when the carrier pulled
out of Australia, leaving his company for dead. Enter Graham Turner
and Flight Centre.

'It seemed the perfect partnership,' Forsyth says now. 'I needed to
reduce my costs, and Flight Centre had this fantastic network of over
two hundred shops that needed accommodation, car hire, etc. I
suggested to Skroo that Flight Centre should take fifty per cent of the
company, and together we could make Flight Centre holidays.'

They agreed on a joint venture. Skinny was ecstatic, but his
bonhomie lasted all of six months. 'It was a bloody disaster,' he recalls.
'Flight Centre consultants wouldn't get behind it unless I gave them a

deal better than anyone else's. I couldn't afford to do that. I was *worse* off than before.' In addition, Flight Centre wanted to run the business its way, despite knowing nothing about the wholesale industry. Or, as Turner puts it, 'We bought a distressed business, then we added to the distress.'

This failure wasn't surprising, as Flight Centre had only just started to experiment with new businesses. Admittedly though, this fact could never stop Peter Forsyth from wanting to retract those twelve words. From Flight Centre's point of view, it would be another opportunity to learn from previous mistakes.

Although the exercise of the late 1980s had been to streamline the Flight Centre outlets into a single, recognisable brand name, by the early years of the following decade, the company was aware that saturation point was looming in Australia. So, as well as considering a return to overseas locations, Flight Centre began looking at other brands that could increase its market share in Australasia.

Still, most of the company's early experiments were with retail brands that grew out of necessity. In 1993 a Flight Centre shop in Townsville was located in a very busy shopping centre and couldn't keep up with demand. Rather than opening another shop or relocating to a larger site, Flight Centre decided to open a new retail brand, Great Holiday Escape (GHE), later rebranded as Escape Travel, that offered clients something different.

The new store was decorated with fake palm trees hung with synthetic coconuts, and had bamboo-edged counters. 'The idea was to attract people wanting to book package holidays,' Skroo explains. 'We would still sell all the other stuff, but the emphasis would be on packages rather than flights.'

Flight Centre's first corporate brand began in a similar way. Some consultants had a lot of business clients but couldn't service them properly in a retail shop. So in March 1993, Geoff Harris decided to trial a Flight Centre Corporate office, in Melbourne. Heather Gilbert was charged with the start-up honours and still remembers Geoff's instructions: 'I'll give you twenty thousand dollars, and you do what you have to do to make it a success.'

Around this time, Turner became interested in getting hold of student fares to compete with agencies such as STA. So in November 1995 Flight Centre opened its third retail brand, Student Flights, in an office in Sydney's George Street. The shop's slogan was 'Cheap Airfares for Students', but the motto was a difficult one to live up to. When the office opened, it only had one student airfare deal, courtesy of Singapore Airlines.

This wasn't the only sort of challenge facing the new retail brands. Skroo admits that it would have been easier if they could've opened on an island where there were no Flight Centre shops, as some simply became poor cousins to the company's main brand. Indeed, consultants from both Student Flights and GHE recall how they would put in the time and effort to quote and advise clients, only to see them head off down the road and make the booking at the local 'red shop'. After all, Flight Centre was the one advertising its 'Lowest Airfares Guaranteed' service on national television.

The brands also had to learn how to specialise in their new areas. When Flight Centre Corporate started, for instance, it didn't even have a credit system – the directors thought everyone should just pay upfront. Technology was another problem area. For whereas Flight Centre Corporate used Apple Macs, as all its parent company's brands did, its corporate clients were on PCs that weren't compatible with them.

These challenges were seen as minor impediments, however. Flight Centre remained enthusiastic about opening new brands, and when the company floated in 1995, it had more cash reserves with which to invest. By 1998 there were three more names to add to the list: 24 Hour Flights, for travellers who wanted to book after-hours; Visiting Friends and Relatives (VFR), a small niche wholesaler that ticketed flights for nationals returning to their country of origin; and Travel Associates, an exclusive brand for clients prepared to pay for quality service and expertise.

By its very nature, Travel Associates was the type of business that FCL had vowed never to set up, although it was a Flight Centre brand manager, Greg Ashmore, who came up with the original concept. Working in a shopping-centre store, he'd been unable to cope with the constant flow of new customers in addition to his existing large client base. In early 1998, Greg decided to leave, to set up an exclusive travel agency in an off-street location, with expensive furnishings and consultations by appointment only. This was the antithesis of the Flight Centre brand.

Geoff Harris was filling in for Turner at the time while the CEO was on long-service leave. He recognised the idea's potential and suggested to Ashmore that he set up the new store under the FCL umbrella. Thus the first Travel Associates office opened in Melbourne in April 1998, using the slogan 'Where Travel is a Lifestyle'. Skroo's first reaction when he saw the store was to fire out a series of questions: 'Why aren't the doors open? Why do you need such big desks? And why do you need a TV and video system?' He would be mollified by the $100,000 profit the shop made in its first year.

Most of these new businesses started in Australia, but there was one new overseas venture. In March 2000 the Flight Centre brand set up a satellite shop in Port Moresby in Papua New Guinea. The idea was to cash in on the large expatriate market flying to and from Australia, and make money for the Far North Queensland FCL area.

But like Vietnam, endemic corruption and bureaucracy hindered this operation. Bribes were required for each step of the set-up, of course, and although the company couldn't get a building permit, it began trading anyway. In an effort to lay down the law on the upstart travel agents, the local building inspector kept coming in and turning the lights off. Ironically, he became their first customer when he booked a package holiday to Phuket.

In the end, the PNG operation was about as effective as the translation of 'Lowest Airfares Guaranteed' into pidgin English was faithful. (The local equivalent of the slogan, *Liklik Moni Tasoal Long Baim Bilong Balus*, actually translates back as: 'Little money that's all you like to buy a ticket that belongs plane'.) FCL realised that one shop was never going to make enough profit to cover the cost of supporting the operation out of Australia. Port Moresby Flight Centre was closed after less than twelve months, with losses of $500,000. 'It wasn't a bad idea,' Turner believes. 'We just executed it poorly.'

Most of FCL's brands proved more successful. Their development followed a definite pattern: they would experience initial losses as they experimented with different systems, but once they arrived at a successful business model, they were consistently profitable. This was true of Travel Associates, Student Flights, Infinity and VFR, all of which were profitable by 2004.

Some brands took more time and effort than others. Great Holiday Escape was one of these. In retrospect, Townsville was probably the last place FCL should've opened GHE. The brand's original marketing slogan was 'Cheapest Tropical Holidays', yet the shop was *based* in the tropics. The first manager, Gina Raccanello, was exasperated at the resulting lack of variation in holiday destinations: 'I sometimes felt that if I booked one more bloody Whitsunday weekend, I would die!'

As time passed and shop numbers grew, GHE continued to lose money. Everyone had a different idea of what the focus should be and the advertising tagline underwent at least five transitions from 'Discount Holiday Specialist' to 'Guaranteed Cheapest Australian Escapes'. It was several years before FCL learned that companies with three-word names are difficult for people to remember.

In 2003, the business which now comprised over 30 stores was re-branded as 'Escape Travel', an iconic name that FCL bought from a Sydney company for $100,000. FCL also changed the look of the stores. Their customers picked the new British Airways–style red and blue colouring, and the consultants came up with a more professional-looking uniform.

The response was promising. By the end of 2003/04, Escape Travel had performed a $1.85 million turnaround on the previous tax year, pulling back the loss to $1.2 million. The brand won the Most Improved Business Worldwide award, the top consultant transferred $3 million worth of revenue, and 59 consultants made over $1 million of revenue for the year. Having felt like the black sheep of the FCL family for so long, former GHE consultants like Tanya Ballard were thrilled: 'This year I was a *1.5-million-dollar consultant in the Achievers' Club*, and I made it to the International Awards Night at Pattaya in

Thailand. It was fantastic!' Escape Travel now has over 100 stores across Australia.

Graham Turner is the first to admit that it generally takes the parent company a while to get it right when it comes to new businesses and brands. Still, one brand broke this pattern and experienced phenomenal success in a very short time. When Danny O'Brien started at Flight Centre Corporate in 1995, there were five offices that made a total profit that year of $40,000. 'In the following year,' he says, 'one office won the Most Productive Business Worldwide award, another office won Most Improved Business Worldwide, and I was Flight Centre Limited's Consultant of the Year Worldwide. We made a total brand profit of $632,000 that year.'

Part of Flight Centre Corporate's success was that it was the first large agency to target small to medium-size businesses rather than going after the major players. But the new brand couldn't attract customers simply by promoting cheap fares. Flight Centre Corporate recruited a team of business development managers to bring in new clients, based on leads generated by a telemarketing agency. These customers were then assigned their own corporate travel consultant to look after all their travel needs. A big factor in the success of this system was that both the business development manager and the travel consultant were incentivised on their client's bookings.

FCL's float raised the brand's profile and attracted more corporate clients, and Flight Centre Corporate received another boost when it changed its name in September 1996. The reason behind this change was that some corporate clients were apparently put off by the 'cheap' connotations associated with the Flight Centre brand. So Skroo 'borrowed' a name from a company he found advertising in a British Airways in-flight magazine, and the brand became The Corporate Traveller.

With a new technology system that allowed it to process accounts more quickly than before, The Corporate Traveller became the company's second fastest-growing brand after Flight Centre. By 2002, its financial performance equalled that of the parent company's New Zealand operation, whose outlets covered Flight Centre and the entire family of FCL brands, of course. The Corporate Traveller had also been replicated successfully in all of the overseas countries, and it set new records in office profitability. For example, in the 2001/02 financial year, one office's six-person team met their annual profit target after only six months. They ended up making $570,000 for the year – an outstanding achievement when average shop profits were $80,000.

The stock exchange float, a name change and state-of-the-art IT were one thing, but it was a decision made in 1999 that had the most impact on The Corporate Traveller. FCL had set a long-range target to have 6000 businesses by 2010 (this would later be revealed as an over-stretch). The directors at the time realised that they couldn't achieve this by in-house growth alone. The company simply couldn't produce the number of leaders required to sustain the pace of development. In addition, the process of setting up new brands and businesses had made them realise that it took hard work, time and perseverance to become a major player in a specialised market. 'The logical solution was to buy other businesses,' Skroo concludes. 'With our share price escalating, we could use our shares as bargaining chips to buy what we wanted.'

In 1999, Flight Centre Limited embarked on the acquisitions trail. Its first purchase was a company that had been started by none other than Dave Tonkin, one of FCL's founding partners. Dave set up Sydney Business Travel (SBT) in 1987 but then sold it to two entrepreneurs, Michael Rudny and Michael Keating. With the help of a revolutionary technology system, Citros, the two Michaels built SBT into a successful enterprise making over $4 million profit per year. It also had a net margin (that is, net profit divided by total transaction value) of 4 per cent, which was rare for a corporate travel company. 'SBT was successful,' Michael Rudny admits, 'but we realised that if it was to grow any bigger, we needed a substantial cash injection and a global partner.'

Feelers were sent out to interested parties therefore, resulting in several offers being made. SBT finally struck an agreement with a large American concern. Five days before the deal was due to be finalised, however, Skroo rang to express interest in the company's Citros technology; Rudny refused to sell it separately so they began discussing the sale of the whole entity. The two men agreed to meet in Brisbane to take the discussions further.

By this time the directors of Flight Centre Limited had decided they wanted to buy SBT, but with the American offer already on the table, there wasn't much room to manoeuvre. 'This was our first acquisition and Michael Rudny was very experienced,' Turner admits. 'We agreed on a price fairly quickly but we were naive when it came to the details . . . We should've been tougher on what was and wasn't included in the business.'

They ended up paying $16 million for the business plus an extra $2 million for the technology, the bulk of which was paid in FCL shares. As these were priced at $6 at the time of purchase, Rudny and Keating made a substantial profit on the deal. The SBT consultants, however, were underwhelmed by the takeover. 'We were having drinks after work,' Mary Gava remembers, 'when someone walked in with a *Travel Daily* and there was an article in it about Flight Centre buying SBT. That was the first we had heard of it.'

The reason for their lack of excitement was the fact that even though FCL was a retail giant, the perception was that it sold cheap tickets on street corners (as Flight Centre Corporate had discovered); SBT, on the other hand, was a top-end corporate. In short, the consultants strongly questioned the wisdom and worth of having a 'lesser' organisation running the show. And the first twelve months did little to allay these concerns.

'We were FCL's first acquisition and there wasn't a lot of effective communication,' Mary continues. 'People would hear snippets of rumours and be terrified about what was going to happen. We lost a lot of people in the first eighteen months.' Eventually even the two Michaels left, which, from the new owners' perspective, was probably a good thing. Rudny and Keating's culture was very different from

FCL's, and it was felt that this had held back some of the change.

Introducing incentives to the SBT consultants was one of the biggest challenges. Many of them took the news that the base wage would be $25,000 to mean that $25,000 was *all* they'd earn. 'We just didn't understand incentives,' Renos Rologas says.

FCL realised that there was no problem in principle with the incentive model, it was just that everyone was nervous about how it worked. In the end, the incentive model was run concurrently with the normal, SBT system, and anyone who moved across was paid his or her last three months of incentives retroactively. Within three months everyone had crossed over.

Over time, as things improved, people's attitude changed. FCL's Family, Village, Tribe system could take much of the credit for this. Prior to the changeover, SBT operated as one large group; then FCL introduced family-sized teams, with the result that each person's level of ownership increased and costs such as the write-off of errors decreased. This was the first sign that FCL's hunter-gatherer tribal structure could be replicated in the 'foreign' model of another business. Mary Gava, who became the SBT area leader, states that now her advice to any employees of a company acquired by Flight Centre Limited would be: 'Don't resist the changes. Just work with them.'

SBT turned out to be a good purchase. It proved a solid performer for FCL, generating substantial profits each year, and the acquisition established the company as a mainstream corporate travel provider. The Citros technology was also a worthwhile investment, as FCL adapted it for use in many areas within the company – The Corporate Traveller being one brand in particular to benefit. But just as critically, the Family, Village, Tribe structure had worked, and the foundation was set for it to be applied to all sorts of other ventures.

In the years following the first acquisition in 1999, FCL's integration process improved, even if some of the newly acquired businesses were bemused by the blind faith that Flight Centre people had in its systems and processes. Alan Spence, managing director of Britannic Travel, FCL's largest acquisition at the time, observed how 'One of the problems is that they buy you, but even a year later they don't see you as "Flight Centre".' 'It wasn't quite a cult, but it was close to it' is another CEO's assessment. Other people were intimidated by FCL's idiosyncratic language – 'What's a BOS?' and 'How do I work out cost-of-seat?' were common questions soon after an acquisition had taken effect.

Despite these drawbacks, there were many upsides for companies acquired by FCL. For some principals, like Michael Rudny of SBT, it was the chance to jump onto a bigger ship. They'd taken their business as far as they could on their own, and needed the money and muscle of a larger company to go any further. For others, it was about growing. Bonnie Tsui, managing director of acquired company Kistend Travel, truly believed that FCL inspired its people to achieve great things (though she loathed having to pay all the head office management fees), while Alan Spence was also satisfied with his decision to sell. 'Overall it's been a good relationship,' the Britannic Travel chief said. 'Flight Centre's strength is that they believe in what they've got and the people they've got, and they let them get on with it. If I had my time over I would sell to them again.'

With the purchase of more businesses and the advent in 2002 of a dedicated Acquisitions team, Flight Centre Limited refined its whole acquisition process. The company focused on businesses that had good track records of profitability and/or were a good cultural fit. This last requirement proved quite difficult, as John Ahern, FCL's then global acquisitions manager, illustrates. During preliminary discussions with one company, he was very excited to hear from its directors that it already had an incentive system in place. It would be a perfect, seamless transition surely. Well, not necessarily: 'When we questioned them further we discovered that their major "incentive" was giving their employees a ham at Christmas.'

By May 2005, Flight Centre Limited had spent $164 million on its acquisitions. The following is a list of those businesses, all of which are Australian-based unless otherwise indicated:

- SBT
- Stage and Screen

- Conference & Incentive Management
- Conference & Incentive Services
- ITG (TQ3 Travel Solutions) – Australia and New Zealand
- AITL – Hong Kong
- Quickbeds
- Cruiseabout/Turramurra Travel
- Overseas Working Holidays
- Shopper Travel
- Sir George Seymour College – New Zealand
- Paula Peterson Travel
- Itchyfeet – New Zealand
- Britannic Travel – United Kingdom
- Kistend Travel
- Contal and Travelthere.com
- 50 per cent of the former Rosenbluth China Comfort Travel – China
- 51 per cent of Friends Globe Travels – India.

Not all of Flight Centre Limited's expansion was through acquisition, of course. As well as the many new brands the company introduced, FCL also formed some joint venture businesses – Peter Forsyth's Infinity being one of them.

A more notable one was with the Fanatics, a patriotic support group that followed Australian sport to events at home and around the world. The organisation had forged close links with Tennis Australia and was already famous for its passionate globe-trotting support of the Australian Davis Cup team, in its trademark yellow T-shirts. By 2005, some 14,000 of the Fanatics' 48,000 members had been on one of the company's memorable tours to events involving sports such as rugby union, cricket, rugby league and soccer.

Years before this, however, FCL saw the opportunity to package up the Fanatics' sporting tickets with flights and accommodation. The

FCL managers were also excited by the thought of being involved with such an iconic Australian product. In mid 2002 they struck a deal with the Fanatics leader, Warren 'Woz' Livingstone: Flight Centre Limited would bankroll the new venture, and he would run it and have a 25 per cent debenture in the business. Thus Fanatics Sports Tours was born.

'I thought it was a no-lose situation,' says Livingstone. 'I would have FCL's six hundred and sixty retail shops to distribute my product, and my only extra cost would be FCL's management fees.'

In the past the Fanatics had bought ticket stock according to customer demand. To cater for the thousands of new customers anticipated from the FCL shops, however, Woz ramped up the business. With FCL's monetary backing he bought hundreds of tickets upfront, for both the Fanatics' core sporting events and many new ones, such as the West Indies cricket tour.

But like Forsythe before him, Livingstone had completely misunderstood how FCL worked internally. Skroo Turner may have promoted Fanatics Sports Tours in his newsletter, but as far as the shops were concerned, it was a very minor part of their business and they had little aptitude for selling niche products.

When Woz bought 30 US Open packages at US$1500 each in 2002 he didn't sell a single one. 'We took risks that we wouldn't normally take,' he explains, 'but only because we thought that with FCL on board we were guaranteed an extra thirty or forty per cent more passengers.' In addition, his management fees turned out to be much higher than he had anticipated.

The results were predictable: Fanatics Sports Tours lost $317,018 in the 2002/03 financial year and $203,268 in 2003/04. The two parties conceded that this was one experiment that hadn't worked. They reached an agreement whereby Flight Centre Limited passed the brand name back to Livingstone, covered the debts for the remaining tours and dissolved the joint venture.

'We should've done a lot more research before getting into bed with one another,' Woz admits. The same sentiment comes through in Turner's thoughts on the short-lived partnership: 'In hindsight, we liked the idea of being involved with the Fanatics but we didn't do the proper due diligence before we started. The whole exercise cost us a lot of money over a two-and-a-half year period, and it was all our own fault.' The Fanatics operation returned to being an independent business under Warren Livingstone's leadership.

On the whole, however, FCL's new businesses were generally profitable. Because many of them were involved in corporate travel, in 2004 FCL decided to consolidate its multitude of both in-house and acquired corporate brands under a single brand name: FCm Travel Solutions. This would be the first global travel management company to be based in the Asia–Pacific region and the largest corporate travel brand based in Australasia.

This new brand enabled Flight Centre Limited to enter overseas markets using licensing arrangements. It started by re-branding its 50-per-cent owned China operation. The first FCm branded agency opened in Beijing in August 2004 and was followed by one in Shanghai and another in Hong Kong. The company also began marketing the benefits of trading under its large FCm brand to external corporate agencies. The first non–FCL-owned licensee signed on in Singapore in December 2004. 'We're looking at more in Asia, India and Europe,' said brand leader at the time, Anthony Grigson, 'and we hope to be in a total of twenty countries in the next twelve months.' FCm now operates in over 70 countries

Despite their maverick origins, FCL's new brands and businesses have been a big success. They would've gone to seed, however, without FCL's culture of rewarding excellence, linking performance to profit, restructuring organisations into hunter-gatherer–sized teams and promoting business ownership. Singapore Airlines' national sales manager, Tom Kenny, is highly surprised at the company's expansion, but no less impressed. 'FCL have managed to diversify so well,' he enthuses. 'I never thought they would be this successful. If you'd asked me when they started, I would probably have said they would become a three- or four-shop organisation.'

People often question the company's motivation for opening all these new brands. Brian Egan, national manager of Malaysia Airlines, for one: 'When GHE opened up I thought, *Why?* Now I can see why, but I couldn't then.' Comments such as 'It seemed like a good idea at the time' foster the belief that these businesses were off-the-cuff operations, almost casual after-thoughts to the main game. But just like the Romans' conquest of Europe, it is the constant thirst for expansion that lies behind FCL's growing collection of new brands, businesses and acquisitions. This is the real driving force behind the company's diversity and the tribal structure is one of the main strategies making it happen.

Chapter 11

WHO'S GOING TO PAY FOR IT?

Humans hate to be accountable and will make many excuses why their case is different.

Graham 'Skroo' Turner, in an FCL newsletter

B y July 1997, Flight Centre Limited had over 300 shops in five different countries, and the result was a distinct change in the shape of the company. Whereas in the past FCL had consisted mainly of retail stores, it now had over 50 so-called 'support' areas – all the divisions that didn't retail directly to the public, such as Banking, IT, Management, Payroll, Ticket Centre and Marketing.

Like a black hole, the cost of these support areas was beginning to swallow up more and more of FCL's profit. For many companies, such 'back-end' expenses were quite normal. When one of Australia's largest travel operations, Traveland, went bankrupt in 2001, it reportedly had a negative $10 million administration account. This was seen as unremarkable at the time. For a company like FCL, however, with an innate dislike of bureaucracy and administration, it was a cause for concern.

Graham Turner identified that the new-look company consisted of two distinctly separate areas: a proven and successful retail business model, and a support area that was running like an overheated engine. With guaranteed income to cover their costs (as shown in the table overleaf), there was no real pressure on support teams to ensure that what they were providing was cost-effective, and they had no impetus

Example of FCL's support area funding	
Marketing costs per year	$2,500,000
Human resource costs per year	$918,000
Finance costs per year	$916,000
Management costs per year	$750,000
IT costs per year	$1,500,000
Total FCL support costs	$6,584,000

$6,584,000 divided by total 306 shops:
    = $21,516 per shop per year
    = $1793 direct debited from each shop's bank account
      per month

to change or innovate. They lacked ownership, a successful rewards and recognition system, small business ideals, accountability – all the key elements in fact that made up the world-class retail model.

The answer, Skroo believed, was simple: replicate the tribal structure, systems and philosophies of the successful retail model across the board. The concept was one that few people in private enterprise had attempted before, but FCL's executive team agreed with him. From here on, the support areas would become back-end businesses, providing products and services to the retailers. All businesses, whether retail or back end, would thus operate under the same principles.

Flight Centre Limited originally called the new policy 'corporatisation', but changed it because of the word's negative connotations. 'Commercialisation' was the term the directors settled on. It was akin to what government would refer to as 'privatisation'; that is, the conversion of traditional 'cost' areas of a large organisation into stand-alone businesses.

Like FCL's retail shops, these new businesses would be broken into team-based units with a manager and a second-in-charge; operate on separate profit-and-loss statements; charge fees for their services; establish key performance indicators (KPIs) and individual incentives; and have a team profit target. Their clients would be the retail businesses that sold travel directly to the public, and other back-end businesses within FCL. Under the heading 'How to convert support areas into commercialised business units', Turner presented the following guide-lines to executives at a 2004 conference:

1. Establish the raison d'etre. Why does the business exist? What is its purpose? What are the main one or two outcomes the business contributes to FCL?
2. Define measurable qualitative and quantitative outcomes for the business or for the internal customer. They are then estab-lished as the KPIs for that unit.
3. From these outcomes how is the income derived? Who pays the fee? Do they agree to this fee? Who keeps the business account-able for the outcomes?
4. Link the fees directly to the outcomes.
5. Link the team and personal incentives to the fees so that incentives are also a derivative of the outcomes.
6. Recognise that business profit is a target achieved from the customer's outcomes and are not a driving factor of the business.

This created an exciting opportunity for FCL's many accountants, payroll clerks, recruiters, trainers, marketers, leasing agents, shop designers, technology consultants, maintenance people and help-desk operators. They would now become entrepreneurs as they turned their operations into small, specialised businesses.

People were less enthusiastic, however, about the way that income was to be generated. Under commercialisation there were three ways that businesses could be funded:

1. **The user pays model** – This meant that a team charged a fee for each service it supplied: that is, user pays on outcomes produced. The fees were expected to be less than those offered by external competitors. (See the table over the page for an example of how this works.)
2. **The management fee model** – Some management teams, such as area leaders and their 'families', offered services that couldn't be

---

FCL's user pays model – IT area

Each area has to negotiate fees for the services that it offers to retail shops. For example, here are some of the services the new IT business offered when it first started up as a commercialised operation:

Server and A4 printer rental	$300 per month per shop
WAN communication	$600 per month per shop
Basic desktop support	$66.40 per month
Email administration	$11.50 per month
Internet access	$12 per user
Remote access dial-up	$3.50 per hour
New shop set-up	$2000 per shop
New user management fee	$30 per user
Shop refurbishment	$1000 per shop
Shop relocation	$1445 per shop
Laptop locks	$55 per item
Laptop carry bag	$55 per item
Laptop short-term rental	$145 per week
CD writer rental	$65 per day
Digital whiteboard rental	$30 per day
DAT back-up tapes	$25 each
Zip disks	$25 each
Home business set-up fee	$1250 one-off charge
Internet domain registration	Registration fee plus 10 per cent management fee
Web development	$85 per hour
Technical engineer	$85 per hour

In this way, shops and other back-end businesses could pick and choose the IT products they wanted, based on their needs and the total price they wanted to pay. Therefore it was felt that commercialisation would be a much fairer system than the old support fees, which were the same across all shops.

---

charged per outcome. In this case each business negotiated a monthly per-person fee with the shops/business teams to cover their cost-of-seat expenses. It was then up to the management team to live within this budget. If their costs went up, they were not allowed to run at a deficit, but had to convince the shops/teams to pay them more. For example, if a management team decided they needed another accountant, they either had to convince the shops to pay a higher fee to cover his/her costs, or wait until their area grew big enough that the per-person fee charged generated adequate income to cover the new accountant's cost-of-seat.

3. **The return on investment (ROI) project model** – Occasionally an FCL team would have to fund a project up-front with the proviso that there was a clear ROI over the next two or three years. In this case they could run a short-term deficit budget for the project, subject to senior management and board approval.

These new funding models meant that all back-end business teams were now expected to run as profitable or break-even businesses. The idea was that if they couldn't justify the cost of an additional service or person to their customers (other teams and the retail shops), then they couldn't have this additional service or person. They also had to be able to offer equal or better products, services and fees than an external competitor in order to survive. There was no guaranteed income and no obligation for people to use a business, except in some areas where the bigger picture was essential, like Branding and Finance. The onus was therefore on senior managers to discipline the model and ensure that margins and prices charged were fair in these monopolistic and semi-monopolistic businesses.

This wasn't all good news for the retailers, by any means. While some support areas had been unaccountable in their costs, others running at cost were simply unable to provide their service at their previously allocated amounts. For instance, the recruitment fee of $1500 was adequate when the area was run as a cost centre because it covered the cost of the in-house recruitment consultants' salaries; but it was insufficient if this area was to run as a specialised operation, because there was no extra cash to develop innovations such as psychometric testing to drive the business forward. Hence, although efficiencies were gained in some areas, others had exhaustive negotiations around repricing structures.

This was another aspect that many people disliked about the whole commercialisation principle. Imagine asking traditional administrators, particularly in the finance and technology departments, to negotiate their services based on outcomes rather than inputs with each retail area. And imagine them having to compete with external businesses for benchmarking fees. For many, the concept of pitching for business was so alien, it was ludicrous. And what if they didn't make enough income to cover their expenses? Who was going to pay for their wage costs, their phone expenses, their office overheads?

'Who's going to pay for it?' This was the crux of the issue for most back-end business people, and it's a common refrain even today. Scott Kyle-Little, FCL's Fit-out leader back in 1997, remembers: 'We felt that the shops should just trust us to do the right thing by them. We certainly weren't trying to rip them off. We all worked for the same company so why did we need to negotiate on everything? It just created a lot of extra work for us.'

There is no doubt that commercialisation was not easy to implement. Leaders were understandably reluctant to convert their businesses across, knowing that they would have to take on the battle of fee negotiations and justify every expense. When Skroo approached Andrea Slingsby in 1997 with a view to 'commercialising' her Human Resources teams, however, she had no inkling of the rollercoaster ride she was about to embark on. Turner convinced her that the new measures would transform the department but, as she says, 'I never realised until much later that everyone else had told him to piss off.'

Andrea's recruitment and training businesses, eventually renamed Peopleworks, were some of the first support areas to commercialise. Up to this point a monthly support fee had been debited from each shop to cover their costs. Following commercialisation, these fees were cut off overnight. The businesses were now catapulted into a new world – one where market forces reigned supreme. 'This was so foreign to most people,' she recalls, 'that for the first four months we didn't make any money at all.'

With no mandate to use services in-house, some retail managers started employing the services of external recruitment agencies and training companies. Because many areas of what became Peopleworks had grown out of necessity rather than strategic planning, there were few standard systems, and these outside companies were more professional. Not surprisingly, they were also more expensive.

By the end of the first year, Andrea's area had lost $670,000, which, to use her words, 'demonstrated how protected we had been under the old fee system'. This was hardly a good advertisement for commercialisation and led people to speculate that perhaps the whole idea was destined to be a failure. One team leader even mooted that commercialisation was like communism – great in theory but not so good in practice.

But just as the nay-sayers were predicting doom and gloom for the new initiative, another factor began to kick in. Following commercialisation, individuals in FCL's back-end operations were incentivised on achieving financial targets, of course. With such a poor year behind them, Andrea Slingsby's people now realised that if they were going to make any money, it was up to them to make things happen.

The first step was to overhaul the old business systems. The Recruitment area researched what worked in other companies and then implemented a whole new brand, called the Recruitment Centre, with standard fit-outs and uniforms, and new processes such as a telephone recruitment line and psychometric testing. The area increased its fee from $1500 to $3000 per recruit, but this was still cheaper than standard market prices and the results were felt to be worthwhile. Vacancies dropped across the company and there was an average turnaround of fourteen days from the time a shop advised it had a position to fill, to the delivery of a new recruit.

It wasn't all as straightforward as it appeared, however. Initially the recruitment consultants were paid an incentive every time they filled a company vacancy. The directors soon found they had rewarded the wrong behaviour. Some recruitment consultants lowered the criteria, simply to ensure they filled every position, and a higher staff turnover resulted company-wide. To counteract this trend, Flight Centre Limited introduced a money-back guarantee that a newcomer to the company would not quit in the first three months of employment, as long as the team leader and area leader fulfilled the obligation of their roles. (Like a new car, the teams had to service their investment properly or the guarantee was worthless.) This ensured that recruitment consultants had to focus on both quantity *and* quality, and proved so successful that the guarantee was eventually extended to twelve months in Australia – a policy that was unmatched in the external market.

The rest of the soon-to-be Peopleworks area also became more businesslike. Accreditation was introduced for trainers, who were incentivised on the commission averages of the people they trained. A monthly customer satisfaction survey rated and ranked every person in Peopleworks on their performance. A customer relations manager was employed to find out what customers (that is, the retail shops) really wanted. Gone, then, were the days when the Human Resources area simply supplied what it thought the stores wanted.

These initiatives paid off. In the second year after commercialisation, the area made a profit of $490,000. This was a $1 million turnaround. More importantly, Peopleworks had created a business environment that made the ongoing development of newer, more efficient business systems a commercial necessity. In effect, it had been forced to specialise or close down.

The success of Peopleworks encouraged other support areas to commercialise. For some, it was a simple process that was highly successful, as shown in the table on page 174. A few even became so accomplished that they began selling their products to companies external to FCL, and thus became even more profitable.

Implementation was difficult for a number of areas. As evidenced by the Recruitment Centre example, finding the right way to measure and incentivise people in alignment with the desired outcome was often the biggest challenge. FCL had its own lawyers and tax professionals, for instance, but most in-house leaders didn't understand how they operated. 'We knew from experience that incentives didn't work unless they were the right ones,' Skroo admits. 'We found over time that the first step was to put an incentive in place, and then generally the people in the business were the first to say how it should be improved.'

Commercialisation also encouraged do-it-yourself merchants. One manager, for instance, decided to buy his own wall map direct from the manufacturer, and asked his brother to help him hang it on the wall. It soon fell down and was so badly damaged, he had to buy another one. The same thing happened with the second map. After this he finally gave up and called in Fit-out – only to find out that he'd ended up overpaying for the first two maps anyway. All up, it cost the manager over $1000, plus the probable $2000 commission he'd lost while attempting to fix the problem himself.

Over time, FCL's retail people stopped trying to do everything themselves and concentrated on bringing pressure to bear on making changes in back-end businesses that failed to deliver. Eventually, some specialties were contracted out to external companies when it was found that outsiders could do the job better and more economically. An example was the Happy Traveller business, whose role was to telephone retail consultants at random, as pretend clients, and score them out of 100 on their sales proficiency. FCL also found that disciplines such as Global Risk Management, which offered legal advice to consultants, needed to employ external specialists. This slightly undermined the company's philosophy of employing from within, but it was a necessity in some areas.

There were other hurdles to overcome, as the Global Financial Reporting (GFR) area discovered. GFR is responsible for consolidating all the financial results for Flight Centre Limited and produces the Annual Report and the monthly board reports; at $1.2 million a year to run, its services are an expensive but necessary part of a public company. Soon after the advent of commercialisation, it was clear that FCL's retail businesses didn't necessarily want to pay for big business strategies, despite the fact that there were many advantages to them in belonging to an internationally branded company.

Examples of FCL commercialised businesses

Example 1: FCL Treasury

Raison d'etre: Invests the company's cash reserves totalling $270 million.

Prior to commercialisation: Treasury funds earned 0.2 per cent over the bank cash rate, and salaries were fairly fixed.

Desired outcome: To get the highest possible return for FCL, within the corporate risk profile.

Key performance indicator: Percentage achieved over the base cash rate of 6.5 per cent.

Incentives: Linked to KPI performance.

Following commercialisation:
- First year – percentage increased from 0.2 to 1.44
- Second year – percentage increased from 1.44 to 2.2
- Third year – percentage increased from 2.2 to 2.5.

Result: This increased FCL's bottom line by $6.2 million; the team made profit and was rewarded in line with the results.

Example 2: FCL Group Buying

Raison d'etre: Negotiate volume deals on purchases.

Prior to commercialisation: Consisted of one individual who looked after the Telstra deal.

Desired outcome: Reduce costs that shops pay for items necessary to run their business; make profit from rebated sales to shops and back-end businesses.

Key performance indicator: Growth in rebated sales; percentage of savings negotiated on merchandise products.

Incentives: Linked to KPI performance.

Following commercialisation: New consultants negotiated deals with suppliers on items such as stationery, computers, mobile phones, office chairs, electronic equipment and uniforms, using FCL's employee numbers as leverage for good prices. The business also invested $250,000 to develop an electronic procurement system called Ezyselect. This allowed retail consultants to order supplies via FCL's intranet and was later expanded to include discounted merchandise for personal use.

Result: Costs of products dropped by up to half the previous amount – for example, the price for an order of business cards fell from $120 to $50. At the same time, FCL's bottom-line profit for this area increased from $600,000 to $10 million in four years. The team members made profit and incentives, and received FCL awards for their profitability.

It is difficult to blame the retail consultants for this attitude. After all, in the incentivised FCL environment, an extra cost could mean the difference between a shop winning or losing a major profit award. When Scott Kyle-Little advised a manager that it was going to cost her $3000 to bring her shop up to the uniform branding standard required, he was told: 'You and your mate Skroo can just fuck off out of here. You're not doing anything in *my* shop!' With their own agendas and profit share to consider, shop managers could therefore potentially thwart a necessary implementation. Turner knew that he and the other executive team members had to draw the line: 'Ultimately we had to force some decisions onto the small businesses, whether they liked it or not.' As the company grew bigger, management by consensus was no longer an option on certain issues. The question became: 'Which measures are non-negotiable?'

This balance is still the subject of fierce debate. When Jim Sturgess took over as chief financial officer from Brian Hickey in January 2001, he felt that FCL had been under-accruing long-service leave. He raised the monthly amount to be debited from each shop to cover the change in policy – which had a negative effect on the projected profits of the Australian operation, run by Danny O'Brien at the time. When O'Brien discovered the change, he and Sturgess had a heated debate in the hallway on the topic.

In Turner's mind, this dissension is essential to FCL's success. 'Our retail people are very important "bullshit" detectors of head office ideas,' Skroo explains. 'If they don't like them and can't be convinced, then they do not happen. This cuts a lot of bad ideas off at the roots.'

While many FCL people might have liked to see the concept of commercialisation similarly nipped in the bud, once put in practice, it was highly effective in getting some managers to think like entrepreneurs. People began to ask themselves, 'What would give added functionality to the company and make me money?' An example of this creative thinking is supplied in the table over the page.

The downside to this was when a few of the new teams pitched to external customers, to increase their profitability, only for it to become apparent that they'd yet to perfect their own systems to a suitable

---

FCL UK's new refunds business

One of the biggest headaches for UK consultants was the fact that airlines took up to six months to refund unused airline tickets. This led to a lot of extra administration in chasing up tickets and was the source of many customer complaints. The Ticket Centre saw this problem as an opportunity and in 2004 found a way to address it. For a £25 service charge, clients can now receive an immediate refund, as illustrated in the following example:

Client's anticipated airline refund	£400
Immediate refund	£375
Airline refund to the Ticket Centre six months later	£400
Difference (i.e. business income)	£25

Thus everyone is incentivised on the correct outcome. The client is happy because for a fee of £25 he or she is paid on the spot; the consultant saves time and energy not having to deal with complaints or chase up the airlines; and the Ticket Centre makes a profit on a service that never existed before commercialisation.

---

standard. The outcome in these cases was that it de-focused the back-end businesses away from the parent company's requirements. Also, as more and more of them became profitable, FCL's own retailers began to question whether some of the former support areas, who had no real competitors within the operation, were achieving their financial goals at the expense of the rest of the company. For, just as the shops could be excused for taking exception to paying for Global Financial Reporting and the like, so it was understandable that back-end entrepreneurs would be doing their utmost to grow their business. After all, weren't they simply following the principles of Skroo Turner's commercialisation?

This was the dilemma that FCL now faced having unleashed the go-getter entrepreneur in each of its accountants, recruitment officers, marketeers and the like. One who could've been forgiven for laughing all the way to the bank was the company's Global IT leader, David Warner. But as his words demonstrate, he saw a far from happy situation: 'When we converted the IT area to user pays, we made *too much* profit. It went to the ridiculous. No one did anything without putting the flag down. The focus became the profit rather than the outcome and people took advantage of their monopolised client by charging the full market rate.'

If nothing else, this at least proved the point (yet again) that what gets incentivised gets done, but it resulted in its fair share of victims. As one managing director of a company acquired by FCL says: 'Everyone in the company was so helpful when I first started, and they all rang up to offer me their services. I thought they were just being friendly – until the bills started rolling in. Now when anybody from a back-end business rings me my first question is: "Am I being charged for this call?"'

The animosity between retail and back-end businesses peaked in July 2001, when the Fit-out business won the Most Profitable Business award at FCL's International Awards Night in Singapore. Several retail consultants booed the team members when they went on stage – an unthinkable act in light of the worship usually afforded such achievers – as they saw them as profit parasites. Flight Centre Limited's response was to place the retail area leader who had been the most vocal in her attack on these back-end businesses, Joell Ogilvie, in charge of them. (It seems the more you criticise an area in the company, the more likely you are to end up running it.)

People's attitudes gradually changed as they realised that many of the profits of FCL's back-end businesses would've gone to external companies rather than stayed within the parent company network. Nowadays, as long as fees are benchmarked to external suppliers, FCL retailers are more accepting of these areas making a profit. This process was helped by the fact that many of the back-end businesses have become more realistic about their roles. As David Warner, company CIO at the time, observed, 'There's been a pendulum swing back, and there's a bit of sanity there now.'

Although in many cases, the initial teething troubles of implementing commercialisation appeared to have been resolved, some of its key opponents simply went underground with their beliefs. Even though it wasn't obvious at the time, by 2004 people had begun to corrupt the commercialisation funding models. 'It just caught up on us,' Jim Sturgess says. 'We were like that frog in the pot of water put on the stove. Because the change is so gradual, it boils to death without realising what's happening.'

Some FCL businesses used separate accounting entries for costs that they felt didn't directly apply to their area. In this way they circumvented the 'user pays' nature of commercialisation. Their rationale was that they were using their entrepreneurial initiative to override the short-sighted attitudes of the shops. In effect though, they created an illegal fourth model of commercialisation.

Turner termed this 'black hole' funding: 'This occurs when the reason for spending the money on extra people or projects is so spurious that there is no hope of any return, no one at team level is prepared to pay for it out of cost-of-seat and no management team will sign off on it as a special project. Hence these operations are funded out of profit.' Because of this last point, FCL's management was unaware of the growing proliferation of these black-hole accounts. Over time, they began to have a serious impact, however. Not only did black-hole funding reduce the profit, but it also led to overspending in many areas. Research costs, for instance, went from zero to a staggering $4 million in just two years – the following table provides an example of how this could happen.

The result was devastating for Flight Centre Limited, of course. In January 2005, the company issued a profit downgrade, announcing that first half (that is, July–December 2004) pre-tax profits would be 10 per cent lower than the previous year. It was the first time this had happened since the 1991 Gulf War. The effect on the share price was immediate: from its trading price of $19 at the beginning of the year, it dropped to $16. And that's just the start of the damage due to rampant black-hole funding, Skroo believes: 'This year [2004/05] lack of discipline in the three commercialisation models could cost FCL thirty million dollars.'

Once FCL became aware of the extent of the problem, it took

Example of black-hole funding

An area leader is incentivised on the profitability of his 25 shops. He decides to spend $300,000 on research to find out what his shop customers want.

Under the correct commercialisation model, he should on-charge this cost to his shops at $12,000 each; however, there is little chance that he could convince the shop managers to approve this fee.

He can't fund the amount as a long-term project, as he knows he wouldn't get approval from senior management. The area leader therefore decides to fund it out of his profits as follows:

Annual profit of his 25 shops	$2,400,000
Cost of research	$300,000
Total annual profits	$2,100,000

Because his area still brings in a profit, he still receives his BOS cheque and his incentives. Management are unaware of the misused funds, and the actual FCL Research business team takes the flak for FCL's overspending, as it is accused of growing too big too quickly.

---

immediate action. Black holes were de-incentivised. If an area leader was found with a black-hole account of $400,000 for the month, his or her incentive would only be paid after double that amount (i.e. $800,000) was taken off the profit figures.

FCL also employed global management consultants Bain & Company to analyse the corporation's performance and find ways to reduce costs. As a result of Bain's review, the company introduced a new strategy, christened 'Full Throttle'. This included ten initiatives, four of which were organisational redesign; controlling black-hole costs (or as CEO Shane Flynn put it, 'getting more bang for less bucks'); transforming the Finance area by improving the quality of financial outputs; and improving cost-of-seat and in-store productivity.

'I've worked with a large number of retailers,' says Tony Duthie, one of the partners at Bain & Company, 'and FCL's commercialisation model is certainly unique. Its true strength is that it focuses everyone on driving profit across the business.' On the downside, however, was that people were more focused on managing revenue, rather than managing costs, and a fair amount of energy was consumed working through this process. 'An awful lot of horse trading goes on,' the management consultant notes.

'Horse trading' and other tribal traditions had become an ingrained part of FCL's unique success, and this observation may have been the first sign that the experiment of bringing in external consultants might not end happily.

Still, even a business analyst like Duthie found it hard to get a clear picture of commercialisation's effectiveness. Part of the problem was that it was still a very young initiative. FCL's successful retail model has been refined over a period of 23 years, whereas the commercialisation model is only seven years old, with most businesses converting in the last five. In terms of development, therefore, the back-end businesses are at the same stage that the retail shops were before standardisation was introduced following the Bangkok conference in 1987. With a complex area involving 40 different specialties, the model still has a long way to go.

Like the acrimonious debates about the direction of the early retail model, there is still a lot of dissension in-house. For every avid supporter like Andrea Slingsby, there's a virulent opponent such as the senior leader who says: 'Commercialisation doesn't work. All it does is add cost.'

Turner, for one, thinks that the detractors in the back-end businesses simply hate having to justify themselves to the front-line shops. He attributes the company's recent cost blow-out not to a failing of commercialisation, but to the fact that the model was not being followed properly, and that adherence to the model wasn't being disciplined. Jim Sturgess, CFO at the time, agreed: 'Many people didn't live within their means. They felt that because their turnover was growing so rapidly, the costs would take care of themselves.'

Despite the setbacks, FCL remains committed to commercialisation for several compelling reasons. Firstly, the process turned traditional organisational hierarchy on its head. FCL continues to have thousands of people questioning the need and value of every service. Management at all levels have become accountable to the people they support, not the other way around – a bottom-up approach rather than the customary top-down strategy.

Commercialisation aimed to take the guesswork out of these back-end businesses. 'In the past we were always having to make judgment calls on how many people should be in each team,' Turner explains. 'We didn't have any rational way to work this out.' With commercialisation, however, the growth of these businesses is determined by what people are prepared to pay for. Quite simply, if they aren't prepared to pay for a service, then the company doesn't need it.

Another factor in FCL's commitment was that commercialisation introduced a level playing field into the company. Correctly incentivised administrative performers can be recognised and paid commensurate with their ability, and receive awards alongside their retail brethren. This makes every single person in the company accountable for what he or she does. Skroo knows this is ultimately a good thing: 'Humans hate to be accountable and will make many excuses why their case is different. Yet people in the shops have no choice – they produce or go. If we are being fair, then the same needs to happen in every back-end business.'

And finally, it added another level of entrepreneurial understanding to FCL, for commercialisation brings the company's ideal goal that much closer to reality. Only in this way can every single person in Flight Centre Limited run his or her own business, within the business.

What's in a name? Top Deck's fleet of colourfully named double-deckers were no strangers to the maintenance yard at Young Stroat Farm in Woking, just south of London.

The very first bus tours, under the short-lived moniker 'Argus Persicus Travel'. **LEFT** *(from left to right)*: The original team of Graham 'Skroo' Turner, Bill James, Steve 'Bombardier' Brown, an unnamed passenger, and Geoff 'Spy' Lomas. **BELOW**: Three Top Deck tours collide at Pamplona, Spain, 1979.

GRAHAM TURNER
Director
TOP DECK
TRAVEL
18 DAWES ROAD FULHAM LONDON SW6 7EN.
Tel. 01-385 8032 OR 01-381 1388. UK.

LEFT: The first business cards were shaped like beer coasters – perhaps a reflection of the partners' preoccupations at the time.
BELOW: The boxing kangaroo hangs proudly over Top Deck Travel's first offices in a prominent location, at 131 Earl's Court Road in west London.

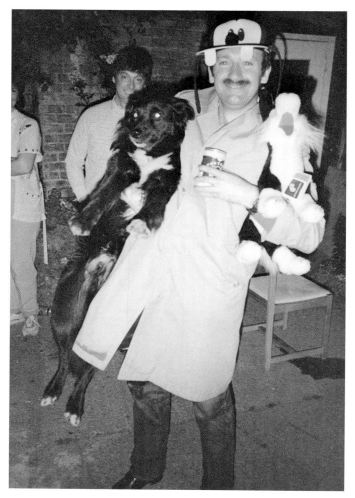

Top Deck 'directors' Bill Barking and Bill 'Speaking' James at a business meeting.

ABOVE: 'Let's have fun' was the company's philosophy at the start. Karaoke enthusiasts and business partners Mick Carroll and Skroo Turner practise what they preach.

BELOW: Hundreds of Australians and New Zealanders gather at the London New Zealand Rugby Club for a day of competition, co-sponsored by Top Deck Travel and *TNT* magazine.

ABOVE: Back in Australia. Bill and Liz James, Mick Carroll, Sue and Geoff Harris, and Jude and Skroo Turner, all dressed up for Flight Centre's inaugural Awards Night, at Jupiter's Casino in Brisbane, March 1987.

BELOW: Turner, finance chief Jim Goldburg and James recover after completing the 1990 London Marathon.

FLIGHT CENTRES	FIRST CLASS
INTERNATIONAL BALL	BOARDING PASS

NAME:	FLIGHT: FC 003	DATE: 29 JULY 89	CHECK IN: 7PM PREFLIGHT DRINKS	SEATING ALLOCATION ON ARRIVAL AT
GATEWAY: MANLY PACIFIC PARK ROYAL		DESTINATION: 55 NORTH STEYNE MANLY - SYDNEY	DRESS: BLACK TIE	FIRST CLASS LOUNGE

What gets rewarded – and recognised – gets done. **ABOVE:** The company's third Annual Awards Night took place at Sydney's Manly Pacific Hotel, while some years later, it would be Flight Centre itself that began to receive accolades for its performance. **BELOW:** Managing director Graham Turner (pictured with wife Jude) was voted Entrepreneur of the Year in 2001.

STANDARDISING
THE FLIGHT CENTRE IMAGE

As most of you may know we have started the programme of standardising all shops and logos under a franchise arrangement from Flight Centres International. There are several areas that will change over the next few months.

SHOP NAMES.

Names will be related always to the actual area that most closely describes where the shop is located. Eg Carillon Flight Centre is in the Carillon Arcade. In suburbs the name will be the name of the Suburb Flight Centre.

GROUP NAME.

The common theme running through all shops will be FLIGHT CENTRE. The Flight Centre part of the name will always be the most prominent feature but all offices will have a distinctive name of their own related to the locality. Some names that don't quite fit like The Flight Shop and possibly Top Deck will be retained but when new signwriting or stationery is done generally it will be

THE FLIGHT SHOP

FLIGHT
CENTRE

SHOP FRONTS.

All shop fronts will now have the Name of the shop eg Adelaide in small black letters above large red with White outline FLIGHT CENTRE.

Underneath this will be the

standard "Discount Flight Specialists " and then the Airfares board. Stuck onto the window will be a discount flight guide holder. On the door will be the Flight Centres International logo with the countries we are operating in and the AFTA sticker and standard credit card stickers all shops will be accepting in future–Visa, Bankcard and Master – charge. No other stickers will go on windows or doors.

In another area of the window

will be a very large Discount Flight Specials with about 6 destinations highlighting special airfares we have to those places.

On the roof will be a very large sign with other destination prices.

INTERNAL SHOP DESIGN.

We will have red trimmed counters not too high nor low and of course red carpet. Behind consultants will be open cupboards and work bench with 3 rows of brochure racks for preferred products above them. The aim is to design shops so staff rarely have to get up from their desk to get things.

It's the look that counts. **ABOVE:** The ideas from the November 1987 Bangkok conference were very specific, as shown by the front page of the in-house newsletter five months later. **LEFT:** The ad hoc nature of the early start-ups since 1982 had led to a diverse range of Flight Centre shopfronts, one of which was the original design for this Queen Street store.

ABOVE: This photo of a shopfront, in Indooroopilly, Queensland, was taken in July 1988. The store still needed some work to bring it up to Flight Centre's new branding standard.

BELOW: The store model as it appears today – the brochure-holding captain at the door, red and white airline counters and interiors, and the ubiquitous Concorde symbol.

Taking on the world. After the bleak years of 1990–91, Flight Centre was ready to renew its attack on overseas markets by 1994. **ABOVE:** Each new start-up area had its own idiosyncrasies to overcome; for South Africa, security was a priority. Brad Jukes, Shane Flynn and Mary Harrison relax with security guards outside Heathway Flight Centre in Johannesburg. **BELOW LEFT:** Gary 'Boxer' Hogan flies the flag as head of the UK operation from 1995 to 2004. **BELOW RIGHT:** Viva Las Vegas. Elvis hasn't left the building – he's here at the 2003 International Annual Awards Night in the form of FCL chief executive officer Shane 'Flynnie' Flynn.

'Buy every Flight Centre share you can. Mortgage your dog, your husband, your wife – anything you have to …' By the mid 1990s, the company was ready to float on the Australian Stock Exchange, a process that required a change to the company name and some official job titles. **ABOVE**: Flight Centre Limited's first board of directors (*from left to right*): Bill James, Marg Mulholland, Norm Fussell (seated), Geoff Harris, Graham Turner, Peter Barrow, Howard Stack and Jim Goldburg. **BELOW**: Harris, Goldburg, Skroo and Chris Greive had good reason for their smiles on 1 December 1995, just minutes before the company's shares started trading.

ABOVE: The three major shareholders of the company. Only Skroo Turner continues to sit on the board in an executive role, Bill James (*centre*) and Geoff Harris (*right*) having relinquished their roles in 1996 and 1998 respectively.

BELOW: Skroo and company president Li Jilie, separated by their interpreters, during the launch of FCm China Comfort Travel in February 2004.

FCL Logo's - Global Gathering

It seemed like a good idea at the time. A sample of logos from FCL's brands, businesses and acquisitions, past and present. Its policy of diversification has been predominantly successful but a few of its ventures were dismal failures and were eventually wound up.

ABOVE: FCL's people-centred policies in action, as retail consultants receive a massage courtesy of back-end business Healthwise. **BELOW:** The company's Family, Village, Tribe philosophy led to the creation of elaborate tribal identities, as displayed in the distinctive dress of these Western Australians from the Quokka Nation.

Flight Centre stores around the world – Happy Valley Flight Centre, Hong Kong; the New York hyperstore on Madison Avenue; the 99Bikes store Newmarket, Australia and the High Street Kensington, London hyperstore.

ABOVE: One of Flight Centre's 'Consultants of the Year', David Austin, feted like an Oscar winner.

BELOW: Promotional vehicle for Flight Centre's India launch.

Chapter 12

METAMORPHOSIS

We had a five-year vision that we were trying to put in place in six months. It was a total unmitigated fuck-up.

Graham 'Skroo' Turner on the development of
FCL's global website

As the turn of the century approached, there were many predictions of disaster. Technology experts warned of a 'millennium bug' that would ravage world computer systems. The economy would be crippled. Airliners would fall out of the sky. Electricity, water and gas supplies would be cut off. Humankind would descend into anarchy.

Even though none of these materialised, in hindsight perhaps FCL should have paid closer attention to the doomsayers. In *Good to Great*, Jim Collins would write: 'As a company grows and becomes more complex, it begins to trip over its own success.'[45] Flight Centre Limited, with 500 shops and nearly 3000 people, had tripled in size in the four years since 1995, and in 2000, it began to lose its footing. The result would be the company's biggest one-off business blow-out ever.

But as FCL's leaders flew into Whistler in Canada for the start of their November 1999 conference, the possibilities seemed endless. In the last year FCL had made a pre-tax profit of $49 million and its share price was now hovering around the $8 mark. All the overseas areas were profitable and most of the brands were well on the way. FCL was now in an enviable position. No longer an underdog, it had the money and resources to accomplish many long-held ambitions. As

Peopleworks head Andrea Slingsby says: 'We did our five-year plans and went "Holy shit!" We were just *stunned* at the magnitude of what could be achieved.'

Unlike at previous conferences, technology dominated the agenda. Internet fever was at its height in the late 1990s, and many FCL people felt that it held the key to the company's future success. A number of ideas were discussed but the most seductive was the concept of a sophisticated global website that would automatically book airfares, hotels, car hire and insurance. The group was excited by the idea and agreed that a new team, Global Online, should be established to develop this flagship site.

Like gold-rush miners, the leaders were keen to be the first to grab market share through the new technology. Under these circumstances, they felt that the company didn't have the time to 'grow' the people necessary to take on this new challenge. Instead it was decided that, based on his presentation on 'first to market', marketing manager Keith Stanley should recruit a team of people to run Global Online, while still overseeing his own large portfolio.

Meanwhile another project was in the pipeline. Unlike Global Online, this initiative was driven by the needs of a specific business. FCL had a four-person team based in Sydney that had been dealing with enquiries from the company's existing small website. With online queries skyrocketing, they could no longer handle the volume. Flight Centre Limited had been toying with the idea of setting up a call centre to handle the excess phone calls; now the managers decided to create a new brand, flightcentre.com, that would run as a 24-hour call centre and handle both surplus web and phone enquiries.

This concept was typical of FCL's 'it seemed like a good idea at the time' style of thinking. And as with Global Online, the Australian management had no available people to run the new scheme. With the mantra 'first to market' resonating in his head, Australian leader Danny O'Brien decided to employ two external call-centre experts to put the project together. This same sense of urgency was responsible for the October 2000 launch date for the new operation, a little under a year away.

The set-up of the flightcentre.com brand proved an expensive business. FCL chose to buck the trend of putting call centres in remote locations, and instead leased premises in George Street in Sydney's CBD, at a cost of $735,000 per annum. This was only the first of many substantial outgoings. A sophisticated phone system, that would divert a phone call *or* email to the first consultant who was free cost another several hundred thousand dollars. It was a big investment, especially when the corporation's CEO had been widely quoted as dismissing the idea of the internet taking over the travel industry as 'a lot of bullshit'. Skroo Turner believed that most customers would rather deal with people than computers or automated phone lines, particularly when they were spending significant sums of money. Needless to say, there were few who agreed with this viewpoint at the time.

There were a number of difficulties to overcome. Ever since the company's inception in the early 1980s, it had had little problem finding new people, but there was an unusual factor to consider this time around, as Danny O'Brien recalled: 'With the Olympics about to start we had four months to recruit one hundred people in a city where no one wanted a job.' As a result, O'Brien had no choice but to lower FCL's normal recruitment criteria. Then, due to a leasing mix-up, flightcentre.com was forced into temporary premises for three months, at a cost of $300,000. The call-centre people would eventually move into their offices in George Street just one week before launch date.

But perhaps the biggest hurdle was that the project managers had designed a conventional call centre that didn't take into account FCL's many cultural differences. Their original floor plans, fit-out and phone system for flightcentre.com were designed around one large team of 120 people. There was no separate 'family' structure, no separate business identities and effectively no small business model.

When Turner got wind of this direction, the project team rejigged its plans to take into account his wishes for a multi-shop fit-out. It was a case of too little too late, however. Much of the infrastructure was already in place and the project became a hybrid mix of conventional call-centre ideas and FCL's corporate ideology.

While the flightcentre.com team grappled with these problems, Global Online also struggled to meet its target date. The new website was to be launched at the opening of flightcentre.com's new offices, in October 2000. Four weeks before the launch, and the website wasn't ready. Three weeks, two weeks, one week . . . still not ready. The site finally went live three hours before the opening.

Joe Ponte, flightcentre.com's marketing manager at the time, remembers the launch night well. 'We held it in our new George Street premises and gave guided tours around the building,' he says. 'There was a big crowd – our industry suppliers, the FCL board, the hundred people that made up the new flightcentre.com teams, and a few media representatives. It was the highlight of my career at that point.' But all his excitement vanished at the press of a button.

When Joe tried to demonstrate FCL's new global website on the giant screen linked to his computer, a message came up telling the world: 'A recursive error has occurred.' He tried several more times and even rebooted his computer, but with the same result. FCL's new website simply didn't work. For Keith Stanley, the humiliation was complete the following morning: 'The next day, a Sydney newspaper – I can't remember which one – ran a story along the lines of: "Flight Centre Limited learned a valuable lesson last night. Never work with animals, children or the Internet." That made us feel pretty small . . .'

Graham Turner didn't need a journalist to tell him what a disaster the whole thing had been, however. 'We had a five-year vision that we were trying to put in place in six months,' he admits. 'It was a total unmitigated fuck-up. It cost us 1.2 million dollars and we had almost nothing to show for it.' The website was canned a few months later – its poor execution would delay FCL's technology goals by several years.

The flightcentre.com operation didn't fare much better. The brand opened with eighteen of the intended 36 teams because of the recruitment problems, and went on to lose $2 million in its first year. This was in addition to the fit-out costs that were double those of a normal FCL shop.

In January 2001, experienced FCL leaders were brought in to oversee the conversion of flightcentre.com over to the company's successful village retail model, as originally intended. Flight Centre Direct, as it was renamed, became a group of small, accountable business teams, with extended opening hours. With this return to the company's key hunter-gatherer philosophy and normal recruitment criteria, the operation became profitable within a year.

Never one to duck responsibility, Skroo came clean at the August 2001 Annual General Meeting. 'We made two big mistakes this year,' he told the other shareholders, 'and it cost us four million dollars.' Flight Centre Limited still finished the 2000/01 tax year with an operating profit of $76 million, 12 per cent up on the previous year, and a share price at an all-time high of $28. But for a company used to 40 per cent profit growth, this was a catastrophe. As Global IT leader David Warner pointed out, standards are high at FCL: 'Global Online cost us less than two million dollars. Other companies spent twenty million with the same outcome. Yet everyone was so pissed off, you would've thought we'd lost *two hundred* million.'

It triggered some serious soul-searching. Turner blamed himself: 'I gave people too much rope. We simply didn't plan and budget big projects enough.' In addition, the company had got carried away with grandiose schemes and failed to apply the usual due diligence approach to its new ideas. It was an important lesson.

Unfortunately for FCL, many of the problems that dogged the technology projects had also dominated the start-up of its new US venture, in the second half of 1999. Having been forced to admit defeat in America back in 1991, at least this time around, the directors were aware that it wouldn't be easy. The USA was a highly individual culture and had been as treacherous as a minefield for many Australian businesses. Country Road, NAB Homeside and Burns-Philp were all big-name companies who'd taken a pounding in the States.

Then again, there had also been some amazing success stories. Sydney-based Westfield Holdings Ltd, the shopping centre giant, had acquired its first US shopping mall in 1977, and by 2004 had over 66 properties with 9300 stores across America, contributing $651 million in property income to the parent company. This was a formidable example of what success in the USA could mean to a business, and for an expansionist like Turner it was very enticing. At the time, the US economy was ticking along very nicely, and the later dramatic company collapses, which would be well recorded, were not on the horizon. Flight Centre Limited had other reasons to be optimistic. Its business model had worked in several locations outside of Australia, and the company's now profitable Vancouver operation could provide back-up support for the new venture.

More importantly, however, US expansion didn't jeopardise the rest of the operation. 'The US isn't crucial to our success,' Skroo says. 'The company is doubling every three to four years anyway. Therefore, it's not important from a financial point of view, rather from a challenge point of view.'

This was just as well, because the operation had a rocky beginning. The company's original plan was to set up a small call-centre environment with two or three teams, and build up enquiries; only when these teams became profitable would FCL open some street-front shops. In reality, however, when the very first US office opened in September 1999, the Wiltshire and Euclid Flight Centre, it was situated right on a main thoroughfare, in the busy Los Angeles suburb of Santa Monica.

Back in Brisbane, although it was obvious to Turner that there'd been a mix-up with his original instructions, he didn't intervene. To people unused to the company's culture, this lack of interference seems incomprehensible. But as previous start-up operators had found, FCL's current managing director holds an unshakable belief that if someone is the right person to lead an area, then the company has to sit back and let the person do it. Although Skroo himself would later admit that this same hands-off approach was partly responsible for the initial failure of FCL's technology projects, by and large, this strategy had worked well for the company up till 1999. Flight Centre Limited was much bigger now, however, and this factor would greatly affect the outcome.

This size issue brought enormous changes to the role of an FCL area leader. Unlike the early company pioneers, Australian area leaders in the late 1990s were 'supported' by teams of profit-motivated accountants, marketers, fit-out consultants, recruiters, trainers, product contractors and the like. Thus it was now a big step-up to become an overseas leader and negotiate property leases, source suppliers, organise fit-out contractors, arrange planning and licensing approvals through local authorities, and be the overall decision-maker and figurehead for every aspect of the operation.

The leader of the new US operation had total autonomy but was used to the FCL world of pre-negotiated prices and volume deals. Starting from scratch in the USA, with little real world experience in negotiation, some of his operational costs blew out. The first shop, with its head-office back room, was so expensive that it set an FCL record. Other shop fit-outs were more than double that of their Australian counterparts. This all had a knock-on effect on the US cost-of-seat, which became the highest in the world at US$12,000 per consultant per month.

The new leader was simply trying to follow FCL's directive to him. 'My brief from Global SWOT [FCL's executive management team] was to roll out nine stores in nine months,' he says. 'So that's what I did.' This was a big ask. Making his job harder was the fact that California was at the height of the dotcom boom and unemployment was reaching record lows. In this environment, Flight Centre Limited found it difficult to recruit and retain quality consultants. With new store openings relying on these internal people for managers, the shops struggled to make money. As revenues failed to materialise in existing stores, the opening of new stores simply compounded the losses.

The US leader also believes that opening without an IATA ticketing licence was a costly error on the company's part. The Ticket Centre was a big part of the FCL's successful business model, yet it took six months to organise the licence and airline deals required to set it up in the USA. In retrospect he feels that FCL should've bought a small travel agency with an existing licence and then built up the business around that.

By March 2001 the US operation had ten shops and a Corporate Traveller office. It had too many overheads, too many back-end businesses, and had lost US$3.2 million in eighteen months. The board of directors felt that this was excessive and the leader returned to Australia. 'It was a roller-coaster ride from start to finish,' he says of his experience. 'Out of all the environments I worked in at FCL, this was the toughest.'

FCL's Global SWOT team had underestimated how hard it was for someone to start up a new country after being an area leader in the much bigger Australian operation. In truth, the US leader had been given little support or direction in one of the toughest markets in the world. (It seems that, for a company that prides itself on learning from past failures, Flight Centre Limited was repeating the mistakes from its start-up days in Canada, when Simon Canning had been left similarly stranded.)

In America, the company paid a heavy price for this, and it would take several years and two more leaders before the business began to get on track. During that time FCL concentrated on implementing its successful business systems. The USA was broken down into smaller communities, and village chiefs were appointed to create local identities. The number of back-end operations was reduced, incentives were increased and the company's Business Ownership Scheme was introduced.

By December 2003 the USA was one of Flight Centre's most improved areas globally. It had seventeen shops and the Corporate Traveller and Infinity brands were profitable in their own right. By the end of the 2003/04 year, the area recorded a $1.4 million reduction in losses (down to $2.6 million) and opened two more new retail shops. It also had a potent incentive in place for when the operation finally made overall profit: FCL's Global SWOT team had agreed to run through the streets of Brisbane wearing nothing but boxer shorts emblazoned with the US flag.

Turner predicted the USA would probably take five to six years from start-up before they got it completely right, and growth would be slow until the venture became profitable. 'This is the same thing that happened in Australia, New Zealand, the UK – in fact, in all of our operations,' he added.

Although the rising share price might have suggested otherwise, the period from 1999 to 2001 was a tough one for Flight Centre Limited. This was par for the course for most companies. The important test was whether FCL could bounce back from these challenges.

In this last regard, the company didn't disappoint – the reaction was amazing in both its effectiveness and the speed in which it was carried out. The Global Online website was closed down after only eight months, and flightcentre.com was restructured in eleven. A new leader was appointed to run the US operation in early 2001, just a year and a half after the first shop opened. This speed saved the company from more serious fallout from its misjudgments.

Many of the difficulties were a direct result of FCL's rapid growth. (See the table below for an example of this phenomenal expansion.) As Flight Centre Limited grew bigger and roles became more specialised, it was difficult to give people a proper grounding in business.

Growth of FCL from 1995 to 2000		
	1995	2000
Profit before tax	$13 million	$61 million
Turnover/TTV	$759 million	$2.4 billion
Share price	Listed at 95 cents	$18 by year end
Number of shops	199	552
Approx. number of people	1100	over 3000

Norm Fussell outlined the problem: 'In a small company people have to do everything so they naturally get the building blocks to build their career. In a big company jobs become more polarised.' FCL would try to ease this burden by employing some external specialists, but this would erode some of the company's cultural ideals.

Flight Centre Limited had already failed to live up to some of its own business basics. Take its standard systems philosophy: 'In our businesses there is a best way and everybody operates that way.' In the case of flightcentre.com and the start-up of the USA, it had become more like 'Everybody does their own thing.' This decay of the standard systems led to other problems during this period, such as an increase in company fraud, as some consultants failed to follow the standardised risk-management procedures.

The FCL directors now understood why many companies didn't manage the transition from a small business to a big corporation. 'The real issue is what you are doing inside your business, not what the competitors are doing,' Skroo acknowledges. 'We realised that a lot of it had to do with changing the structure and re-engineering.'

Danny O'Brien, for instance, had been struggling with over twenty direct reports in his role as head of FCL Australia. The result was that his operation's profits had begun to suffer. In February 2001 this area was restructured into five more manageable units, called 'nations'. Where there had only been one person focused on Australia, there were now five, all reporting to Skroo Turner, the overall CEO. Sue Rennick, who became one of the nation leaders, remembers: 'It happened virtually overnight. It was extremely controversial at the time, but now you can see it was definitely the right thing.'

The new nations were as follows:

- Flight Centre Nation (including the Flight Centre brand), run by Sue Rennick
- Holiday Nation (including the Escape Travel brand), run by Melanie Waters-Ryan
- Corporate Nation (including the Corporate Traveller brand), run by Danny O'Brien
- Youth Nation (including the Student Flights brand), run by Marg Mulholland
- Product Nation (including the Infinity Holidays brand), run by David Burns.

A sixth one, the Cadre Nation, was added a few months later. It encompassed FCL's back-end businesses, and because of its specialist areas, Anthony Grigson was brought in from Caltex to oversee it. Apart from Grigson, all the new leaders were FCL pioneers. They met with Skroo once a week and ran their nations as independent units with total accountability for their areas.

The results from this change in corporate architecture were striking. Whereas many accountants might've predicted that five extra leaders would blow out FCL's cost structure, in practice the reverse was true. The extra expenses were more than compensated for by the fact that Flight Centre Limited now had an incentivised leader driving each area of the Australian businesses. Family, Village, Tribe again. Cut, cut, cut into smaller areas. Over a twelve-month period, each nation's profits showed a marked increase, as shown in the table below.

Operating profit comparisons from before and after FCL's nation split		
	February 2001	February 2002
Flight Centre Nation	$2,157,063	$4,597,632
Holiday Nation	−$190,903	$96,017
Corporate Nation	$698,211	$1,503,805
Youth Nation	−$49,393	$36,617
Product Nation	$140,073	$143,546
Cadre Nation	$94,710	$246,142
FCL group overall	**$4,604,476**	**$8,108,762**

This was only the start of FCL's metamorphosis, however. The executive team also identified that one of the company's biggest weaknesses was its lack of succession planning. A Future Leaders Programme was developed, with the idea that no one person should be crucial to any business within the company. At the executive level, however, CEO Graham Turner was still very much a linchpin of FCL, and he had no trained successor. If anything happened to him, it could potentially jeopardise the whole operation.

Flight Centre Limited decided to employ a chief executive officer who could concentrate on the operational side of the business. Turner now retook the title of managing director and was able to focus more on the expansion of the company – in particular, acquisitions, new brands and new countries. This would give someone a chance to grow into the CEO role and allow for a suitable handover period.

The board of directors agreed that the new CEO had to be an internal candidate who had run a successful FCL business. This narrowed the list down to the national and brand leaders. In August 2002, Shane Flynn, with 75 stores, over R18 million in annual profit, and 8 per cent of South Africa's market share under his belt, was appointed to the role.

This came as something of a surprise to those who had only known him at the start of his career. Flynnie himself was the first to admit that his early track record had been less than exemplary: 'In my first two years as the Queen Street Flight Centre manager, I was terrible. The showdown came one day when Skroo told me that I had forty-eight hours to justify my position. In fact, he already had my replacement lined up.' Work was not a priority in Flynn's life at this point. Juggling coaching for Brothers Rugby Club with managing a Flight Centre store, his performance had been lacklustre at best.

Turner's ultimatum was the wake-up call he needed. That year Flynnie's office won Most Improved Business Worldwide. He then set up Queensland's first Corporate Traveller office before moving on to seven years of success as South Africa's country leader.

One of Flynn's first tasks as chief executive officer was, in his words, 'to try to work out how we were going to keep our people'. The company was now a large, complex organisation in seven countries and with three pillars: retail, corporate and back-end businesses. Despite FCL's best intentions, some of its ideals such as Family, Village, Tribe were being undermined from within. This led to an increase in management layers, worsening communication and a lack of transparency and accountability.

From about 2000 onwards the company began to lose some people, hence Flynn's concern. It is difficult to put an exact figure on this, as the 32 per cent staff turnover reported in 2003 included consultants and leaders who had transferred to back-end businesses and overseas areas. What is a given, however, is that the increasing recruitment expenses and the lack of in-shop experience were beginning to impact on the operation.

This effect was also noted by Murray Dempsey, a research student studying quality systems at Christchurch University. In 2001 he noticed that the service offered at his wife's Flight Centre store lacked consistency. Dempsey approached Chris Greive, who was then the New Zealand leader, with an idea. As a result, FCL introduced the Baldridge criteria – a US system for evaluating organisational management of quality in seven major areas.

The Baldridge system gave FCL a means of measuring its percentage of delighted and dissatisfied customers (45 and 12 per cent respectively in the Australian retail area, as of September 2004). This was important because as the company had grown, its senior leaders were more and more removed from the voice of the customer. The new initiative also enabled Flight Centre Limited to track its progress in quality systems improvement. FCL's new research team conducted facilitated workshops across a large cross-section of the company; it scored 369 in July 2003 but by September 2004, after the recruitment of business improvement managers in many areas, it had improved its quality score to 452.[46]

The company admitted that even though it experienced some improvements in this area, there was still a way to go. 'The theory is that if you can measure it, you can manage it,' says Dempsey. 'But it can be difficult to make changes in such a large, autonomous company like FCL.' This last statement would prove prophetic after World Class was cut within two years.

In other areas the company was having greater success. In 2001 Turner came up with a new initiative – strangely enough, after telling an area leader that a position she'd aspired to had been filled. 'But where's my *brightness of future*?' she asked him, and left the company shortly afterwards. Although she would return a year later, the phrase 'brightness of future' lingered in Skroo's head. He began to understand why in some areas where FCL was no longer the underdog the business had begun to suffer. Conventional thinking would suggest that market domination should lead to greater profits, but this was not the case.

Take Queensland, for example. In the late 1980s and early '90s it had been the highest performing FCL region. By 2001 though, profits had stopped increasing in some inner-city areas and staff turnover was rising. Flight Centre Limited realised that in Queensland people's brightness of future (BOF) was all about growth and rapid promotion. In the areas where the company had saturated the market, it had stopped opening as many shops. People felt they had nowhere to move to, which had a dampening effect on morale.

FCL leaders now understood that money and prestige were inconsequential without this important factor. Team leaders were given the task of coming up with a BOF vision for their shop. This included setting goals to increase market share, and spelling out career opportunities. Each area came up with new initiatives, such as 'Flight Centre Seniors' and 'Flight Centre Groups', so that people would feel they were at the cutting edge of business. By 2004, with this BOF focus, Queensland had become FCL's Most Productive Nation globally.

The process proved so effective that it soon became a company philosophy:

> We believe our people have the right to belong to a Team, Area and Nation that provides an exciting 'Brightness of Future'. Our people need to see a clear pathway to achieving their hopes, aspirations and dreams. FCL is the vehicle for this journey.

Perhaps the greatest realisation to come out of these years, however, was that the key to FCL's success did not lie in some spectacular new project or an exciting new initiative. All the company had to do was stay faithful to its existing philosophies. These were the real engine behind Flight Centre Limited. Yet knowing this and living it were two different things. FCL would double in size once more between 2002 and 2005, and the company's ideals would again come under sustained attack.

Chapter 13

RIDERS ON THE STORM

The impact of September 11 has reached nearly every sector of the world economy, touched lives far beyond ground zero and claimed hundreds of thousands of jobs in the process.

Robert Milton, president and CEO of Air Canada, 15 January 2002

G eoff Harris, one of Flight Centre Limited's executive directors, woke up and looked out of the window. The sun was just coming up and it looked like it was going to be a fine day. He jumped out of bed and padded to the bathroom, switching on the radio as he walked past. With the shower running, he began thinking about his plans for the day, until a news bulletin caught his attention. The announcer said something about a war in America. That can't be right, Geoff thought. Wrapping a towel around himself he walked back into the living room and turned on the television. What he saw astounded him.

All around the globe, people were seeing the same shocking images, as two hijacked planes and their 156 passengers slammed into the twin towers of the World Trade Centre. A short time later the buildings imploded into the streets of New York, with thousands dead beneath the rubble. Another hijacked aircraft crashed into the Pentagon, setting it ablaze. The White House was evacuated. Washington was sealed. Airports, roads, government buildings, petrochemical plants and nuclear power stations were closed down. Global panic ensued. For FCL, it was only the first blow in a conflict that would change the very face of travel.

'The airports were like ghost towns,' remembers Vicky Astley, leader of Flight Centre Limited's US operation in late 2001. 'There were no planes in the air. People just couldn't believe it.' Across the border, things weren't much better. The Ontario operation, whose main traffic was from Toronto to New York, only had a handful of passengers that entire week.

The financial effect on the company was instantaneous. As the table below shows, FCL's profits dropped radically in September. The North American operations, consisting of cells in the USA, Western Canada and Ontario, went straight into the red, while profits halved in FCL's businesses in Australia, New Zealand and South Africa. A bigger factor for the fall in the Australian figures was the collapse of Ansett Airlines, one of the nation's major domestic carriers. It went into receivership three days after the terrorist strikes.

Effect of September 11 on Flight Centre Limited's monthly profits, by international area			
	August '01	September '01	October '01
Australia	$6,203,000	$3,266,000	$4,024,000
New Zealand	$1,129,000	$698,000	$728,000
South Africa	$444,000	$217,000	$160,000
UK	$122,000	$114,000	$334,000
USA	–$156,000	–$332,000	–$298,000
Western Canada	$112,000	–$65,000	–$62,000
Ontario	$173,000	–$118,000	–$49,000
All areas	**$8,027,000**	**$3,780,000**	**$4,838,000**

One of Flight Centre Limited's businesses was almost unaffected, however. The UK, buffered by its large volume of intra-Europe traffic, reported a September profit only $8000 lower than the previous month. The October figures showed a big resurgence. It appeared that many clients had simply switched their trans-Atlantic holidays to destinations closer to home.

Falling profits aside, it was a very stressful time for the company's salespeople around the world. They had to rebook and refund hundreds of airline tickets and deal with many upset clients. One US customer even picked up a computer and threw it at a consultant in response to the news that his plane had been grounded.

At the same time, these consultants had to contend with their own fears that their jobs were at risk. 'Everyone in our office had brand new mortgages,' Tony Freedman, a Melbourne consultant, recalls. 'We thought it was the end of the world.' Up in Brisbane, Terry Patterson felt the same. On 10 September he'd bought a block of land, but was soon calling the real estate agent to cancel the deal. 'I was convinced the industry would die,' he says.

FCL had been through the same thing before, of course, ten years back, and survived. Skroo sent out emails reminding everyone of the company's experience in the Gulf War. 'We knew that there would be a tidal wave of business in a couple of months once people started travelling again,' he explains. This helped determine a lot of FCL's strategy. It increased its advertising, opened new stores and recruited more people.

By focusing on the things that could be controlled, such as increasing its market share, the company avoided the negativity that consumed other travel companies. People found positive ways to occupy themselves. The Ontario operation organised a candlelight vigil in New York, as a result of which it booked 400 people. Consultants gradually began to relax once they worked out their jobs were safe. Terry Patterson got back on the phone and bought that block of land after all.

This was all good strategy, but many of the ripple effects of September 11 were yet to come. America declared its 'War on Terror', and it appeared more and more likely that it would attack the Taliban regime in Afghanistan. This acted as a damper on travel; in fact the total air traffic worldwide for that year would decrease by 6 per cent, a loss of 60 million people. The corporate area was hit particularly hard. Many businesspeople stayed home and teleconferenced instead.

There was also the problem of what Graham Turner termed 'unhealthy airlines'. The International Air Transport Association calculated that in the first week after September 11, $10 billion was lost in flight cancellations alone. With an economic downturn at the start of 2001, many airlines were already struggling to survive. Now they were pushed to the brink of bankruptcy.

Flight Centre's Canadian operations would take the first hit. Aileen Bratton, who was working in Vancouver, remembers Skroo asking her in November 2001 how secure she thought local airline Canada 3000 was. 'I told him they were rock solid,' she says. 'We had no idea they were in trouble. Two days later, of course, they collapsed.'

Many of the 40,000 passengers who were stranded around the world following Canada 3000's collapse were FCL clients. As a goodwill gesture, the company paid for many of them to get home. Because everyone who was booked on Canada 3000 was rebooked on Air Canada, however, there were no seats left for people to buy during the holiday season. The result was a major slump for six weeks and losses in both FCL's Western Canada and Ontario operations.

And worse was yet to come from this particular airline's collapse. Flight Centre Limited found out two months later that it was liable for all the losses for people who had paid for the Canada 3000 flights by credit card but hadn't actually travelled. Because the passengers hadn't received the product they had paid for, the banks held FCL accountable for the credit card payments.

This would be an ongoing problem. FCL had lost money after the Ansett collapse for the same reason, so it now decided to refuse credit cards as payment on airlines it deemed a financial risk. In the current economic climate, however, it was difficult to determine which airlines this boycott applied to. Swissair and Sabena, two European carriers, had gone bankrupt in October 2001, and the press was full of rumours that one of the big American airlines could be next. If this was the case, FCL could be liable for a very large sum of money.

But this threat went beyond the company's finances. If another airline did go under, then consultants would have to repay the personal commission they'd made on each booking. Naturally, people worried about how this would impact on their salaries. In the US, where the problem was most pronounced, FCL started a 'belly-up' fund whereby consultants paid the Ticket Centre an extra $2 on every ticket. If an airline went bankrupt, this money would be used to repay the consultants' commission. It was a good idea to boost morale, but in the end the fund wasn't needed. The US government spent billions of dollars to bail out the struggling airlines.

Overall, the financial fallout from the events surrounding September 11 and the collapse of Ansett and Canada 3000 lasted for about six months. As Skroo had predicted, bookings went mad in the second half of the 2001/02 financial year. FCL policy of staffing up and opening more shops now paid off. In the January to June half-year, the company recorded an operating profit of $59 million. To put this in perspective, the entire profit of the previous year was $65 million. The amount was also two-thirds of the $90 million profit that FCL would post for the entire year. It was a truly impressive result, as Queensland's major newspaper, *The Courier-Mail*, acknowledged: 'Flight Centre Ltd has sailed through the most difficult twelve months in the aviation industry's history with ease, posting a 45 per cent increase in net profit to $62 million.'[47] Much of this success could be attributed to FCL's decision to diversify into different brands and geographical areas in 1995, but in large part, it was down to the resourcefulness and initiative of the company's people.

Flight Centre Limited had withstood the effects of the September 11 terrorist attacks, but that was merely phase one. The next instalment occurred on 14 October 2002, in Bali, one of the islands that make up the Indonesian archipelago. A horrific attack was carried out in a crowded nightclub, where 178 people, mainly Western tourists, were killed.

Even though this attack had less effect on the travelling public (FCL only experiencing a small drop in profit in November, for instance), the fallout would have serious repercussions. America increased its anti-terrorist rhetoric and began sabre-rattling against what it called 'the Axis of Evil', specifically Iraq, Iran and North Korea. After several months of high-profile coverage, the USA and its coalition partners invaded Iraq on 19 March 2003. War had begun.

Almost simultaneously, the first case of a deadly pneumonia outbreak labelled SARS (Severe Acute Respiratory Disorder) hit the newspapers. With words like 'severe' and 'acute' in its title, and rumours that it spread via sneezing or touching an elevator button, it was no surprise that panicking travellers began to cancel their flights by the thousands. Soon the disease had spread rapidly through eight countries, and World Health Organization alerts were trumpeting around the globe. Once again the travel industry almost shut down.

These two events had very different impacts on the travel industry. The Iraq war made a small impression, but it appeared that, in just eighteen months since the tragedy at the World Trade Centre, many people had become used to the dual threats of war and terrorism, and were almost immune by this stage. 'It didn't affect us as much as I thought it would,' Ontario leader Grahame Hubbard admits.

To Skroo Turner, SARS was the real issue. With some airline staff wearing surgical masks, and heat detectors installed in airports to spot passengers with fever, travel via Asia came to a virtual standstill. Singapore Airlines' Tom Kenny was another to feel the impact: 'SARS was so terrifying because there was no cure. The first quarter of 2003 was the only time Singapore Airlines has made a loss in its entire history.'

In Toronto there was a major SARS outbreak, with 250 cases and 35 deaths. People from that city were banned from cruise ships and conferences, and quarantined from the rest of the world. Global corporate travel was also hit hard, with an unprecedented number of conferences cancelled.

Over in Australia, SARS had a very big effect, although many FCL consultants felt that the press blew it way out of proportion. 'The influenza in Hong Kong killed more people than SARS,' one consultant points out, 'but you hardly heard anything about that.' With their clients refusing to fly via Asia, FCL had to reroute them all via Africa and the USA.

Ironically, Flight Centre Limited's two-year-old Hong Kong operation had a record month following the SARS outbreak. Unfortunately, the sales came from expatriates and their families who were leaving in droves. This would be the last good month the Hong Kong business had for some time.

In the USA there was little impact. Most Americans travelled domestically, and as far as they were concerned, Canada could've been on the other side of the world. As for South Africa, which would finish the year with profits of R10 million better than the previous year, it had already proved it was immune to many world crises. 'South Africans are a little more resilient in tough times,' area leader Dominique Pomario explains. 'From our perspective, we're probably more at risk within South Africa than when we're travelling overseas.'

But these encouraging signs could never hide the fact that, overall, the financial impact of SARS and the Iraq War on FCL was substantial. The company's April profits were less than half the budgeted amount. This time around, however, the resurgence in travel was much faster than in 1991. In May, the 'tidal wave' of enquiry generated an operating profit of $11 million, in June it was a record $17.7 million. FCL finished the 2002/03 financial year with a net profit of $69.9 million – an increase of 12.9 per cent over the previous year. This was a good result when compared to those of other major industry players, such as Thomas Cook, which ended the year with a $272 million loss and more than 1000 redundancies.

Behind the scenes, these losses were changing the shape of the industry. Bankruptcies had decimated travel agencies. In just three years the number of travel agencies in the USA dropped from 43,000 to 20,000. Many airlines were struggling to stay afloat as flight routes were slashed, regional offices were shut down, and staff were retrenched. Low-cost airlines such as easyJet in the UK were the winners in this more frugal environment, and grew enormously.

Unfortunately for FCL, one of the first things to go was travel agents' commission. The company thought this was very short-sighted. 'If airlines turn their backs on travel agents they are ignoring the cheapest distribution network available to them,' Skroo wrote in a newsletter. 'Unhealthy airlines that choose this route do so at their own peril. Many of them will go broke by following this path.' The

Ansett administrators reportedly said that this was one of their mistakes when they tried to revive the ailing airline.

Cutting out the agent seemed like an attractive option to many airlines, particularly the US carriers, who were struggling to find ways to cut costs after their revenues had plummeted. In March 2002, after months of rumours, the top five American airlines axed all travel agents' commission within 48 hours of each other. This halved FCL's North American profits overnight. Air Canada followed soon after.

To avoid panic, the leaders of Ontario, Western Canada and the USA continued paying their consultants commission for those airlines, but paid it out of their support accounts instead. This gave them some breathing space while they worked out what to do.

With the media giving the story wide coverage, public sentiment was with the travel agents. In this environment, the Western Canada and US operations decided to charge an airline commission fee on all tickets. Americans and Canadians were used to these, so the areas didn't feel it would antagonise any clients. Still, Western Canada leader Margje de Groot was prepared for some backlash: 'I told the consultants that if anyone questioned the commission fee, then they shouldn't charge it. We never had a single complaint.'

The team members of the Ontario operation took the opposite approach. They decided to differentiate themselves from other travel agents by advertising that they charged no booking fees at all. 'We decided to make a stand and be faithful to our claim of "no service fees",' Grahame Hubbard admits. 'In hindsight, this brought us no benefit. We should have stuck to the "Lowest Airfares" guarantee instead.'

Toronto's gross profit margins dropped from 14 to 9 per cent, which was hardly a surprise considering that consultants now earned $5 on tickets that would have netted them several hundred dollars before. After six months, Ontario was forced to introduce a commission fee after all. This caused uproar from consultants who had turned the whole 'no service fee' issue into a major campaign against the airlines. By dropping it, they felt they had lost some integrity.

In contrast, the introduction of airline commission fees in Western Canada and the USA had seen a 1 per cent jump in those operations' margin over a 12-month period. They actually made more money out of the fee than from their previously capped commission.

By the end of 2004 many travel agencies saw the airlines' commission-cutting policies as a fact of life, and service fees had become an established part of their business model. Even though Flight Centre Limited also changed some of its practices in this area, Skroo said he believed that 'commission is coming back. Air Canada is paying nine per cent again. They knew it was a fucked idea in the first place.'

To prove his point, in September 2004, FCL undertook a global review of the commissions paid by airlines in all its overseas operations. The research contradicted suggestions in Australia of a global trend towards reduced payments. The main change was in the way that commissions were being paid. Many airlines no longer paid base commissions, but once a travel agent reached a certain target level they paid the same or sometimes even more commission than before, retrospectively. American Airlines, one of the first to introduce zero commission, was one who now offered what it referred to as 'commissions to travel agents on special revenue programs',[48] in order to compete with other carriers offering comparative payments. This type of structure, similar to a passenger's frequent flyer program in that it rewards loyalty, obviously favours large and growing travel agencies such as FCL.

Commission-cutting was only one of the challenges facing Flight Centre Limited in the post-September 11 environment. The airlines, desperate to cut any expenses they could, also stopped paying for joint advertising costs and new marketing initiatives. Instead the carriers began feeding this money into the development of internet booking engines. As one senior representative from the travel company Cendant told an FCL conference in 2002, 'The world of co-opetition has begun.' By this he meant that companies that had previously been travel agents' suppliers and business partners were now also squaring up as their direct competitors.

Airline commission comparisons based on research in September 2004 of FCL's international operations*

USA
Domestic flights	5–12 per cent
Charter operators servicing Mexico and Hawaii	12–15 per cent
Trans-Pacific flights	15 per cent

Canada
International flights	15–30 per cent

By Australian standards, Air Canada pays comparable upfront and back-end overrides for domestic, cross-border and other international flights. In recent times, Air Canada has clearly been working on developing good agent relationships. The smaller domestic carriers are now generally following suit.

United Kingdom
Short-haul European flights (minimum)	8 per cent
Long-haul flights	12–18 per cent
Charter holiday packages to the Mediterranean or Caribbean	12–18 per cent

South Africa
Domestic flights	5–8 per cent
International flights	from 5 per cent plus targeted overrides, to 10 per cent

South Africa is FCL's only overseas market where margins are clearly less generous than those available in Australia.

New Zealand
Domestic flights (very small market)	3–8 per cent
Trans-Tasman flights	8–14 per cent
International flights	17–19 per cent

*   *The figures in this table are taken from an FCL press release and include the commission paid retrospectively once the company reached its set target.*

American Airlines, Continental, Delta Airlines, Northwest Airlines and United had already joined forces to set up Orbitz, an online travel company. It would expand rapidly, with 455 airlines, 45,000 lodging properties and 23 car rental companies by 2004. Others quickly followed suit with their own sites. By 2003, travel accounted for 43 per cent of total online sales, in terms of dollar value, while the next largest category, 'computers/peripherals/PDAs' represented only 17 per cent on online sales.[49]

Even though in Australia internet sales of international flights were still a very small percentage of the market – just 1 per cent for British Airways and 2 per cent for Singapore Airlines, for example – some investors felt that FCL's bricks and mortar strategy, which had made it a market darling, was now obsolete. With airlines offering cheaper airfares, extra frequent flyer points and many other incentives to encourage people to book via the internet, they saw online bookings as a serious threat to the company's viability.

FCL's 'Lowest Airfares' guarantee was one of the first things to come under attack. The domestic airlines in Australia began advertising that the cheapest fares were those booked on the internet. Feeling the need to change the public's perception, the company responded with a big marketing campaign guaranteeing that its fares were 'Cheaper than the internet'. Flight Centre Limited trumpeted this slogan on television, inserted it into all press ads and even plastered it on the side of council buses. In addition, the company backed the guarantee with its price-beating account. Prior to the campaign, enquiries had dropped by 30 per cent; within two weeks they were up 30 per cent.

FCL's retail consultants bore the brunt of the pressure from the airlines' new internet strategies. As well as looking up flights in the Galileo reservations system, they now had to search many individual airline websites as well. In effect they had to do more work to make the same amount of money. The knock-on effect was that by 2004, retail areas such as the original Flight Centre brand were experiencing higher levels of staff turnover as some people left to pursue easier roles. (The company's smaller brands such as Student Flights and Escape

Travel escaped this effect, once again demonstrating the strength of Nicholson's hunter-gatherer Families and Villages philosophy.)

In response, Flight Centre Limited began to invest more in technology as evidenced by its purchases of online hotel and airfare booking engines Quickbeds and travelthere.com, in 2003 and 2004 respectively, and the employment of a dedicated e-commerce leader. This has had some effect: according to Hitwise, the company's website was the most popular travel agency site in Australia in 2004, receiving over 700,000 hits and 30,000 enquiries per month.

In 2005, FCL announced a new 'clicks and mortar' strategy that involved directing point-to-point enquiries such as domestic bookings from Brisbane to Melbourne via its website, with the aim of freeing up its consultants for more complex itineraries.

FCL chairman Norm Fussell discounted some of the hype around the impact of online travel bookings: 'Following September 11 we picked up a lot of clients. In times of crisis people don't want to deal with computers and phone systems.' The company's positive attitude had also helped. Always best in the underdog role, FCL's trials had led to more creative pricing and an improvement in its processes and deals on things like car hire and hotels. In fact, Flight Centre Limited discovered that its margins on land products were actually 50 per cent higher than those on airfares.

But it was FCL's purchase of Britannic Travel that really demonstrated its attitude to adversity. In April 2003, at the height of the two-part storm that was SARS and the Iraq War, when investor confidence was abysmal and the stock exchange was at a five-year low, FCL decided to buy a company. Not just any old company, but its most expensive one to date. Britannic Travel was a licensee of TQ3, one of the five largest corporate travel providers in the world. If FCL could buy Britannic, it would become one of the biggest players in the UK corporate market.

There was a catch, however: to Britannic owner Alan Spence, Flight Centre Limited was a foreign company, an unknown – he wanted cash, not shares. The estimated purchase price was $100 million, which meant that FCL would have to raise $80 million in share capital. To the underwriters, ABN Amro Morgans and Wilson HTM, it seemed like mission impossible.

Rather than ignoring the external threat during the necessary presentations to major investment groups, FCL decided to attack it head-on. This was another idea the directors had borrowed from Jim Collins, one that Turner had already put to good effect when fronting up to shareholders after the poor results of the technology projects in 2000/01.

Skroo explains the approach the Acquisitions team took: 'We began our presentation with "What are the greatest things that threaten Flight Centre and what are we doing about them?" Then we outlined all the negatives, such as the world crises, unhealthy airlines, and the encroaching internet.' Most companies were reporting declining profits, and FCL was upfront with the fact that its profit could be well down too.

On the upside, the company pointed out that during the 1991 Gulf War it had lost $300,000; by 2003 however, there was $200 million in cash reserves. It had also diversified with different brands and overseas businesses.

FCL could withstand a hit in any one area. It was staffed up, ready for the business resurgence that the directors knew was coming. In comparison, much of the competition would disappear in this tough climate.

And finally, it didn't hurt that the four founding directors had agreed to put in $18 million themselves. This was seen as a refreshing change from a host of floats of the same period.

It was a fairly close call, by some accounts, but the board got the money. Flight Centre Limited bought Britannic, and simultaneously catapulted itself into the big league.

FCL's decision to stand up and face the music – or 'confront the brutal facts', to borrow Jim Collins' phrase – paid off. The company was included in the books *The Most Promising Companies in Australia* and

100 Great Businesses and the Minds Behind Them,[50] and by the end of the 2003/04 financial year, FCL had again increased operating profit by 20 per cent, to $121 million.

There were more challenges ahead, however. In late 2004 the Australian Competition and Consumer Commission (ACCC) forced Flight Centre to change its slogan from 'Lowest Airfares Guaranteed' to 'Price Beat Guarantee'. The problem was not with the actual guarantee – a third-party survey showed that the company honoured its guarantee and price-beat international fares 100 per cent of the time – but with the wording. The ACCC was concerned that one possible interpretation of the 'Lowest Airfares' guarantee was that customers would automatically be quoted the lowest airfare all the time, without the need to tender a competitor's quote. This was in spite of the fact that the guarantee was always accompanied by a dominant tagline that read: 'Bring us a competitor's quote, and if it's available we will beat it.'

On receipt of the ACCC's concerns, Flight Centre conducted focus groups with its customers. Some were fervent supporters:

> When is a correction not a correction? Flight Centre travel chain has been forced to change slogans. 'Price Beat Guarantee' replaces 'Lowest Airfares Guaranteed'. To me, they are the same. Only to the eggheads at the Australian Competition and Consumer Commission do they seem to be different …
>
> C.D. O'Keeffe, Toowoomba[51]

Others indicated that they would prefer the company to change to the term 'Price Beat Guarantee'. For Flight Centre's company secretary, Greg Pringle, the choice was clear: 'The bottom line was that if there was room for misunderstanding by our customers, then we needed to remove that misunderstanding, because if we didn't have their full trust and confidence, then we wouldn't have their business.' In November 2004, the company changed all its branding to 'Price Beat Guarantee'.

Turner certainly didn't take the ruling personally: 'I think the ACCC's real issue was that other companies such as Bunnings hardware and Retravision had also begun to offer 'lowest prices' guarantees. They wanted to stop this proliferation, and because we were perceived as the main player we were the first target.'

Despite all the chaos of the four years to 2004, the company collected a raft of awards. In 2002, FCL entered the Employer of the Year Awards in Australia (sponsored by the Australian Graduate School of Management and *Boss* magazine) and Canada (*The Globe and Mail*). The organisers sent out hundreds of questionnaires to people working in all areas of each company; their answers were given a point value. For FCL to win, it had to score the highest number of total points.

In its first year of entry, FCL won Employer of the Year in both countries. The company's business model had prevailed against the best. This was understandable in Australia, where FCL had a long and successful commercial history, but in Canada, where the company had only been trading for seven years, it was truly remarkable.

In 2003, Flight Centre Limited again participated in Australia and Canada, as well as entering competitions in the UK (where it was sponsored by *The Sunday Times*) and New Zealand (*Unlimited* magazine) for the first time. As in the previous year, the results were incredible. FCL won Employer of the Year in Australia and New Zealand, came first in the Leadership category and third overall in the UK, and placed third in Canada.

For one retailer to win these awards all around the world was a staggering achievement, and the business community duly took note. In the UK, where FCL's eight-year-old operation was up against retail giants with over 50 years of successful business experience, *The Sunday Times* reported: 'More than nine in 10 staff say their team is fun to work with. 88 per cent feel they make a valuable contribution to the firm's success – both scores are the highest in our survey.'[52]

The results put the company squarely on the recruitment map. Add this success to the company's global operations, its strategic acquisitions, its 7600 people and more than 1500 businesses, its Travel Agency Group of the Year awards (FCL won again in 2003 and

2004), its crossing of the $100 million profit barrier and its consistent ranking in Australia's top 100 companies, and there is no doubt that Flight Centre Limited had come a long way from its humble beginnings in a Munich beer hall in 1973.

Chapter 14

FULL THROTTLE

Skroo once said to me founders are forgiven many sins. He's right.

Shane Flynn, Flight Centre CEO (2002–2006)

T he size of the prize was more than $100 million over three years. But there was a whole lot more to Flight Centre Limited's internal overhaul, called Full Throttle, which dominated late 2004 and 2005, than the size of its prize and its kick-ass *Charlie's Angels* connotations.

In the story of Flight Centre Limited, Full Throttle was a titanic jolt.

Always able to emerge stronger than ever from crises and conflicts that wreaked havoc on the travel industry, the company was left scarred, though perhaps wiser, from one of the most significant growing pains it brought upon itself.

It was the moment Flight Centre Limited, despite its determination to learn from mistakes past, gave strategies introduced by an external consultancy priority over the distinctive FCL way, its culture and its people.

And it was when 'outsiders', those who hadn't done their time as travel consultants on the front-line, were endowed with the power to direct and effect internal change.

Given the result and bruising legacy of the experiment, perhaps Skroo's initial project appellation, Purple Dog, would have been more apt, even if it was actually meant as a nod to Seth Godin's business-transforming bestseller, *Purple Cow*.[53]

'Normally we make the same mistake a number of times before we learn. I'll be pretty pissed off if we make this mistake again,' Turner said.

It remains difficult for the company to explain quite why it pursued the culturally out of kilter elements of Full Throttle. It was as if it suffered temporary amnesia about the lessons of its own success and the guiding concepts of Jim Collins' *Good to Great* that had been such a manual to FCL during its process of maturation. Collins had found that in the pathway to success in great companies, progress was constant, focused and incremental; there was 'no single defining action . . . no wrenching revolution'. Wrapped in a single package, Full Throttle confirmed the pain and damage one counter-cultural, turbocharged wrench of the flywheel could cause.

With the lure of an estimated $100 million benefit at a time when FCL's profit and share price were slumping, Full Throttle clearly may have 'seemed like a good idea at the time'. There is little dispute that something needed to be done. Growth in Australia and internationally had pushed the company to more than 1500 businesses. All markets had expanded and Flight Centre employed 7600 people from consultants through to senior management. Ruminations were growing in volume that change was required to deal with the size of the business and the evolving nature of the industry. Of particular concern was that while frontline growth continued apace, support costs, even with the commercialisation model in place, had gone rogue. The company's financial results just weren't stacking up.

Chief executive officer Shane Flynn said that in the combined years of 2003 and 2004, Flight Centre Limited's turnover had grown by 56 per cent, but profit grew by only 32 per cent. 'This is a sign our costs grew faster than our income. This means we need to adjust the way we do things,' Flynn said.

For founder Geoff Harris, the problem was simple: 'We'd got fat at head office.' Harris said the company had 'too many bureaucrats producing fancy reports that no one reads. We even had our own research division. We were moving away from our core business. When this happens, companies have to purge themselves and become more efficient.'

One head office research project had already identified potential efficiency improvements. The Baldridge Quality Program had been entrenched as Flight Centre Limited's business improvement framework since the company first used the US quality management tool in 2002, to measure and evaluate quality across seven key areas. Geoff Lomas, who worked on Baldridge assessments after the initial analysis, said the research team found that FCL's scores had generally improved, ranking it a world-class company. But what the company wasn't so hot at were systems – quite a paradox given that standard systems and 'One Best Way' were of extreme importance and part of the FCL philosophies, said Lomas. 'I think any long-term successful business gets a degree of arrogance. We identified that change was needed and that the problem was with systems. But the research calling for changes to systems, from accounting to sales to IT, wasn't acted upon despite commitment to continuous improvement being part of the same philosophy,' he said.

Around the same time, FCL was jostling with cultural issues around leadership teams laced with 'outsiders' from recent recruitment drives to bring in external executive blood. People with industry expertise in their fields were recruited into top roles to strengthen the company's corporate backbone and provide diversified skill and experience ahead of potential problems. 'It was a period when we were looking for easy solutions,' said Turner. 'We were looking for silver bullets in terms of hiring people.'

The strategy of absorbing outsiders meant that by mid-2004, six out of the ten members of FCL's global executive team were external appointments – all of whom were experienced and expert in their fields, but who hadn't previously proven themselves in the FCL structure or culture.

But research, quick fixes and easy solutions weren't producing the results the company should have been generating. In Turner's words, the much-desired silver bullets turned out to be lead.

Deeming that an alternative approach was required, Turner spoke with Ron Malek of corporate advisory firm Caliburn (subsequently Greenhill Caliburn), who had forged a close working relationship with the company through deals including the takeover of corporate travel specialist ITG in 2002 and the $119 million acquisition of Britannic in the UK in 2003.

Malek introduced Flight Centre Limited to Bain and Company as an external consultancy to assist with issues surrounding stalled profit growth.

A shake-up wouldn't have been unexpected at Flight Centre. Greg Pringle, company secretary in 2004, said that Skroo orchestrated reform every few years because it was required, or maybe just to keep people on their toes. The difference this time and one of the reasons the Full Throttle shake-up was so distinguishable, Pringle said, was that this fiercely self-sufficient company was prepared to give an external consultancy 'the keys to the front door and allow them to change the locks'.

In November 2004, Bain conducted an eight-week investigation into FCL. Bain partner Tony Duthie said the diagnostic turned up results that indicated many issues being experienced by the company were 'a blip' and could be turned around. It compared Flight Centre Limited with the performance of other companies on the Australian Stock Exchange Top 200 list and showed that FCL had been in the 'legendary' category for the previous four years. 'Because of the massive growth necessary to become "legendary", it is impossible for a company to stay in that box all the time,' Duthie said. FCL had hit a point where it needed to pause and potentially look at different ways of working. 'It's not unusual for a company that grows that fast to experience a bit of a slow down.'

Bain proposed a program of work to be implemented over a three-wave process of savings and productivity improvements. It said the 'size of the prize' that could be delivered by the 2007/08 financial year was $100 million. At a retreat at Turner's Spicers Hidden Vale property, Full Throttle was given the go-ahead and declared to be the most important change program ever undertaken at Flight Centre.

With board support, CEO Shane Flynn and Steve Becker took charge of Full Throttle for Flight Centre and Tony Duthie had oversight of the project for Bain.

Flynn recalled that at the outset, Bain advised that two things

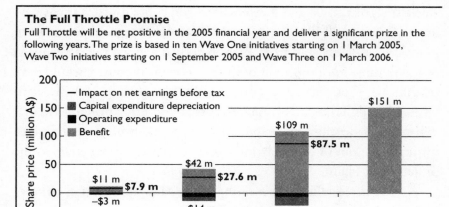

The Full Throttle Promise

Full Throttle will be net positive in the 2005 financial year and deliver a significant prize in the following years. The prize is based in ten Wave One initiatives starting on 1 March 2005, Wave Two initiatives starting on 1 September 2005 and Wave Three on 1 March 2006.

usually happened during the process. Firstly, the company would say that it did not dig deep enough and it should have gone harder to make all possible changes. Secondly, the CEO wouldn't last.

'We thought, this is Flight Centre, this won't happen to us. Well, that's what I thought. I would like to think at the time we all thought that,' Flynn said.

On 13 January 2005, FCL advised that its pre-tax profit for the six months to 31 December 2004 would be 8 to 10 per cent below the same period in 2003, rather than matching the previous first half as expected. The day after the profit downgrade announcement, shares fell $2.86 to $16. The 15 per cent slide was the biggest since the company's 1995 listing.

A month later, FCL announced its official half-yearly results. The results, as the company had advised in January, when it warned of an 8–10 per cent drop, were plain awful. Profit for the first half of the 2004/05 financial year was $30.5 million, a 10.6 per cent downturn on the previous year's net result. It was a time in which there were no major crises in the industry, no major incidents affecting travel and tourism worldwide. Just bad results.

Full Throttle preparations hit high gear. With the brutal thud of profit and share price slumps resonating in its ears, the company was desperate for a potential panacea. An entire floor was set aside in FCL's

Adelaide Street, Brisbane, headquarters for Full Throttle, as thirteen Flight Centre people were seconded from their regular positions to join about as many staff from Bain. Bain had advised that in order to get good value for money out of the project, the company would have to dedicate a number of senior people to the process 100 per cent. Given that FCL operated more on a trial and error principle than a research and development model, it was most out of the ordinary to move people out of their day job, where they were productive, to the project, said Flynn.

At the project kick-off meeting on 1 March 2005, ten priority initiatives were green-lighted for Wave One, including an organisational revamp and changes to bring about quick cost savings. A review of costs found numerous instances of duplication, overspending and waste. It was discovered that annual savings of $750,000 could be made by buying printer toner in bulk, rather than via separate orders for each division. 'People embraced those kinds of savings, and embraced that part of Full Throttle in typical Flight Centre fashion,' said Steve Becker. 'Signs went up: "Give Skroo a Boner, Consolidate Purchasing of Your Toner!"'

Other low-hanging fruit gave the project early savings and results. Greeted with less enthusiasm by the masses, monthly Buzz Nights – the heart of the Flight Centre social and recognition structure – were targeted for not following guidelines.

Flynn said some areas were spending $5000 for a Buzz Night and inviting guest speakers. 'That's not what they're meant to be, it's about getting together, having a few drinks, talking about results and where improvements can be made, training and a bit of celebration. You should be able to run a good Buzz Night in a car park.' Along with enforcing guidelines for conference attendance, the crackdown on Buzz Night spending over six months reduced costs by $6 million – a figure so surprisingly big it was audited four times.

Flynn said one of the elements of Full Throttle that he had particularly high hopes for was improving systems to reduce errors made by consultants. Better systems and fewer errors meant fewer unhappy customers and fewer staff members losing confidence, feeling

Full Throttle Wave One	
Under Full Throttle it was envisaged that ten key initiatives would run at any one time. Some initiatives would run for six months, others for as long as three years. As some finished, others would be added. The list below is the starting point.	
Initiative	**Purpose**
Organisational redesign	To remove complex reporting lines and more effectively support an efficient front-end business
Compressible costs/blackholes	To control and optimise the company's spending habits to get more 'bang' for less bucks
In-store productivity	To boost retail consultant productivity by reducing administrative load, staff turnover and time required to quote and book by simplifying systems
Transform finance	To reduce the cost of performing financial tasks and improve the quality of financial outputs
Multi-channel strategy	To align each retail channel's offer with its users' requirements and service customers' needs in the most cost-effective manner
IT capability review	To increase IT's ability to provide competitive advantage by delivering solutions on time, within budget and with the functionality required to achieve business objectives Operate and develop a cost-effective and reliable technical infrastructure for business users
Ticketing solution	To reduce cost, improve efficiency and enhance reliability in the ticketing process.
Marketing effectiveness	Detailed design of future marketing organisation covering: • Structure/accountabilities • Measures • Processes and tools Develop process for forecasting and measuring marketing effectiveness
Optimise margins	To optimise margin outcomes by improving supplier relationships and improving business coordination
Corporate business strategy	To define business goals and identify the best opportunities and strategies to compete for and win accounts.

Source: Shane Flynn memo to staff, 'Project Full Throttle'

unrewarded for their efforts and leaving the business as a result. 'I was so excited. I saw that if we could reduce staff turnover in shops from thirty-five per cent to twenty-five per cent, then that would save millions. It would be a bonanza,' said Flynn.

That Full Throttle wave never came. Wave One's restructure of the organisation swamped Flight Centre's head office like a tsunami.

With the shockwave of the first round of redundancies and job losses, a new level of condemnation was directed at the 'suit-wearing outsiders' of Bain and Full Throttle. Bain was already being accused of corrupting the Flight Centre culture and its core philosophies by introducing otherwise commonplace business practices, such as PowerPoint presentations, waterfall graphs and referring to people as FTEs (full-time equivalents), which was seen as undermining Flight Centre's valuing of people. The buyback of many of the company's hugely popular Business Ownership Schemes (BOSs) to stop people making too much 'lazy money' from their investment, despite being proposed pre-Full Throttle, upped the anti-Bain sentiment. The BOS had long been the key motivator in getting people to run shops as their own businesses. Supporters of the scheme warned that scrapping it would shatter the building block of the company's philosophy that each person had the opportunity to own part of their success. This rupturing of the Flight Centre way caused friction enough, but when FCL people began to lose their jobs – for the first time in the company's history – the trauma and outrage sent morale plummeting to new lows.

On the advice of Bain, the restructuring was displayed with people's names in boxes showing their job prospects. Everyone was spilled from their roles and they either had to reapply for the job they already had or apply for an alternative position – or they found themselves not in a box.

Melanie Waters-Ryan, Australian wholesale leader at the time, said she believed it was a mere formality that she would get a newly created global wholesale role. 'Then I was called in and told that I didn't have the job, but also that I didn't not have the job. I was told they wanted to see first if there was anyone better out there. I remember saying that

I certainly wasn't going to be their date for the prom until they could get a better one.' The Flight Centre 'lifer' was so incensed she almost walked.

Alissa O'Connell, who was running the company's Australian operation, was called in amid the stress-inducing void of internal communication to be told her name wasn't in a box. 'I was sat down and told they were doing away with the structure. I was told: "You don't have a job." Then none of them spoke to me for two weeks. Shane Flynn wouldn't even return my calls,' she said.

Rachel O'Brien, global PeopleWorks executive, sat in on many Full Throttle strategy meetings only to find out in the restructure that her own name wasn't in a box. Perhaps worse, she said, she knew friends who were going to be 'Full Throttled' and couldn't tell them. Among them was her future husband. 'Full Throttle is a blight on our past. It was a dark time. It was totally unaligned with our culture – we were put in the position where we betrayed our friends. I'd never do that again.'

Yet the Flight Centre culture meant people worked to find a way of dealing with circumstances that were unsettling and depressing. To the infuriation of Bain and many in the Full Throttle team, signs began appearing around the office highlighting the ludicrousness of senior leaders not knowing if they had a place in FCL's future. As quick as the 'Is your name in a box?' or '[just deceased] Yasser Arafat's got a box, why don't I?' banners were erected, largely by Flight Centre brand leader Joell Ogilvie's team, they would be torn down by Throttlers. Police crime tape and chalk outlines of slain bodies appeared around the office in reference to the culling going on by the Full Throttle razor gang. And people came dressed in pyjamas and threw Full Throttle parties on the day redundancy slips were issued, commiserating over highly intoxicating 'Shane Flynn Snakebite' punch.

PeopleWorks chief Mark Aponas, who had been seconded to the Full Throttle team, said the staff cuts – numbering 67.5 FTEs, including those made redundant, people who resigned and weren't replaced, and contractors whose expired contracts weren't renewed – were, in fact, 'very mild'. The cuts represented less than 1 per cent. They saved

FCL $5.2 million. However, subsequent global PeopleWorks leader Michael Murphy said that within a year, as the roles excised from the business built up again, the net result was only about ten fewer people working for the company.

Aponas said the number of people removed was vehemently challenged by Turner at the time. 'He [Turner] wanted two hundred. He might not be seen as the bad guy of Full Throttle, but I knew who was loading and firing the gun.' Flynn said he was staggered at Turner's demand for more staff retrenchments and warned that deeper cuts would take out the muscle with the fat.

Turner confirmed that a cut of 200 FTEs was the aim, but ultimately it was irrelevant. Full Throttle, he said, was a shambles. It was at this point that tension over ownership of Full Throttle – indeed the dual leadership model that had been in place at FCL since 2002, when Turner became managing director responsible for strategy and Shane Flynn was appointed CEO handling the day-to-day operations of the business – came to a head.

Board chairman Norm Fussell had long pushed Turner to invest in succession planning for the company. Rather than following Fussell's plan of putting a preferred candidate through their paces in a senior position in the Australian business, Turner said Flynn was appointed CEO in 2002 based on his success running the South African operation. 'The funny thing is, I was only ever interested in keeping my job in South Africa. That's all I ever wanted to do. Nothing more than that,' Flynn said.

The model resulted in a splitting of the realm and even created two separate leadership teams – Turner's X Team and Flynn's Y Team. It meant a lot of crossover and a lot of mixed messages. It meant staff could and would 'play Mummy off against Daddy' if they didn't like a decision. It also created the potential for decision-making inertia, lack of ownership and fissures in the structure – a brittle base from which to stage Full Throttle, with its capacity to cleave gaping fractures in morale and trust in the company's leadership.

Turner said Full Throttle was clearly Flynn's project. 'I admit to agreeing and pushing for it, but it was Flynnie as CEO who had direct responsibility for it,' he said. Flynn maintains he was unfairly cast as the villain. 'I didn't start the Full Throttle process. I just took it on because I was asked by my MD to do it.'

Co-founder Bill James said that in the middle of Full Throttle he went to see Flynn to offer support. Asked how he was feeling, James recalled Flynn replying that he was tired of second-guessing Skroo. 'As soon as he said that I thought, mate, you're gone. He was the CEO and was implying that he was trying to predict what Skroo would do in a certain situation. That's just not the way you do it.' Flynn denied he meant to convey to James that he was trying to behave like Turner. Rather, he said he was highlighting the farcical result of two distinct leadership styles forced, at a time of immense pressure, to co-exist in a dual leadership model.

The end came quickly. Turner stepped in to disband Full Throttle. The big changes scheduled for the second six months of the program under the 'Full Throttle Reload' Wave never got rolling. But the project did leave a lasting legacy.

Melanie Waters-Ryan said it's likely that Full Throttle will forever be seen as the era in which the company completely lost its mind. 'When culture is such a critical part of your success, you just can't put that in the hands of strangers,' she said.

Yet many agree that Full Throttle introduced some valuable changes, including an increased level of measuring and discipline, and a cleansing that forced the company back to its fundamentals. And while it was unpleasant for some, it was the right thing to do by share-holders. But the across-the-board program of change was too much, too fast, and the scarring on morale was too deep for it to continue.

Immediately after Turner stepped in to disband Full Throttle, Flight Centre revealed a full-year profit for the 2004/05 financial year of $67.91 million, down 17 per cent from the previous year's mark of $81.93 million. The company said sales were up 17 per cent to a record $6.9 billion, but profits were affected by increased overhead costs and margin pressure.

Turner and Flynn went for coffee at a Brisbane Starbucks.

Flynn said Skroo told him the split leadership model of MD and

CEO wasn't working. 'I knew there wasn't another option. I was gone. Like the movie *Highlander*: "In the end there can be only one."' Flynn walked out of Starbucks and out of Flight Centre, ending the almost twenty years of his life that had been dedicated to the company. His resignation was announced on 1 September 2005.

Turner said he saw no option. 'In the end, Full Throttle didn't achieve what it was supposed to. I tried to let him [Flynn] have a run on that. It didn't work, so he paid the price, I suppose.'

Whether it was fair or not, Turner said, the joint MD and CEO leadership model, exacerbated by the Bain and Full Throttle program, hadn't worked and had caused problems both internally and externally. 'In the end, you've got to have one person, total responsibility,' he said.

Turner put a new executive team in place – externals were out and long-timers were back in, with the new X Team boasting almost 60 years combined experience in the company. One of the new executive general managers, Rob Flint, had been busy drafting a letter of resignation, thinking he had been sidelined and had no real future with the company following the shake-out of Full Throttle. Before sending it he went to lunch. 'Something in me said, just think this through a little bit more,' Flint said. 'When I came back everyone was saying congratulations. I had no idea what happened. It was bizarre.' While Flint was at lunch, Turner had sent out an alert about a leadership restructure of the company, which named Rob Flint one of the first executive general managers of the Australian businesses. To Flint's further surprise, the email said he was to be moving 1700 kilometres away from his Brisbane home, to Victoria.

Turner said the move away from the dual leadership structure he and Flynn had unsuccessfully trialled signalled a return to a leaner and simpler leadership system, more in line with the company's philosophies. The philosophies themselves were tweaked to reflect lessons learned from the experience. 'Promotion and transfers from within will always be our first choice' was added to the company's sixth philosophy, 'Brightness of Future'. The updated philosophy reads:

We believe our people have the right to belong to a Team (family), a Village, an Area (tribe) and a Nation (hierarchy) that will provide them with an exciting future and a supportive working community. They also have the right to see a clear pathway to achieving their career goals. Promotion and transfers from within will always be our first choice.

Turner remains sanguine about the episode and the lessons it imparted. The tempest that was created by the combination of the split leadership model, the dilution of the company's ethos through slotting outside recruits into key leadership positions, and allowing external consultants to dictate a program of internal change would endure as an important lesson in strategy, leadership and morale. 'I've accepted it was a mistake,' he said. 'Everyone survived and I don't think I need to say sorry. I will accept guilty as charged.'

Chapter 15

THE CAPTAIN, PINEAPPLE AND CRUSH

Skroo might have been able to pull it off; he's an extraordinary leader. But the global financial crisis hit not long after. Many people have asked Bruce and me if Skroo has thanked us yet. We're still waiting.

Howard Stack, Flight Centre director (1995–2007)

With Turner and the back-to-the-future executive team in place by late 2005, FCL pushed to move beyond Full Throttle in 2006. Rebuilding began, but having glimpsed the company's unmasked corporate side in its pursuit of profit at the expense of its people during Full Throttle, many said they forged ahead led by their heads, no longer their hearts.

There were other considerable issues that had to be dealt with. One was the company's ill-fated loyalty program. RewardPass had been launched in December 2004. The program was based on the loyalty program of the world's third largest retailer, UK supermarket giant Tesco. The program was picked up after the book *Scoring Points: How Tesco is winning customer loyalty* by Clive Humby, Terry Hunt and Tim Phillips was passed around FCL. As with other wisdom applied to FCL from assorted business books, the loyalty scheme seemed to have synchronicity with Flight Centre and, on the face of it, seemed like another good idea.

RewardPass allowed travellers to earn one bonus travel point for every dollar spent at Flight Centre Limited's retail stores or websites. As with Tesco's Clubcard, the savings on offer were expected to generate high buy-in to the scheme. With data about customers' travel shopping behaviour, FCL hoped to better target their promotions. Such targeting has been one of the reasons Tesco's marketing has been so successful – registering a 20 per cent response to campaigns compared to an industry average of 0.5 per cent.[54]

Where Tesco got real value out of the program, and which no Australian loyalty program operator had at that stage tapped into, was the on-selling of aggregated information (non-identifying and privacy law-compliant information) about their customers to suppliers and other corporate entities.[55] Selling the data, or customer 'insights', would have been a real boon of the loyalty program. But Flight Centre's RewardPass never got that far. All the program did was cost millions. In January 2006, after no sign of recouping its losses, it came to a shuddering halt. In the 2006 financial year alone, RewardPass cost the company $13.1 million to operate and close down. After the debacle of Full Throttle and its write-off costs, there was no room for delicacy in its axing.

But the losses associated with RewardPass were small fry compared to the two-pronged attack of plummeting airline commissions and increased competition from the web that hit Flight Centre.

Qantas and other major airlines started the attack, making massive raids on agency commissions by adding fuel surcharges and levies to ticket prices, but refusing to pay commission on those surcharges. Fuel surcharges had originally been introduced to the price paid by air travellers to cope with spikes in fuel prices. However, the surcharges remained long after fuel price hikes levelled out, and by 2006 they were permanent fixtures that were wrapped into the price of an airline ticket. The problem for Flight Centre was that the company earned no commission on about a quarter of the price a customer paid for most airline tickets. Flight Centre argued that airlines should reflect the fuel surcharge in their pricing or they should suck up commission being earned on the collection of the surcharge as an ordinary business expense. Flight Centre claimed the impact of commission not being paid on the surcharges short-changed them about $60 million a year.

Anatomy of an Airfare

Turner and Flight Centre were livid about airlines including the surcharge in the ticket price, not as one of their own operating costs, as it meant an increase in the cost of a ticket with no corresponding increase in commission for agents.

In 2005 a typical Qantas Sydney–London return flight with a Singapore stopover cost $1558 gross, plus $509.48 surcharge, meaning the total cost to the customer was $2067.48.

The $509.48 surcharge was made up of Australian departure tax ($38), Sydney noise levy for arrivals ($3.40), fuel surcharge ($312), Singapore passenger service levy ($18), UK passenger service charge ($32.80), UK air passenger duty ($50.40), and Australian international passenger services charge ($42.88) and safety and security charge ($12).

Flight Centre earned zero margin on $509.48, or about 25 per cent of the fare.

As surcharges and levies increased, so too did the non-commission percentage of each sale Flight Centre made.

By 2012 a similar Sydney–London return ticket cost the customer $2438.08. The fuel surcharge alone cost $760 and combined surcharges and levies a massive $1176.08, almost as much as the $1262 fare price. The hike in non-commission charges per ticket justified Flight Centre's campaign.

And then there was the internet. Just as increasing airline surcharges bit into revenue and profit, online bookings began making rapid inroads into the FCL profit model. With the airlines' internet strategies – borne through the period of 'co-opetition' in 2002, when airlines and other suppliers went into direct competition with their agents via the web – and internet travel booking start-ups becoming more prominent in the travel booking space, FCL again found itself having to fend off the online onslaught. In a short space of time, customers had become confident and accustomed to booking their own fares online. They had become accustomed to researching destinations and deals. FCL had to answer the question: Why would anyone bother going into a travel agent anymore?

'The press was full of stories saying that bricks and mortar travel agencies were dead in the water. Everyone in the industry was shit scared that the Flight Centre model wouldn't last,' said co-founder Bill James. 'Skroo wasn't. But I had my doubts, to be honest.'

The doomsayers became even more pessimistic because FCL's reported profits remained in the doldrums. The half-yearly results for July to December 2005 showed $33.6 million net profit. The share price that had grown like Topsy since listing a decade earlier, save for a few fluctuations, had by December 2005 tumbled to $9.06. By the time FCL reported its full year profit growth in August 2006 of $79.9 million profit, a small comeback that was up 4 per cent on the previous year's figures, the share price struggled to bob above $12.

The share price woes meant that far from its long-held mantle as Queensland's glamour stock, Flight Centre Limited was the worst performer on the S&P/ASX 200 Index in 2005/06.[56]

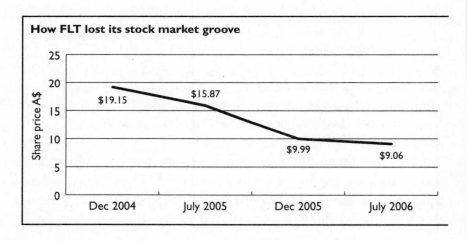

It was in this environment in September 2006 that assistant company secretary Stephen Kennedy and a small Flight Centre Limited contingent were called to the Brisbane offices of ABN AMRO Morgan (now RBS Morgans), where they met with representatives of Pacific Equity Partners (PEP).

Founded in 1998 by former Bain and Company partners, PEP was the largest and one of the most active private equity funds in Australia and New Zealand. In the eight years prior to 2006, PEP had completed transactions with a total value in excess of $3 billion in acquisitions, including Frucor Beverages, electronics manufacturer Startronics, marketing company The Communications Group, book retailer Angus & Robertson/Whitcoulls, Collins Foods Group and cleaning products manufacturer Godfreys.[57]

Some of the PEP faces were surprisingly familiar to the Flight Centre people, from Bain's former engagement during the Full Throttle project. Tony Duthie was the most recognisable crossover, though he said he was not the primary person running the new deal for PEP.

'They were all in their three-piece suits from Sydney on one side and we were all in our uniforms on the other,' Kennedy recalled of the first meeting with the PEP players. 'It was marble and mahogany meets polyester and laminate. They probably thought we were such yokels.' But the yokels, whose uniforms meant they were actually far more suitably attired for Queensland's sunny spring conditions, had what PEP wanted.

PEP laid out a proposal to privatise Flight Centre Limited with an offer to minority shareholders of $17.20 a share. Turner backed the proposal, which was codenamed Project Captain after Flight Centre's ubiquitous airline captain marketing image. He felt the dramatic fall in share price undervalued the company. He was frustrated that the business was hamstrung by the short-term demands of the share market. He believed such share market constraints on long-term strategies meant FCL was less likely to realise its true potential as a public company than as a private one.[58] In short, he and the other founders, who together were 57 per cent shareholders, wanted the company back.

Quietly, with PEP as financial partners, Turner, Geoff Harris, Bill James, Jim Goldburg and Chris Grieve formed a consortium to buy back Flight Centre Limited from shareholders. Turner, who would stay on in the top job, was particularly motivated by the potential return to him of decision-making power, such as playing hardball with airlines over major gripes like the payment of commission on surcharges and levies, without being constrained by quarterly, half-yearly and annual performance obligations. For the founders it meant they finally had the option to liquidate or take money off the table – $435 million would go to the founding shareholders while allowing them, in partnership with PEP, to remain in control of the company.[59]

Turner's arguments were a colossal backflip on his rationale for taking the company public. Back then, floating was about involving more people in equity. It was about giving more people tangible company ownership. It was about putting the company among a new league of players. It was about the value of publicly listed shares being the only genuine measurement of the company's success. Now he wanted it all back. Perhaps an even greater about-face, however, was that Turner, who had always had a strong distaste for liability, was prepared to leverage the company to the hilt. The PEP privatisation meant substituting about $700 million of minority shareholder equity for up to $1 billion debt. 'It was a good deal,' he said. 'The downside, of course, is that we could have gone broke.'

The business environment at the time was conducive to the move. The bid was smack in the era in which privatisation was all the rage around the world and particularly in Australia. From 1 June 2006 to 31 May 2007, Australia registered 43 private equity trans-actions valued at US$25.9 billion – a 389 per cent increase over the corresponding period the previous year.[60] Deals during the time included Newbridge Capital's $1.4 billion buyout of Myer depart-ment stores, the sale of 50 per cent of PBL Media to CVC Capital Partners Asia Pacific, and the Seven Network's sale of its media assets into a joint venture with Kohlberg Kravis Roberts. Not all bids during the Australian privatisation stampede succeeded. Airline Partners Australia, a private equity consortium led by Macquarie Bank, failed in its $11.1 billion buyout of Qantas Airways. The bid by Irish billionaire Tony O'Reilly and his private equity partners to take APN News and Media private was also turned away by share-holders. But in this silly season of private equity takeovers, each operated off the same blueprint: ramp up debt and leverage on the extra money to grow the company.

On 25 October 2006, barely a month after Project Captain was first proposed by PEP, Flight Centre's independent directors, chairman Bruce Brown and director Howard Stack, supported the proposal to re-privatise Flight Centre, dependent on a review by inde-pendent expert Ernst and Young.[61] The other director, Peter Barrow, who had been close with the founders since he joined as Top Deck's original accountant, said he had a conflict of interest, as he advised the founders on tax matters and was always going to have an allegiance to Turner, and so abstained from the decisions.

Brown said he and Stack supported the proposal because they believed it could unlock significant value for minority shareholders. Turner, who confirmed he would remain chief executive officer and managing director of Flight Centre after the transaction was completed, said he believed the price that valued the company at $1.62 billion was fair. Inside Flight Centre, people were told little would change under the re-privatised scenario. 'For most businesses there won't be much difference,' Turner assured staff.[62]

Many Flight Centre 'lifers' weren't convinced. Particularly after the chopper incident. PEP's compatibility with the Flight Centre culture was always going to be an issue. To help alleviate the problem, and as part of their immersion in the company, PEP representatives attended an FCL executive general managers conference in Whistler, Canada, in January 2007. The Flight Centre executive team all shared a bus from Whistler to Vancouver International Airport for the trip home. 'There was all of us plebs sitting on the bus and the PEP guys went and hired a helicopter,' said global marketing EGM Colin Bowman. Then the bus hit a landslide on the way down. As the FCL team huddled, shivering, waiting for the bus to resume the journey, they watched as the helicopter whizzed by, filled with the company's potential new 'partners' being delivered safely and comfortably to their destination.

For the vote to privatise to succeed, it required a super majority of 75 per cent of minority shareholder support. The founding shareholders could not vote. As proxies began to arrive ahead of the 28 February 2007 vote it became clear the deal was in trouble. Ron Malek of Caliburn Partnership, who was advising the consortium of the founders and PEP and became known as 'Red Cross Ronnie' due to his role trying to appease all the different stakeholders, said institutional investor Lazard Asset Management, with a 12.45 per cent stake, had the numbers to block the deal.

Former CEO Shane Flynn, with a 0.42 per cent holding of 400,000 shares, was the largest single shareholder apart from the founders and institutions at the time. Flynn said he believed the offer was too low. He said he and others anticipated a profit surge the following year. 'I could see at least one profit upgrade coming three to six months away,' said Flynn. 'I thought the whole thing was a disgrace. It was mum and dad shareholders being ripped off.'

Lazard also believed the offer chronically undervalued Flight Centre shares and refused to accept the deal. Tim Crommelin of ABN AMRO Morgans Corporate, who was advising the independent directors Brown and Stack, said it became obvious the plan was doomed to failure unless Lazard was on board. 'It is possible there was some underestimation of their [Lazard's] resolve,' Crommelin said.

The vote failed.

The failure was pegged on the price offered to shareholders being too low. Stack revealed he and Brown had reservations about the price and the timing, but reluctantly supported the offer in the interests of all shareholders. With the Full Throttle writedowns behind it, drains like RewardPass gone and battle plans readied for the internet and commission wars, there seemed validity in the expectation of an upsurge in profit. 'We were not happy that the offer arrived just as FLT's profit was recovering strongly, which made FLT hard to value and made PEP look opportunistic to us,' Stack said.

Co-founder Bill James rejected claims the offered price was dodgy and that the founders and PEP were 'trying to buy back the farm at rock bottom price'. Rather it was an opportunity that had to be pursued given that 'everyone was having doubts about what future there even was for Flight Centre', James said.

But PEP was not deterred by the shareholder rebuff. Nor was Turner. Within one month PEP made another approach. On 29 March 2007, just a month after shareholders rejected Project Captain, PEP and Turner launched Project Pineapple.

By buyout standards, Project Pineapple was an even pricklier proposition than Captain. Under the deal, PEP and FCL would enter a joint venture. All operational assets would be transferred to a lever-

The share price illustrates both cause and effect of the attempted privatisation of FCL. The floundering share price triggered Project Captain. But FCL's own signs of recovery, as well as news of the buy-out, contributed to a share price rebound. This recovery made the buyback price appear less attractive, contributing to the deal's failure.

The following chart shows the share price and corresponding events that were either caused by market movement, or a result of it.

Ties to trading

aged joint venture at an enterprise value of about $1.4 billion (or about $15 a share). Flight Centre would initially hold a 70 per cent interest and PEP, with an investment of $195 million, would hold 30 per cent, eventually moving to 67 and 33 per cent respectively. And this time the buyback wasn't compulsory. Shareholders would be given the option of taking a payout or remaining with the restructured and aggressively geared company.

But little augured well for Pineapple from the start. The deal soon proved even more problematic than Project Captain. 'Howard [Stack] and Bruce [Brown] were like the Mad Hatter's tea party,' Turner said. 'Howard was a very conservative lawyer and Bruce wouldn't make a decision without Howard. That was the thing that really annoyed. It was a painful process.'

Brown said the process wasn't the problem. It was the price, the lopsided joint venture carve-up and the excessive gearing. The negotiations over a deal that 'made no commercial sense to me' were tense and controversial. 'Howard Stack and I, we didn't have a lot of respect for that second offer,' Brown said. 'It was a mediocre offer in terms of valuation and control. I couldn't understand why Skroo supported it.'

The deal was too complex, there were too many questions on the valuation, it involved a lot of debt and didn't get the shareholders out, Stack said. 'It got pretty willing at times between Skroo and us – he threatened to sack us and sue us. We said go ahead. But that did not worry us or make us in any way think the less of him because he was just focused on the outcome he believed in.'

Crommelin, again as advisor to Brown and Stack, said watching the two directors face off against Turner was like watching three dogs go at a bone. 'These are all strong, focused individuals. None of them are easy to shift and they all thought they had a particular job to do,' Crommelin said. At one board meeting, involving PEP, the directors, advisors and lawyers, Turner growled about the meeting going nowhere, packed up his papers and started to march out. Brown, considered a master of one-liners, bellowed: 'Turner, are you an only child?' It was a tension diffuser at a time when there were not a lot of laughs.

At another board meeting, crowded with the Brisbane investment and legal community involved in the deal, Turner became so enraged at the lack of progress that he virtually lost the ability to communicate. 'He just is the most laconic, relaxed individual under seemingly extraordinary pressure. I'd never seen him lose it in my life,' said former chief financial officer Shannon O'Brien. 'But he lost it so badly. It was incomprehensible. I looked to see if we recorded just how many times he said fuck. I got about thirty-two.'

The deal seemed stalled in a Mexican stand-off. But with pressure from both sides Project Pineapple did manage to progress and in May 2007 FCL and PEP announced they had reached an in-principle agreement. Then, as had been predicted by many, including those who said the pricepoint of the Project Captain privatisation plan was too low, the company revealed its profit was rallying. In June FCL revealed it was anticipating its 2007 full-year pre-tax profit to be 25–30 per cent above the previous year's result. On the back of such rosy profit expectations, shares were trading at $19.20 by the end of the week – a bump from the $14.30 mark when Project Captain was crushed.

So confident was PEP that Pineapple was in the can, executives including managing director Rob Koczkar and founder Tim Sims headed off as guests to the Flight Centre Global Ball in Dublin, Ireland, in July. All that was left before the deal was sealed were the final trimmings of an independent evaluation, as requested by the Flight Centre Limited directors, and the shareholder vote.

But Barrow, who described himself as the 'meat in the sandwich' during the wrangling, said he realised the other founders were not entirely locked in to the deal. It was the morning before the Global Ball (featuring guests Bob Geldof and Ronan Keating) when Barrow and Turner went for coffee in Dublin. Barrow said while the other founders supported Turner, it wasn't a good deal for them. 'The other founders will support Skroo 'til the end of the world. And Skroo was incredibly focused to try and make it happen,' Barrow said. 'But someone had to have a talk with Skroo.'

Turner was well aware before the coffee with Barrow that Pineapple was bruised. He said he told Koczkar before leaving for Ireland, and again in a taxi in London before arriving in Dublin, that there could be issues with the privatisation going ahead. 'I don't know if he believed me,' Turner said. David Smith, who was then head of global acquisitions and was also in the taxi, said he saw shock register on PEP faces when Turner told them there were doubts Pineapple would come to fruition, but then saw them carry on to the ball as if there were reasons to celebrate. 'I don't think they fully believed it because they partied like the deal was done,' Smith said.

It wasn't. Just days after the Global Ball, on 31 July 2007, Ernst and Young released their independent expert's report into the proposed transaction, concluding that it was 'neither fair nor reasonable'. Ernst and Young valued the company at $1.9 to $2 billion – about $400 million more than the value applied under the joint deal with PEP. It also showed Flight Centre Limited would be hit with a capital gains tax bill of up to $430 million if the transaction went ahead.

Flight Centre dumped the deal outright. PEP was livid. There was to be no third time lucky. Privatisation was dead.

Geoff Harris, who left the FCL board in 2008, said he remained 'personally glad' the deal fizzled. 'I think we took the right course,' Harris said. 'I think Bill, Skroo and I as founders and the current board would all now say we were glad that didn't go ahead.'

Turner said the second deal was just too hard for the punch-drunk board to handle. But he remained convinced it was worth pursuing. 'We would be in a pretty good position now – if we'd survived.'

Brown and Stack didn't survive the ordeal quite so well. After the privatisation drain, both said their positions as chairman and director respectively became untenable. At the Flight Centre AGM on 1 November 2007, Brown was replaced as chairman by Peter Morahan, chief of an events hire company, and Stack as director by resort owner Gary Smith (known locally as the King of Fraser Island).

Stack said he remained convinced the deal was not right for the shareholders, particularly those who may have opted to stay with the heavily geared joint venture. As controversial, as difficult and as pressured as the board was to approve it, killing it was the right thing to do for the future of the company, he said. In hindsight, Stack said, the decision looked even better. Soon after, the world plunged into the global financial crisis. With the extreme gearing in place, it could have made business extremely tough for Flight Centre Limited. 'It has certainly caused Bruce and I to say we haven't got a phone call yet from Skroo to say thank you,' Stack said.

With the deal scuttled, Turner tried to put the episode to bed, reporting that there were to be no further buyout attempts. 'Now we are back to normal with nothing else of the kind on the horizon,' he told staff.[63]

Except for one last attempt at shaking things up: Project Pineapple Crush. All the work undertaken during Project Captain and Project Pineapple had shown Flight Centre Limited that it needed more flexibility in the way it funded future growth. The company wanted the option of equity raising or external debt funding. To do this, it determined it needed structural change. It had seen the gearing and growth opportunities proposed by PEP and wanted more.

But due to regulations imposed when licensing and the Travel Compensation Fund (TCF) were imposed upon Australian travel agencies in 1986, the company's debt capacity was capped at $100 million. Under Project Pineapple Crush, FCL made moves to ensure it could get around these debt-capping restrictions. It meant a massive restructure of the company that involved transferring all of its travel agency assets and operations to a subsidiary.

The attempt to skirt the cap was yet another rule-challenging move in FCL's long battle with the TCF, which it saw as a cost-ineffective and overly restrictive organisation. The TCF had become the bane of FCL after the company fell foul of the body right from the start. The TCF had forced the partners to remortgage their homes in order to cough up the $1 million required to keep their travel agents licence.

Project Pineapple Crush was worked on for months, but then it was parked. There were a few reasons. One was that there were indications the TCF could soon be abolished – and with it the debt capacity restrictions.

The end of the privatisation projects and Pineapple Crush was a line in the sand. After all the internal turmoil and change wrought by Full Throttle, after the confusing and contentious buyback attempts of Projects Captain and Pineapple, Flight Centre was back to business. From top to bottom, from staff to shareholders to management, Flight Centre had been stirred by shake-ups that rocked even a company accustomed to frequent change. It had emerged giddy, though perhaps fortified, from the experience. But it was about to face even more testing times. And, having played its best privatisation hand, it would have to do so in the full warts-and-all glare of the public.

Chapter 16

A NEW ERA OF GROWTH: THE GOOD, THE BAD . . .

*We are a business in Dubai. No one here is used to a workplace like
this. Yet our local people have taken to Buzz Nights, to incentives, they've
been to global balls, we took them skydiving over the Palm Jumeirah. The
guys here are probably more Flight Centre now than a lot of our
Australians.*

Andrew Boxall, managing director, FCm Travel Solutions Dubai

Melanie Waters-Ryan wasn't so much concerned that PEP representatives on the privatisation prowl were at Flight Centre Limited's executive general managers' meeting in Whistler, Canada. She was far more bewildered that her audience started yelling 'Bingo!' while she was outlining a move she was passionately convinced was crucial to the future strategic plans for the company.

Waters-Ryan wanted to acquire a company called the Travel Spirit Group. She was unaware her laser-like zeal for the project was causing such mirth among her colleagues. She was also oblivious to the back-room book they had run on how many times she would use the term 'product powerhouse' in her presentation to get the cash for the purchase approved. Her bafflement when they started yelling 'Bingo!' as she got into the groove of selling her 'product powerhouse' vision may have meant the joke was on her. It wasn't. She got the money.

Using the Travel Spirit Group (TSG), Waters-Ryan wanted to create a direct contractor – a company that could make deals with suppliers for accommodation, tours and car hire that FCL's Infinity

Holidays, or any of the group's sixteen other wholesale brands around the world, could bundle into package deals to sell to customers. By creating such an entity, FCL would no longer have to rely on a third party such as Qantas Holidays to purchase and consolidate deals.

As was the case when FCL excised the traditional middlemen between airlines and retailers by deciding to do its own ticketing – dumping consolidators and setting up its own Ticket Centre in 1989 – the company wanted control. This time it wanted control over every aspect of the package holiday process. The new business, renovated out of the bones of TSG, would be the final link in the chain, allowing FCL to procure deals directly from suppliers for non-flight elements like accommodation and tours, construct the package holidays and, of course, sell the package holidays to customers.

FCL wanted TSG in particular for two reasons. Firstly, TSG's product range – Explore Holidays, Venture Holidays and African Traveller – could be aligned or absorbed into FCL's Infinity business. Secondly, its wholesale reservations system, Calypso, would be a high-tech gain for FCL, which was notoriously sluggish in adopting new technologies. TSG's operational Calypso system had the potential to leapfrog FCL years ahead in the development of a procurement business – and it could operate globally.

Flight Centre Limited acquired TSG in February 2007 for $10 million. With scarcely more experience in procuring and consolidating non-flight deals than it had in airline ticketing when it embarked on the Ticket Centre project, FCL turned the TSG business into Flight Centre Global Product (FCGP). And then, in one of the most ambitious turnarounds in the company's history, FCL implemented Calypso and FCGP's direct contracting of the non-flight package holiday elements internationally, just four months after the purchase.

Of course, under the FCL commercialisation model, the company's businesses were not obliged to purchase through this newly created internal wholesale and corporate product procurement division. In fact, the system suffered immediate teething problems as a result of being implemented too quickly. But despite a few crashes, the technology worked. The model, tweaked in the intense environment of going live with precious little preparation, also worked. FCGP offered products that FCL wholesale businesses such as Infinity snapped up. And just as the FCL Ticket Centre transformed the traditional travel agency ticketing process, the new Flight Centre Global Product machine took off.

FCGP global leader Nick Lucock said FCGP was 'a business on speed'. When Flight Centre Limited bought TSG in 2007, it had a $56 million annual turnover. By 2012, FCGP turnover was $1.4 billion – in other words, it turned over every fortnight what TSG did in a year. In the first five years of FCGP's operation, it went from recording $760,000 profit to $51.5 million. In the 2011/12 financial year, FCGP put about 10 million room nights a year through FCL corporate and leisure businesses. It has been projected to hit $140 million profit by 2020. Such has been the rapid-fire success of FCGP, it is poised to take its product beyond the Flight Centre Limited realm and sell to non-FCL wholesalers.

FCGP has become the powerhouse behind Infinity. Infinity, which started its Flight Centre life as a problematic joint venture in 1993 and was just an hour from being closed down in 2000, was in 2012 the highest net profit margin business in the company.

The unrivalled cash-generation capacity of the FCGP business also made it a winner with FCL. As customers pay upfront for their holiday, but FCL does not have to pay the hotel or supplier until after the customer has stayed, it creates significant cash holdings for the company. 'It's a beautiful business, it's like a dream,' Waters-Ryan said.

FCGP is the result of one of the more fruitful purchases made by Flight Centre Limited since it embarked on the acquisition trail in 1999, when it picked up the high-end corporate Sydney Business Travel for $16 million. It is also the product of some of the lessons the company has learned in the process. FCGP's success could not have been achieved in such a short timeframe were it a start-up business instead of a renovation of an existing company. It couldn't have been remodelled into such a powerhouse of the global operation if FCL did not take full control of the company from the moment of purchase.

Acquisitions, renovations and the Flight Centre-isation of businesses it has purchased have been instrumental in taking FCL beyond its core strength as an Australian-based leisure travel specialist. In its quest 'to be the world's most successful travel company', a key pillar of the FCL approach to growth has been global expansion through strategic acquisitions, renovations and local partnerships. But FCL does it its own way.

Acquisitions Good and Bad		
Below is the complete list of FCL acquisitions. Many have been successfully transformed under FCL ownership. Some have failed or been relegated to the 'seemed like a good idea at the time' pile.		
Date purchased	**Name of company**	**Current status or brand**
1993	Infinity (joint venture)	Infinity
1999	Sydney Business Travel	FCm Travel Solutions
1999	Stage and Screen Australia	Stage and Screen New Zealand and North America
2000	Conference and Incentive Management	CiEvents
2000	Conference and Incentive Services	CiEvents
2000	Overseas Working Holidays	Folded
2001	Shopper Travel	Folded
2002	Sir George Seymour College, New Zealand	Sold
2002	Paula Peterson Travel	Folded
2002	Internet Travel Group (ITG, TQ3 Travel Solutions)	FCm Travel
2002	Fanatics Sports Tours (joint venture)	JV dissolved
2002	Cruiseabout/Turramurra Travel	Cruiseabout
2002	Quickbeds	Quickbeds

Date purchased	Name of company	Current status or brand
2002	AITL Hong Kong	FCm Hong Kong
2003	Britannic (TQ3 United) Kingdom	FCm UK
2003	Kistend Travel	Campus Travel
2003	Itchyfeet	Folded
2004	China Comfort (joint venture)	FCm China
2004	Contal and Travelthere	Travelthere.com
2005	Friends Globe Travel India (51 per cent)	FCm India
2006	Bannockburn	FCm USA
2006	Nation Wide Currency	Travel Money
2007	Garber (25 per cent)	FCm USA, Travel Associates USA and Corporate Traveller USA
2007	Travel Spirit Group	Flight Centre Global Product and Explore Holidays
2007	Dubai	FCm Dubai
2007	Liberty Travel and GoGo Vacations USA	Liberty Travel and GoGo Vacations USA
2008	Employment Office	Employment Office
2008	99 Bikes (joint venture) Advance Traders (joint venture)	99 Bikes Advance Traders
2008	Intrepid (joint venture) Back Roads (joint venture)	My Adventure Store Back Roads Touring
2009	Balance of Friends Globe Travel	FCm India
2009	Balance of Garber	FCm USA, Travel Associates USA and Corporate Traveller USA
2010	Air Services Singapore	FCm Singapore
2010	Gap Year UK	Gapyear.com Gap Year Travel

Expanding through acquisitions is one of the reasons that corporate travel is no longer the 'ugly sister' to leisure in the Flight Centre Limited organisation. It was through acquisitions, particularly the company's takeover of Internet Travel Group in 2002, that FCL broke into the lucrative travel management services (TMS) market. Upon entering the TMS arena, which provides strategic travel services for top-tier corporate entities, FCL found no reason or desire to dance to the tune of the traditional industry mainstays. 'Flight Centre is really not terribly good at answering to whomever. It's a common theme. Instead, we decide we'll do it ourselves,' said company secretary and mergers and acquisitions chief David Smith.

True to form, FCL decided it could create its own TMS network to take on the incumbent players in the market, consolidating and expanding its corporate travel operations to launch FCm Travel Solutions. From seven businesses in 2004, FCm Travel Solutions soon became a global network that could compete, rather than work with, the major TMS networks of the time – including the once-dominant TQ3. FCm Travel Solutions aimed to have its own businesses and licensees in twenty countries within its first two years of operation. Within eight years, it had operations and licensees in 75 countries and was among the top three TMS companies in the world.

FCL's Corporate Traveller – with its distinctive model of a dedicated travel manager, or buddy, who is available to the customer 24 hours a day – complements FCm in the corporate travel sector. It also operates globally, specialising in the small to medium business (SME) sector. It has developed to become a market leader in the SME travel sector in most countries in which FCL-owned business operate. Flight Centre Business Travel, an offline retail business, provides travel services to smaller businesses that spend up to $1 million on travel. By 2012, FCL's combined corporate operation turned over $4 billion and drove just under 50 per cent of the company's profit.

While acquisitions and partnerships have driven FCL's geographical expansion, particularly in corporate travel hotspots like China, Singapore and Dubai, some FCL businesses – such as Flight Centre Canada, South Africa and UK – are start-up operations that have predominantly grown organically. In each location, the Flight Centre brand has evolved within its own market, in both the corporate and retail arenas.

However, it is acquisitions that have proven to be the most significant chapter in the modern Flight Centre growth and diversification story. Through acquisitions, FCL has undergone a crash course in operating in different countries, cultures, currencies and time zones. For a company that is so focused on its own culture, it has had to wrestle with issues such as cultural fit, local recruitment, whether to impose rapid or gradual change, and whether to operate jointly with local operators or pursue total ownership. By 2012, FCL-owned businesses operated in ten countries outside Australia, stepping the company up into the class of a truly global enterprise. Each country was operating profitably by the end of the 2011 financial year. In getting to this major milestone, the tales from abroad show that each country has had its own distinct evolution.

FCL global operations		
Country	**Businesses**	**Turnover**
Australia	1230	$7.8 billion
United States of America	271	$1.7 billion
United Kingdom	215	$1.2 billion
Canada	215	$836 million
New Zealand	172	$602 million
South Africa	172	$409 million
India	44	$337 million
Greater China (incl. Hong Kong)	29	$118 million
Singapore	10	$63 million
Dubai	4	$46 million

Note: Figures are accurate at 30 June 2012

It was only her determination not to fail that stopped Suyin Lee packing her bags and leaving the joint venture FCL entered into with China Comfort Travel in 2004. The deal, sealed over much drinking of cognac with the Chinese partners, was the acquisition of Rosenbluth International's 50 per cent stake of a previous joint venture with China Comfort Travel, which became available after Rosenbluth was taken over by American Express in 2003. Entering into the joint venture meant Flight Centre would pay China Comfort US$1.25 million and each JV partner would inject US$750,000 of equity into the business.

The early days working in China were 'incredibly difficult' said Lee, former FCL China executive general manager. It wasn't just the rat-infested offices, finding out that the phones were tapped and suspected of being monitored by the government, or the discovery that someone was selling access to the company's internet connection, which meant customers were surfing porn on the FCL online system and dime. It was that doing business in China and building a relationship with the company's Chinese partners was such a steep learning curve that at times it seemed an insurmountable struggle.

Lee said expectations on both sides of the joint venture were out of whack. It quickly became obvious to both partners that FCL was not going to magically transform the business into a successful template of its other corporate operations. It was very much a case of 'same bed, different dreams', Lee said.

For FCL, the purchase of the stake was aimed at developing the company's Asian and global corporate network. Rebranded as FCm Travel Solutions (the first FCm-branded agency to open), the task was servicing Rosenbluth's former global and regional clients, such as Disney and Reuters, as well as growing the business among companies attracted to the economic hub of China.

China was a key player in the world's new emerging business economy known as BRIC – Brazil, Russia, India and China. FCm Travel Solutions was one of the world's fastest growing corporate networks by 2005, and it needed a solid foothold in China. After opening in Beijing and then Shanghai, the strategy was to tap into a market that was already huge and destined to increase. FCm's targets were small national and mid-sized multinational companies that required expertise in managing their travel requirements and consolidation of reporting. But China was a very raw business – the systems were a shambles, there was no electronic ticketing (which meant tickets were handwritten in quadruplicate), getting cash into China was highly problematic, and due to changes in local regulation the company was unable to hold a domestic ticketing license, forcing it to be entirely reliant on the local operator.

Still Lee persisted. Staff positions were culled and a new phase of recruitment and selection began. The company waited a year before it even introduced the notion of incentives, one of the company's core philosophies. As it turned out, the concept that 'what gets rewarded gets done' was embraced by the Chinese.

FCm expanded beyond Beijing and Shanghai to open in Guangzhou in 2007. Trying to staff FCm Asia's centralised after-hours support service in Guangzhou presented its own problems and demonstrated some of the recruitment challenges international FCm Travel Solutions operations had to deal with, especially in relation to the special requirements of jobs and the available pool of people to fill them. The Guangzhou support service job required people who could speak Mandarin, Cantonese and English. 'People with those language skills don't want to work for a travel agent, let alone night shift for a travel agent,' said Greater China managing director Dave Fraser. Many Chinese employees had not travelled much themselves, there was not necessarily one common language among staff – making conferencing particularly challenging – and it was difficult to implant the Flight Centre culture. 'Booze is just not enough,' said Fraser. 'But I do remember at the 2009 annual ball, all the local staff were up dancing on the table. It was when I thought we'd finally got this right.'

In 2005, China merged with FCL's Hong Kong operations to form FCm Asia. Flight Centre Limited had been in Hong Kong since the 2002 acquisition of the American International Travel corporate travel company from Hong Kong businessman Joseph Kao. As FCm's share of the Asian corporate market grew, FCL saw an opportunity to take the business beyond corporate to develop a leisure travel operation targeting the large Western expat community. But first it had to get the feng shui in its new Hong Kong head office right.

'It's one of the things about being a foreigner in an international business in another country. You try to do things according to the local culture. And seemingly simple things aren't always simple,' said Fraser.

In deference to Chinese culture, FCm Asia called in a local feng shui master. The 6000-year-old Chinese art of feng shui aims to increase the positive energy or 'qi' in a space and avoid the negative energy. Feng shui masters position objects – especially buildings, graves and furnishings – based on the power of yin and yang (cold and hot energy), to channel the flow of qi.[64]

What it meant for Fraser was a fit-out like no other. Renovation of the new Hong Kong head office had to start on a lucky date, calculated using his date of birth, and he was required to put a nail into the floor to signal the start of the change before sprinkling eleven grains of rice into each corner of the office. 'It wasn't a straight rectangular office. There are sixty corners in this office. I had one of the consultants sitting with a big pile of rice on her desk and a letter opener, trying to make sixty piles of eleven grains that I could then sprinkle in each of the corners,' he said. Teams were then positioned in the office to facilitate the flow of qi, Chinese symbols were placed all around the finance team and a lucky gold coin was glued to the floor under the carpet.

But it has been a hard and emotional, rather than lucky, ride for the Asian business. 'We nearly shut down China,' said global corporate leader Rob Flint. 'We didn't see how we were ever going to survive in a market where our business model clearly wasn't in place.' But from facing real questions as to whether the business could ever work in China, being forced to implement make-or-break rescue plans and even having Suyin Lee transfer her Asia expertise from China to FCL's Singapore operations, FCm in Greater China has managed to grow in line with expectations. As Rob said, 'We're pretty happy that our plan succeeded and that we didn't have to fall back to our second option of finding a licensee.' By 2012 there were 25 businesses in Greater China, including three retail shops.

It started so well. Smoking Havana cigars and slamming shot glasses of Moët & Chandon over due diligence deliberations should have signalled a match made in heaven between Indian Friends Globe Travel founder-owner Rahul Nath and Flight Centre Limited.

The agreement between Friends Globe Travel and FCL was signed in February 2005, when the Indian business and legal delegation came to Australia and holed themselves up in a meeting room for a week with FCL representatives to nut out the deal. As soon as agreement was reached, the lawyers were sent home, fifteen Indian friends were flown in for the deal's official announcement and partying began, climaxing in a crazy table dancing celebration in Brisbane fine dining establishment Restaurant Two.

The deal, which would become FCL's third largest acquisition, involved FCL entering a joint venture agreement with the Indian company. For $8.3 million, FCL invested in a holding stake of 51 per cent of Friends Globe Travel, with a plan to buy a further share of 26 per cent.

FCL was eager to gain a significant foothold in another of the world's emerging markets and aimed to become a market leader in the mid to large TMS business in the region. 'We certainly didn't want to buy it all immediately,' said company secretary David Smith. 'If we needed a local partner anywhere initially, it was India.'

The business grew and appeared to be well aligned. With his larger-than-life personality and wise Indian maxims, Nath wooed his Australian partners with parties at his twelve-bedroom mansion (complete with bespoke disco room) and prestige car collection. Nath also started up an operation with FCL in Dubai in 2007 to create a Middle Eastern hub for FCm Travel Solutions.

But within a year the relationship with Nath started to fray. Nath was knocked back by the FCL board numerous times on a luxury car business that would have required a significant capital outlay. FCL also became increasingly concerned as it continued to fund working capital for the Indian business for little return. Costs were blowing out and the partnership began to crack.

In September 2008, FCL sent in the internal audit team to investigate. The move sent the relationship haywire. FCL quickly engaged

Dubai

The story of the Dubai operation has been a stand-out example of FCL integrating its systems and culture into a foreign social, cultural and economic environment. Rahul Nath set up the business in 2007 following the acquisition of Friends Globe Travel. This timeline shows the impact of FCL imposing its own culture and systems two years later.

1 July 2007: Operations commence, managed by FCm India. Single office with sixteen staff.
2007/08: Operated at loss of $1.2m.
2008/09: Operated at loss of $1.4m.
May 2009: FCL's Andrew Boxall dispatched to Dubai with instructions to 'come back in two weeks with the keys or a plan to make it work'. Boxall determined Dubai was a viable business, but needed stronger leadership, motivation and FCL systems.
September 2009: Four months after Boxall arrived and Flight Centre systems were implemented, the business recorded its first trading month profit.
January 2010: Incentives introduced.
2009/10: Operating profit of $400,000.
2010/11: Profit of $1.2m.
2012: Sales up more than 300 per cent, staff numbers up by 126 per cent and $3.1m earnings before tax (EBIT) a new record for the business. At the 2012 Flight Centre Global awards, Dubai won some of the company's most prestigious honours: Globally Most Productive Nation, Globally Most Productive Area and Globally Most Profitable Corporate team.
2013: First Flight Centre leisure travel shop opened in February.

local lawyers after Nath shut all Flight Centre representatives out of the business.

According to Flight Centre, Nath refused to cooperate, branded Ben Barnes, head of the FCL audit team, 'cuckoo' and walked out on mediation meetings with FCL representatives. In one instance, Flight Centre chief financial officer Andrew Flannery flew to New Delhi to meet with Nath. At the lobby of a hotel in central Delhi, Flannery opened the conversation with allegations of mismanagement in the order of more than $5 million. Nath stormed out. Flannery had no option but to declare the meeting a failure and get straight back on a plane home.

As the JV deal involved Flight Centre Limited gradually buying Nath out, the company brought the issue to a head by withholding a payment. With Nath enraged, FCL lost all ability to see what was going on inside FCm India. The audit team agreed not to consolidate the 2008 Indian results because FCL just didn't have control. The company reported the legal dispute to shareholders.

The dispute did give FCL's legal team an insight into the Indian legal system. To find a legal solution to the impasse, FCL brought proceedings before the Company Law Board – a quasi-judicial body set up in 1991, with powers to regulate its own procedures and oversee company regulations relating to the operation of businesses in India. Appeals relating to Company Law Board decisions can be made to the High Court of India.

'I remember being over there and going to court. We had our barristers, we were all dressed in suits. We marched into the court precinct and this guy walked past us with a large monkey on a leash. We were so accustomed to India by then, none of us batted an eyelid,' Smith said.

On another hearing date, Smith was reading the newspaper over breakfast before the court session was due to begin. Reported in the paper was the revelation that a member of the Company Law Board – the member who was hearing the Flight Centre and Friends Globe Travel case – had been arrested for corruption involving another matter.[65] The FCL hearing was delayed. The legal team flew home – again.

Global corporate chief Rob Flint said FCL needed to stay in India. 'We're in there for the long haul. We'll make it work,' he said. 'The future should be in this market. We do need to spend the time and the money to be there.' FCL made the decision to pay Nath $14 million for the remaining 49 per cent of the Indian company – compared to the $8.3 million for the first 51 per cent. The deal meant Nath left the company. He exited with the payout in April 2010.

'We were concerned we could have lost the forty million we had tied up in the business at that time,' said Andrew Flannery. 'We paid fourteen million for the privilege of buying him out.'

Flint said there was still debate about whether Flight Centre should take over acquired businesses more quickly. Flight Centre Limited often kept owner-founders around after acquiring businesses due to their expertise and relationships in the region. FCL legal counsel Chris Gavras-Moffat said there were definite advantages to having local knowledge, expertise and contacts in an overseas operation like India. The departure of Friends Globe Travel management meant FCL was operating in a completely foreign environment with cultural and language challenges, and applying Australian business principles to a market that operated significantly differently, he said. 'Now that we have one hundred per cent control and are operating it ourselves, the question has to be asked if it is as successful as it would be if we had someone like him [a local entrepreneur such as Rahul Nath] involved. I know that might be quite a controversial view.'

Naren Nautiyal, chief executive officer for FCm India since 2010, said it had been difficult to make FCL-aligned changes, especially to the culture of the corporate business that had been operating as Friends Globe Travel as far back as 1987. The operation still adhered to the model pioneered by Friends Globe Travel of an 'implant' system, with an FCm travel desk based in corporate customers' offices. Corporate business consultants were also still lukewarm on the incentive model.

Under Geoff Lomas, the company had opened thirteen leisure stores called Flight Shop (the name Flight Centre is owned by another company in India) in 2007. In the leisure sector, the culture of incentives and Buzz Nights had been more readily embraced, Nautiyal said. The Indian contingent were so excited and imbued with FCL culture when they arrived at the 2007 Global Ball in Dublin that they stormed the stage – and broke it.

Trying to replicate the Family, Village, Tribe model in India had presented challenges because there were so many layers of staff in the system, Nautiyal said. While management were attempting to remove layers and adhere to the lean company structure of a maximum of five reporting levels, sometimes decisions were made differently about which costs could be stripped. This shows that while FCL's principles and philosophies can be applied, the company does not take a cookie-cutter approach to international business. There are local market nuances to be respected. One of the staffing layers in India and Dubai includes the pantry or tea boys. The company has tried to upskill employees performing tasks like getting the tea for the benefit of the people holding such positions. 'The average cost of wages is so low and they are so dependent on the wage. There are moral and ethical obligations you need to consider with these roles in the overall model,' said Andrew Boxall, managing director of FCm Travel Solutions Dubai. 'These are the types of decisions best made in the country in which we're operating, not at head office.'

Sometimes the unforeseen side effect of an acquisition can be its innovation and growth-creating legacy. In the case of Flight Centre UK's operations, one corporate acquisition was to have considerable consequences for the organically grown retail operation.

Flight Centre Limited's gutsy purchase of UK corporate travel manager Britannic Travel Limited in March 2003, during the SARS outbreak and the Iraq War, had a massive impact on FCL's corporate operations in the country. At the same time, the acquisition unexpectedly and perhaps just as significantly revolutionised the Flight Centre UK retail operation that had been in place since 1995.

FCL merged Britannic Travel with Flight Centre UK's Corporate Traveller brand to form FCm Travel Solutions UK in 2005. The move left the retail operation floundering. The swift amputation of corporate left the formerly combined business without the profit driver that had largely fuelled expansion over the decade to 84 retail stores in London, Bristol, Manchester, Glasgow and Edinburgh.

Taking over the ailing retail operation in 2005 was Chris Galanty, recruited back in 1995 as one of the UK's first Flight Centre consultants. Galanty said it was obvious the traditional Australian growth model of opening retail shops just wasn't working. Flight Centre UK's retail sector was losing money.

The retail operation needed a point of difference. To specialise in premium long-haul travel rather than being a generalist travel agent, Flight Centre UK launched new sub-brands. As well as the Flight Centre 'Airfare Experts', Flight Centre UK's retail operation offered 'Flight Centre First and Business', 'Round the World Experts' and 'Flight Centre Business Travel', focused on the small and medium-sized enterprise travel market.

Then Galanty went further. The UK retail operation began a strategy that bucked the accepted physical growth model of opening new shops. Instead, Flight Centre UK began bundling multiple teams into the one shop. Instead of having six employees per shop, each shop would have twelve to eighteen people – a team of six out the front and two teams of five or six out the back, dealing directly with email or phone enquiries.

The success of these multi-team shops led to the creation of the Flight Centre UK hyperstore and megastore models in 2008. The seven hyperstores stand as Flight Centre UK's flagship retail outlets. They house as many as 60 people in teams from the different sub-brands and are open seven days a week for up to fourteen hours a day. In London, the Flight Centre hyperstore on Kensington High Street contains more than 30 people across different sub-brands and the Oxford Street store has eight teams over four levels.

The hyperstore model means property costs per person are usually lower than the single-team shops, despite the hyper- and megastores' prime retail locations. The look of the hyperstore is modern and dynamic, with large window and internal merchandising space. The stores host on-site events and create a travel research and purchase experience for customers. The combined effect is an in-store experi-ence for travel customers that echoes those found in flagship stores of some of the world's most celebrated modern retail giants, including the famed Apple Stores.[66]

From 84 stores in 2003, Flight Centre UK increased to just 85 retail locations over the subsequent nine years. Flight Centre UK did not open any single-team shops in the five years from 2007. Of the 85 shops open in 2012, twenty were multi-teamed. Despite this virtual standstill in the number of actual shops, Flight Centre UK's retail operation more than doubled its turnover between 2005 and 2011/12.

In late 2007, the corporate FCm Travel Solutions UK reintegrated with the retail arm. Britannic Travel owner Alan Spence, who had been managing director of FCm Travel Solutions UK, left the company. Galanty was appointed managing director of both retail and corporate for Flight Centre UK.

Flight Centre Limited's acquisitions almost always try to fit the strategic growth plan. But sometimes the temptation can be a bit of fun, maybe even a dash of sentimentality.

Still in the UK, FCL acquired Back Roads Touring Company – a London-based bus touring company – for just under $3 million on 31 October 2008. It was quite possibly the acquisition most in need of renovation that the company had ever chosen. It was also to be one of the greatest turnarounds of any of its acquired businesses, and one that hooked Turner right back into the London-based overland bus touring business.

In 2003 Turner convinced his then twenty-year-old daughter, Jo, to head to Europe to take a Topdeck tour – the company that began it all in the 1970s and which Turner and the other founders had sold out of in 1986. He wanted to know if Topdeck tours were still any good. Jo reported back that they were, so Turner flew to London. It was time to rescue the company that had been so integral to the Flight Centre story, but was now teetering on the brink of collapse. A consortium of Turner, Geoff Harris, Chris Grieve, Bill James and Peter Barrow bought back Topdeck along with partner James Nathan, who was appointed Topdeck managing director. Thirty years after Top Deck began, the crew was back together on the buses and keen to grow in the overland touring niche.

Nathan worked to restore the almost 40-year-old company to its former status as a market leader in the youth tour sector. He was not unfamiliar with the industry. Not too long after Skroo and Geoff 'Spy'

Lomas set off across Europe in double-deckers with paying passengers in tow, Nathan started a similar type of company. Originally called the Camping Connection and later rebranded as Connections Adventures, it offered youth tours in Australia and New Zealand. He sold Connections Adventures in 2000. With his experience and the new Topdeck owners' investment, he has made enormous headway in the market. The award-winning new Topdeck provides specialist tours for eighteen-to-thirty-somethings in Europe, Africa, Egypt, the Middle East, Australia, New Zealand, Fiji, the USA and Canada. Its buses are a far cry from the famous fleet of double-decker rattlers like Belch and Grunt that started the Topdeck story back in 1973. In 2012 Topdeck won Favourite Big Tour Operator, Favourite Tour Operator in Western Europe and Favourite Winter/Ski Operator at the TNT Golden Backpack UK awards. To complete the circle, the Topdeck board purchased Connections Adventures in April 2010. It now operates as Topdeck Australia & New Zealand.

Meanwhile, Back Roads Touring Company was being run by Bruce Cherry, a London university lecturer in marketing, tourism and transport. Cherry was a senior leader at Topdeck in the 1980s. He set up Back Roads in 1986 as a teaching aid for his marketing students, but for most of its 22 years he also ran it as a commercial venture.[67] Following the consortium's re-entry to the Topdeck scene, Cherry approached Turner and the new Topdeck owners with a proposal for his Back Roads company.

'I didn't want any part of it,' said James Nathan. 'But Skroo was unbelievably determined. He has a way of getting people to go along with him.'

In Back Roads, Turner saw ingredients that could be a recipe for success. And he thought taking the business on and turning it around would be enjoyable. It tapped into that underlying nerve that has driven much of his business interest: a combination of intellectual challenge and commercial thrill. 'It was a bit of a risk. A bit of fun,' he said.

Nathan, busy on the Topdeck front, still wasn't so sure. He said that on walking through the red doors of Back Roads, down an alley off London's Ealing Broadway, he felt he'd entered possibly the worst office ever. The company had no systems in place. Students were doing the marketing. When the buses were not on the road, they were left uninsured so as to save money. 'Jimmy thought at the start it was pretty rough and ready,' Turner said. 'We found in reality, when we went in there, it was far worse.'

Somehow, Nathan was convinced. He put money into a joint venture with FCL to take over Back Roads from Cherry and became the company's managing director.

Emma Jupp, who had previously been a vice president of FCL's Canadian operation, moved to the UK to handle the Back Roads changeover and make the business work.

She was eager to see the transition of the business to a Flight Centre company. She said she was confident the embracement of the FCL way could turn the operation around. 'One Best Way allows us to achieve consistency,' Jupp said, though she admitted the business she was confronted with in London was a far greater challenge than she'd anticipated.

New Flight Centre chairman Peter Morahan also paid the Back Roads acquisition a visit. He thought it was a disaster. However, he was slightly appeased that it wasn't one of Flight Centre's more costly acquisitions. 'I knew it wasn't going to hurt us, so I wasn't sweating blood over it,' he said. It was at this juncture that Morahan came up with a new rule for all Flight Centre acquisitions: an FCL non-executive director must visit all acquisition targets before final sign-off.

The Back Roads experience shows that the FCL formula applied to acquired businesses has been honed and improved over time. It also shows the results that can emerge when the plan is followed. In Jim Collins and Morten Hansen's *Great by Choice* (HarperBusiness 2011), the follow-up to Collins' *Good to Great* and equally as influential for FCL leaders, the authors discuss the concept of SMaC. SMaC stands for Specific Methodical and Consistent. Collins says the more uncertain, unforgiving and changeable the environment, the more important it is to be SMaC. Back Roads has diligently adhered to its SMaC recipe, as described above. From a loss of GBP£616,000 in 2009/10 it returned around GBP£250,000 profit in 2012/13.

Back Roads' recipe for success

Goals

YEAR	PAX	TURNOVER	P&L
2015/16	4000	£9.0m	£1m profit

<u>Hedgehog</u>: (In Jim Collins' *Good to Great* the Hedgehog Concept is defined as 'a simple, crystalline concept that flows from a deep understanding about the intersection of the three circles: What you are passionate about? What can you be the best in the world at? What drives your resource or economic engine?')

To be the best small group, off-the-beaten-track coach travel provider in the UK, France, Spain and Italy for the discerning middle-aged (60+) traveller who can afford not to be part of large impersonal groups. Tours are led by educated people who are passionate about the concept, the business and the features, history and culture of these countries.

<u>The key ingredients</u>

1. Small groups (maximum fifteen people in the UK and eighteen people in Europe) and suitable transport for those groups.
2. Leisurely pace (generally no starts before 8.30 am, only two hours in coach at a time, majority of two night stays in the trip).
3. Off the beaten track (generally no motorways, rather accessing small country lanes or medieval cities that large coaches can't reach).
4. Food and drink experiences (more than just good food – preferably with a regional or traditional element; could also be an iconic restaurant such as Rick Stein's).
5. Quality hotels – wow factor could include location, history, or the owners/hosts.
6. Knowledgeable, educated, passionate and personable guides (suitable travel companions for clients; culturally aligned with the company; organised in order to create a hassle-free experience; professional and safe).
7. Unique local experiences (activities at least every other day such as thatching, bagpipe making, wineries and fishing).

The SMaC recipe approach to FCL businesses across the globe has also proved vital, especially in times of high volatility and uncertainty. It would never be tested more than in the economic instability of 2008 and the ensuing years.

Chapter 17

(AND) AN UGLY TIME TO TAKE ON AMERICA

Give us five years and everyone will be claiming Liberty was their idea.
Dean Smith, president USA Flight Centre Group, ahead of the October 2012
opening of the first US Liberty hyperstore on Madison Avenue, New York

A
t their first board meeting, Flight Centre Limited's non-executive chairman Peter Morahan and director Gary Smith signed off on the purchase of FCL's largest ever acquisition, an American company called Liberty Travel. Morahan had just become the fourth Flight Centre Limited chairman after Bruce Brown, Norm Fussell and Graham Turner, who had briefly performed the role.

Five days later, on 12 November 2007, Flight Centre Limited announced the US$135 million acquisition of the privately owned Liberty Travel. The deal was formally settled on 8 February 2008. The timing was rotten.

Just as FCL signed off on their largest ever acquisition, at what was considered a top-of-the-market price, the world plunged into financial meltdown. The US subprime mortgage market and related financial markets collapsed and the housing bubble in other industrialised economies disintegrated, sending a ripple effect around the world that caused reallocation of capital, loss of household wealth and a drop in consumption. The subsequent collapse of Lehman Brothers in September 2008 saw the largest and sharpest drop in global economic activity in the modern era.[68] FCL's Liberty purchase suddenly looked a whole lot less inspired.

The timing of FCL's acquisition of Liberty Travel in the United

States meant it was integrally connected to the company's handling of the global financial crisis. FCL had survived major external catastrophes before, such as the Gulf War and September 11, when it was feared the industry might never recover. The company had always stuck to its guns with the mantra that you could never blame external circumstances. Keep doing the internal things well and business would return bigger and stronger once people started travelling again. It was the FCL version of the strategy Jim Collins labelled SMaC and it had triumphed before in adversity. But this time, FCL was being hit with a one-two punch. With the critical worldwide financial failure it was facing an external blow to every brand across every geographical location of its diverse business. The impact was compounded by an internal decision – the $135 million purchase of Liberty Travel – that itself contained unforeseen problems. Many feared the combination left the company open to a knockout.

Liberty Travel was one of the United States' largest and most recognisable travel agency groups, credited with the invention of the packaged vacation. It was founded by Fred Kassner and Gilbert Haroche in 1951, with the Kassner and Haroche families maintaining leadership and ownership of the company continuously up until the FCL purchase.[69] Liberty was an iconic brand in the US, with an equally iconic marketing position as the second longest-running weekly advertiser in the *New York Times* behind Tiffany.

Liberty was coveted as a way to salve a longstanding thorn in FCL's side. Flight Centre Limited had been thrashing away at the American market since the late 1990s, with retail stores on the West Coast and in Chicago that were based on the Australian model. The brand just never took off. What needed to be changed to make FCL a success in the US market remained a source of curiosity within the company, even if Turner had always claimed that the US wasn't critical to FCL's success from a financial point of view, but 'rather from a challenge point of view'. Reasons for the failure may have included the inability to get brand cut-through with just thirteen shops in a city the size of Los Angeles, and the cultural differences between the way Americans and Australians travelled and shopped for their travel. Yet for years FCL persisted in the US, trying to make it work.

Even if the leisure stores failed to make money, FCL was determined to have a corporate presence in the US. The company spent a long time in 2004 and 2005 looking at corporate opportunities. In March 2006, FCL acquired Chicago-based Bannockburn Travel Management for $13 million. The profitable company, which turned over US$93 million in 2005, was FCL's eleventh corporate acquisition to be wrapped into the FCm Travel Solutions fold and the first in the United States.

The Bannockburn purchase gave Flight Centre Limited some presence in America, but not as much as the company was seeking. In January 2007, FCL bought a 25 per cent stake in Garber Travel Services in Boston for $7 million. Garber was a larger corporate travel management group, with offices in Massachusetts, California, Rhode Island, Illinois, Vermont, Virginia and New Hampshire, as well as Toronto in Canada and London in the UK. The profitable family-owned business generated about US$350 million in turnover in 2006 and gave FCL a reasonable footing in the US East Coast. FCL was alerted to the sale through its strong relationship with its German partners in FCm Travel Solutions, Deutsches Reisebüro (DER) group. FCL wanted to buy a greater share in Garber, even though prices were high in the 2007 boom, but it wasn't for sale. (In December 2010, after the crash, FCL paid $10.5 million to acquire the remaining 74 per cent of Garber.)

Throughout this time, a large team from FCL was assembled to investigate the business case for the purchase of Liberty Travel. From July 2007 the team identified a lot of appeal and synergies with FCL, but also plenty of red flags. Some of these included declining turnover, cost structure overruns and an IT system upgrade that was not living up to expectations. The FCL team identified potential cultural clashes between the way things were done in the US business compared to Flight Centre, including transparency of results and even the

American formality (compared to the Australian lack of it) of the annual awards night. They also identified a multi-million-dollar cash deficit. 'But we really thought we could make it work,' said mergers and acquisitions chief David Smith.

FCL said the purchase would fast-track its global expansion and transform North America into FCL's largest international market outside of Australia by sales. It would also add 193 leisure travel shops to the Flight Centre stable along the US East Coast and in Florida and Chicago, as well as 40 wholesale locations in 22 states. Liberty actually had two business units: Liberty Travel, which was the 193-store retail network, and GoGo Worldwide Vacations, a wholesaler of leisure vacation packages servicing 18,000 US travel agencies. One of the attractions and synergies for FCL was that GoGo could potentially service the entire FCL network with package holiday elements, particularly for the Americas and Caribbean.

By combining FCL's existing businesses in the US with the new Liberty leisure, wholesale and corporate business, FCL would go from being less than a crumb in the market to being the tenth largest travel group in the USA. It also didn't hurt – and was in fact a strong attraction for the acquisition – that FCL could see the potential of putting a northern hemisphere version of its gung-ho Sydney-based Flight Centre Global Product (FCGP) procurement operation behind GoGo as a way of creating even more value in the purchase.

After months of discussions, FCL agreed to the purchase on 12 November 2007. Members of the due diligence team, Dean Smith, Sue Rennick and Natalie Benson, jetted off to Aruba in the Caribbean to attend the Liberty team leader conference at which the acquisition was to be announced. After missing their connection in Miami, the trio arrived just in time for the conference close. They were exhausted. They were also nervous at the reception they would encounter, anticipating that the staff of such an iconic US company might not be entirely enamoured at being taken over by an upstart Aussie travel group that was anything but ordinary. The Liberty crew welcomed them like rock stars.

In announcing the deal, Turner said FCL had experienced a strong start to the 2007/08 financial year. He said he saw positive signs for FCL's leisure travel model and the $180-billion-a-year leisure travel sector in the US, despite the emergence of worrying economic factors such as the subprime housing crisis and the relative weakness of the US dollar.

He rationalised his argument for investing in bricks and mortar agencies in the US rather than going online in the following way. Of the US leisure market, travel agents held about $70 billion of the value, while the rest (more than $100 billion) was online. But of the online business, travel agents held only about $25 billion, while the rest went directly to airlines and hotels. The offline bricks and mortar travel agents had been stable at about $70 billion for the previous four years. The Liberty Travel bricks and mortar agencies were clearly part of the better pie of which to grab a slice, he said.[70]

However, the positive outlook, the acquisition rationale of Liberty fast-tracking FCL's growth in the difficult-to-crack American market and learning from acquisitions past by taking immediate control of the new business from the owner/founders did not entirely impress Morahan, who had ticks of regret about delivering board approval. 'I knew deep in my heart it was not a great idea, but I was very young in my chairmanship,' Morahan said. Sue Rennick, the former FCL Australia brand leader and West Canada president who was given the role of Liberty integration team leader, said Morahan asked her just before she left for the US whether she would have made the Liberty purchase if it were her money. 'I said no,' Rennick said. 'But I'm not likely to have one hundred and thirty-five million.'

When the deal was formally settled, on 8 February 2008, FCL discovered a few more surprises. The multi-million-dollar cash deficit that the due diligence team had identified ahead of the November signing of the deal had blown out to $60 million. The hole in cash holdings was blamed on the cyclical nature of the business, plus a trading downturn that was sharper and more severe than anticipated. The startling blow-out was to take on even more significance with the imminent shock of the global economic crunch.

As it happened, in August 2008, just one month before Lehman Brothers filed the largest bankruptcy in US history and the world slid into a new calamitous phase of the economic crisis, Skroo went on long service leave.

Peter Morahan had been tenacious in discussing the issue of leadership succession, or what he termed 'the number one question in Queensland business, maybe Australian business', with Turner. Turner said he thought the experience of the senior executive team and the good shape the company had been in throughout 2007 and early 2008 meant his departure wouldn't cause FCL to miss a beat. Morahan said, 'prove it – take six months off and see what happens'. So, reluctantly, Turner did.

Appointed to the role of chief executive officer was CFO Shannon O'Brien. The appointment was particularly satisfying for O'Brien, who had been on the way back up since he was thrown out of a job under former CEO Shane Flynn during the Full Throttle period. Turner told staff that the CEO appointment was not a caretaker role and that O'Brien was the 'standout current successor in a strong field'. Turner also made it clear that his stepping back from the organisation would not mean a return to dark times like the 'unmitigated disaster' of Full Throttle, as had happened the last time he handed over to a CEO. 'With the current X Team I know mistakes like this will not happen,' he said.[71] Turner said he genuinely did not like the idea of leaving his team and that 'life would have some empty spaces for a while'. He said he would return in February 2009.

But Turner did not stay away. It was a standing joke in the office that, though banned from the building for the duration of his long service leave, he continued to operate from the nearby Mondo Coffee shop on Adelaide Street, just metres from the front door of FCL's Brisbane headquarters. He held meetings at the coffee shop, he did business from the alfresco tables, he summoned people from inside FCL headquarters and he even assembled his former X Team for a chat. 'I'd sometimes wonder where people were, then realise they were with Skroo, who was supposed to be on leave,' O'Brien said.

It wasn't just his physical proximity to the business that caused frustrations. 'He never left in his head or his heart,' said Jude Turner. The long service period was a jolt for the entire Turner family. Jude said she believed her husband was shocked by the realisation of how much he needed Flight Centre, and the family by the fundamental dawning that he couldn't and wouldn't ever leave it. 'It is his being,' she said.

But then the global financial crisis kicked in. Turner effectively returned full-time in November 2008, even though he was not officially due back on board until 2009. In one of the worst economic shocks in history, it was unthinkable – for Turner and the company – not to have the organisation's key player and managing director with at least one hand on the wheel.

With O'Brien elevated to the position of CEO in Turner's supposed absence, Andrew Flannery was appointed to the chief financial officer vacancy. In the highly volatile global financial environment, it was possibly the most intense, hair-raising and demanding time to be thrown in as CFO of any company, let alone one that had just taken such a risk on a massive purchase – one that not only had the potential to make or break its assault on the United States, but, if it failed, could impact the company's strategic global network.

From the moment he became CFO, Flannery said it felt like a new monster came crawling out from under the bed every day. 'It was disaster after disaster after disaster. Every day there was something that had some unexpected implication for us.' When international insurance organisation American International Group (AIG) looked like it was going down, FCL feared major implications. AIG underwrote FCL's directors and officers liability insurance. This meant that if AIG failed, Flight Centre's executives would have been without protection – a major risk in the highly unpredictable travel industry. AIG survived with a US Government bailout in September 2008. Meanwhile, FCL took a $15 million hit on its collateralised debt obligations

(CDOs) – the sophisticated financial scheme based on packaging loans and selling them to investors that triggered large losses for banks during the economic collapse. Luckily, FCL's CDO investment was only a small component of the Australian head office's conservative investment portfolio.

Even worse, as the economic turmoil destroyed consumer confidence, people stopped travelling, businesses tightened their belts by slashing corporate travel budgets and sales slumped. Fortunately, the Flight Centre remuneration model provided some in-built cost savings, as major costs such as wages were linked to incentives on revenue. 'When profit share is down, wages are down. We have the inward mechanisms to cope in a lot of ways with a contracting economy,' said Geoff Harris. But this incentive model was not yet in place in America. It was just one of the reasons that the business, in its first year under FCL ownership, was haemorrhaging money.

The Flight Centre team dispatched to the USA to sort out Liberty moved quickly, thanks to the support of forward-thinking incumbent Liberty leader Cathy Paleaz. With the undercurrent of financial disaster caused by the global economic ructions and the knowledge that Liberty finances were far less healthy than when the deal was reached in November 2007, urgency was key. 'It's fine to do the due diligence, but when you get there you still have to understand how the business is working, get to know the individuals and understand the history,' Sue Rennick said. However, the pressures of the global financial crisis and the problems that were present in Liberty meant there was little pause for reflection. There were obvious savings and decisions that had to be made.

While FCL was conservative in its approach to cash and investments, it turned out that Liberty wasn't. FCL was faced with tough decisions regarding Liberty's investment portfolio as the stock market hit its stomach-churning drop on the roller-coaster. FCL decided to sell what they could of Liberty's investments, which were worth around $60 million at the time of the November deal. FCL took a $24 million hit by offloading what they could of the portfolio.

Liberty's next-generation travel IT system, which had been under development at a cost of $80 million, was dumped and had to be written off. In the first week, 100 IT positions were also gone.

Every Liberty retail store had an assistant and a team leader who acted as greeters and didn't sell. This arrangement went against the Flight Centre model. About 160 assistants were removed from the shops and the team leaders were sent back to selling. Incentives were revised and teams placed on new key performance indicators (KPIs) that included outgoings as well as commission. Performance criteria had never been so transparent at Liberty and the change caused distress among many consultants, especially those whose results were seen as less than stellar under the KPIs in place in every FCL operation around the world.

Some changes sparked significant pushback. As had been the case during numerous past acquisitions, many staff members were appalled at the requirement to wear uniforms. Surprisingly, one of the most emotional changes was coercing consultants to use calculators instead of adding machines. 'It was kind of crazy, but it was a colossal change,' said Billy McDonough, USA FCm Travel Solutions and Travel Associates president. 'Every consultant had one of these retro adding machines on their desk with rolls of paper tape coming out of it. It was very old-school, but they had used them forever and were very reluctant to give them up.' Of course, there were plenty of people delighted to embrace the new ways, including 82-year-old consultant Marie Borchert, who happily put on her uniform and threw away her adding machine.

As was the case in all FCL acquisitions, not everything the company tried to change worked. 'There was a little bit of arrogance on our behalf that Flight Centre knows best,' said Flight Centre USA group president Dean Smith. Trying to shift the Liberty brand from a package holiday brand to a flight brand was one example of a misfire from Flight Centre in terms of reading the market and understanding its own people. 'We didn't understand that our [Liberty] people didn't really have the knowledge or desire to be flight specialists, they wanted to be vacation specialists. We should have taken a little bit of time to assess the situation a bit more deeply. But the pace was incredible.'

The global financial crisis meant the cuts had to go deeper and harder than just the obvious savings. More than 40 shops were closed. In the first round of closures, called Project Odyssey, 36 Liberty stores were closed. The follow-up round of closures, Project California Dreaming, saw ten Flight Centre stores shut down in Chicago and Los Angeles, including those 'legacy stores' opened back in the '90s, when Flight Centre arrived as a start-up company in America. 'At that point it was a matter of survival. Closing stores is so foreign to our business model and our culture, it was not a decision or strategy enacted lightly,' said McDonough. A total of 700 positions were terminated.

Dean Smith said the team never waivered in their belief that Liberty would be profitable. But it was going to take time and it was being carried out in the ugliest of financial environments. 'It was about getting the business to where it needed to be,' he said. With the $24 million equity writedown, $20 million restructure and a $16 million trading loss on top, Liberty recorded a $60 million loss in its first year as an FCL business.

Liberty was far from the only FCL business suffering during the financial crisis. The new economic reality meant Flight Centre operations worldwide felt the pain. About 200 support positions were cut from other countries, including 100 from Australia. The 100 job losses in Australia – which exceeded the number of cuts that caused such trauma during Full Throttle – caused barely a protest. 'It was a good thing to reflect on the lessons learned from Bain. It happened humanely,' said Australian executive general manager Rachel Miller. The message to the company's leaders that savings needed to be made, however, was delivered without compassion. In order to convince them that trying to ride out the financial crisis without significant cost cutting was not an option, Flannery presented the company's executive general managers with a graphic image of Flight Centre's possible future. He said that rather than using a series of diagrams and numbers to model the potential decline and ramifications for the business, he felt he had one shot to get his point across. He presented the image of Flight Centre past as a healthy cow, then Flight Centre future as a slaughtered cow. It served to spark debate in the room over whether the image was in fact a cow or a goat. 'To this day it is still considered that it was the slaughtered cow, or goat, that convinced them to take action,' he said.

The Perfect Cash Storm (aka the Death of the FCL Cow)

Combined threats

1. Growth businesses including Liberty, Corporate, Travelmoney and Back Roads are working capital hungry
2. Trading downturn means reduced cash earnings
3. Funds via banks, fund markets and equity markets are hard to get and very expensive
4. Big commitments such as IT projects, dividends and taxes require large outflow
5. Travel Compensation Fund rules require maintenance of certain cash level.

Action plan

1. Cash plan and expenditure cutbacks demanded from all businesses
2. Internal target set to achieve $300 million in company funds
3. Pull back on capital spend, including IT projects and office accommodation blow-outs.

Flannery may have used shocking imagery to convince his colleagues that drastic change was needed to avoid dire consequences for the company, but his own actions didn't help matters. On the release of half-yearly results, the slump that had hit Flight Centre Limited's performance and share price deteriorated further. It was made worse by what Flannery admits was a massive blunder on his part. It was February 2009 and the investment community was on a razor edge. Flannery prepared to announce the company's unedifying results. Liberty Travel and GoGo in the US had just been wrapped into FCL, as had FCGP North – the northern hemisphere sister operation of the FCGP procurement business. These businesses operated a little differently from others in the FCL stable in that they collected most of their cash from sales in the latter half of the financial year, held it, then spent most of it on product in the first half of the following year. The trend had not been seen in the FCL business before because the acquisitions were so new. This was to be the first reporting period in which the cash was paid out. The average cash outflow reported by FCL for the first-half period was normally around $20 million. In the first six months of the 2009 financial year, largely due to the impact of the new businesses, it was almost $300 million.

'What I did wrong was that I didn't explain it to the business community leading up to the announcement,' Flannery said. Confusion swamped the market. There was no explaining away the result once the figures went live. 'The results were pretty average. But the cash looked horrible,' said head of investor relations Haydn Long. Investors and commentators, alarmed by Flight Centre's seemingly abrupt downturn, pronounced that such a big drain meant the company was floundering.

FCL shares plummeted. For weeks the price tumbled, bottoming out in early March at $3.39. From trading as high as $32.06 in January 2008, the crash was catastrophic. 'I remember going to buy a cup of tea one day and seeing three dollars fifty and thinking I should be buying Flight Centre shares instead. They cost less than a tea or coffee,' Flannery said.

Public misconception about the company's financial state was far from the only damaging issue it was dealing with. The impact of the economic slide was biting hard. Airlines struggling to fill seats during the economic crisis engaged in unprecedented price discounting. When Virgin Australia's long-haul carrier V Australia entered the market in February 2009 with discount flights to the US, airlines were forced to slash prices. V Australia offered flights from Sydney to Los Angeles from $975.[72] In March, US airline Delta revealed it was launching a Sydney to Los Angeles route with return trans-Pacific flights from $777.[73] Just four months earlier, in October 2008, Flight

Centre was advertising return fares from Sydney to Los Angeles for $1685.[74] Qantas also sparked a price war with a $2 million seat sale on domestic routes.[75] The discounting impacted on FCL results through lower yields, or lower base commission. Even though the cheap flights meant volume didn't suffer, the lower yields made it more difficult for Flight Centre to meet the revenue tiers required to earn its more lucrative back-end commissions from airlines.

Tough times were made even tougher for the Canadian leisure sector when a swine flu epidemic created panic across the country and caused travel to nosedive. In July 2009, the Public Health Agency of Canada reported 10,156 confirmed cases of swine flu and 45 deaths in the country.[76] Mass fear about swine flu severely curtailed travel, particularly from Canada to Mexico, where the outbreak began. It was a massive hit for the Canadian travel industry, as Mexico had become the most popular non-US international destination for Canadian travellers, with about 1.14 million Canadians travelling to Mexico in 2008.[77]

Widespread belt-tightening meant FCL's corporate travel businesses hurt badly during the global financial crisis. The businesses in India, China and Hong Kong suffered and the newest FCm Travel Solutions brands in Singapore and Dubai slumped.

Dealing with banks became extraordinarily difficult. The FC board realised that if things kept going downhill then the company's covenants might be at risk (its promises to the banks that gave it loans that the company's financial position wouldn't dramatically alter). There were three possible solutions. Firstly, FCL could go to the market to raise cash. The second option involved the founders raiding their own kitties and coming up with around $100 million. The third option was for the board to hold the line and do what was required to get the business back on track. 'What the board did was make the tough decisions and cut the cloth, trim the sails,' Harris said. 'It became a much healthier company, a leaner company and a more focused company.' Director Gary Smith said it was important FCL did not succumb to pressure to go to the market to raise capital. FCL was one of few companies that did not dilute earnings per share by raising funds during the global financial crisis. 'The fact that we didn't was really an achievement.' It was perhaps this decision that put the steel back into FCL's deter-mination to stick to its business recipe and ride out the storm.

The economic disaster bit even deeper across the board in the UK than in Australia. Despite this, UK managing director Chris Galanty said the operation had 'a fantastic recession', turning over $1.1 billion in 2008. In the middle of the most dire economic times in recent memory, the UK team came up with a plan to double their turnover by 2014. 'So we had this "Billion Pounds by 2014" goal that we created in 2008, during the beginning of the great recession. In a way, that really fortified us. It gave us a road map of where we were going,' Galanty said. Despite the UK still reeling from economic uncertainty across Europe, by 2012 the UK operation's turnover in the four years since they made the pledge was up 8 per cent to £788 million, and was considered on track to reach the £1 billion mark in total transaction value by the end of 2014. It was a result that epitomised the FCL mantra that while you can't change the world, you can change how you respond to it. It was an example of the company's obligation to look within to fix problems, even if they were created externally. It was a successful test of the company philosophy on taking responsibility:

> We take full responsibility for our own success or failure. We do not externalise. We accept that we have total ownership and responsibil-ity, but not always control. As a company we recognise and celebrate our individual and collective successes.

Turner said the global financial shockwave had focused the company on cash and cutting costs. It also sharpened FCL's thinking on negoti-ating with suppliers for more guaranteed margins, rather than going for the big carrots that required top-tier sales growth and put some FCL revenue at risk. One of the bonuses of the economic crisis and the accompanying desperation among airlines and suppliers to fill seats was that it put FCL in a position of strength to use its bargaining power in negotiating for better deals. Flight Centre Limited recorded a $38.2 million profit in 2009, a 72 per cent slide on 2008. But there was, Turner said, 'positive momentum'.

Chapter 18

THE EVOLUTION
OF THE TRIBE

*You can call someone a bastard in this organisation, but don't ask them
to do your photocopying ... the culture, the model, it's just very different.
I can't really imagine it working anywhere else.*

Andrew Flannery, Flight Centre CFO and former investment banker

The global operations of Flight Centre Limited reached a
milestone in the 2010/11 financial year. For the first time,
each of the ten countries in which FCL operated fully owned
businesses was profitable.

Having suffered its unsightly growing pains, Liberty had blos-
somed into a significantly more attractive creature.

After two years of considerable losses, the 257 businesses across the
USA returned record corporate travel results and significant improvement in leisure to log $10 million profit (before tax and interest).
With the US$10.4 million purchase of the remaining 74 per cent
interest in Garber in December 2010 , FCL finally had its long sought
after foothold in the world's largest corporate travel market. The
purchase meant FCL had 48 corporate travel businesses in New York,
New Jersey, Chicago, Boston, Seattle, Los Angeles, San Francisco,
Dallas, Phoenix and Washington, DC. Corporate Traveller was introduced in the US, alongside the established FCm Travel Solutions
business, to service the SME market. While still performing below
initial expectations, the 169-shop Liberty Travel retail network was
cashing in on increased levels of enquiry and was supported by a stable

of online leisure travel brands to suit the shopping style of the American travel customer.

Elsewhere, record earnings were generated in Australia, Canada, India and Dubai, and advances were made in Greater China and in Singapore, which opened its first Flight Centre-branded leisure travel shop to complement the corporate business. Despite dire and ongoing economic volatility, the UK was FCL's second largest profit contributor behind Australia.

In South Africa, there was a marked recovery from the country's biggest ever drop in profitability two years earlier. Managing director Janine Salame said it took two years to bounce back from the effects of the global financial crisis, which had been exacerbated by soaring costs and lack of planning in the business. South African turnover plunged $45 million between 2008 and 2010, scrambling back up $37 million to $426 million in 2011. Leading into 2008, there were over-complications, support cost blow-outs and disregard for FCL's One Best Way at all levels of the South African business, Salame said. She put the turnaround achieved in 2011 down to a return to FCL's fundamentals.

Turner said there was no mysterious methodology to the company's 2010 rebound or 2011 across-the-board performance, which surpassed forecasts – even with a goodwill writedown of $28 million on the Liberty purchase. 'We went back to basics.' He believed that with airlines still offering discounted airfares, customers were bound to find reasons to travel again. Even in tight times, a holiday was not considered discretionary spending. It was a ritual. The business needed to take advantage of the inevitable rebound, just as it had following previous crises. It proved yet again that the FCL SMaC recipe should never be ignored. And Turner was more certain than ever that FCL's Family, Village, Tribe structure, its philosophies and its growth business model were its recipe for success.

By 2013 there were 16,000 people in Flight Centre's global operations and 2500 shops and businesses across 36 brands – half of which were located outside Australia. In any FCL shop, in any part of the world, if you scratched beneath the surface there was no doubting the people who worked there were part of a Flight Centre Limited business. There were four basic but universal features of the company's business model. They had to be applied totally, or it would not work.

Firstly, the business was driven by growth – 'always was, always will be,' said Turner. The company aimed to grow organically by 10 to 40 per cent every year. From the 8820 selling staff and 1718 businesses and shops before the Liberty purchase in 2008, the company grew in number and business diversity to 12,130 selling staff and 2362 shops by June 2012. Even more extraordinary was that this growth happened during the global financial crisis. In the 2012/13 financial year, the company aimed to add a further 1000 people to its workforce and open its 2500th shop. In addition, it planned to have 3400 businesses by 2017.

Secondly, the company's Family, Village, Tribe structure of decentralised teams – with each separate team accountable for its own profit and loss accounts – was central to its success. The company had always given the team leader and team members intellectual and emotional ownership of their business, and the Family, Village, Tribe concept had cemented this even further. The teams were the engine room of the overall company, which had a simple and lean structure of no more than five layers: the team of up to seven members; the area or tribe made up of 20 to 30 teams, including as many as six villages; the brand (formerly the nation); the country, such as the UK or USA; and the X Team/board and Taskforce (the top-level strategic team formed in 2012, made up of Turner and FCL leaders Waters-Ryan, Flint, Flannery, Galanty from the UK and Smith from the USA).

Incentives were the third tenet and were based on rewarding simple outcome-based results, usually profit or commission, or sometimes sales growth. Incentives were not normally applied to volume and never to behaviour. The model was about empowering, motivating, measuring and rewarding individuals in the small business teams on the clearly measured outcomes they produced.

The fourth feature was the egalitarian idea that team members should be multi-skilled, taking care of their own administration as well as sharing team administration and business activities. Or, 'team members share the team's shitwork', according to Turner.

The business model in conjunction with FCL's guiding philosophies has created its unique company culture. It is a complete package
that others have cherrypicked from, yet few have emulated or
managed to impose so absolutely. 'Unless you've got someone who
fundamentally believes and is prepared to live and breathe those values
themselves, you can't sustain it,' said CFO Andrew Flannery. Co-
founder Bill James said it worked because Turner was prepared to
delegate and empower others in the organisation. 'He's not like a lot of
chief executive officers, who cling to power and micromanage the
business,' James said. Former CEO Shane Flynn said it took 'real guts'
to run a business the way Turner did. 'Others can know it and understand it, but you can never copy it. It's inculcated into the way they
think. It's magnificent.'

The Flight Centre Limited business model continues to be cited as
one of the world's most specific and dedicated applications of basic
human instinct and the psychological theories of human evolution to
the corporate arena. It is routinely borrowed and copied by businesses
eager to tap into the magic formula that has helped deliver the
company ongoing growth and success. Former FCL people who have
gone on to consult for such businesses cite problems introducing the
necessary changes to their clients' operations. Businesses adopt bits of
the blueprint they like, such as conferences or incentives, but discard
others like profit share schemes. Some apply the philosophies, but
rework them to suit their existing values and goals. Some tack on hits
such as staff benefits in the hope that they'll provide a simple cure-all.
What the businesses can't add on, and this is the fundamental flaw
in the cherrypicking or simple supplement approach, is culture.
Implanting a Flight Centre-style culture into any other business
requires an entire corporate rethink. However, the benefits may be
worth it.

London Business School psychologist Nigel Nicholson, who in
2001 said Flight Centre was the first company he knew to have
consciously applied evolutionary psychology theories to its business,
more recently said the company's application of human instinct was
not only a reason the business functioned so gainfully, but also a

reason its customers were so loyal. He said the genuine feeling of belonging in Flight Centre, through its Families, Villages and Tribes, was so strong that the customer also felt part of the community. 'You form a relationship with a particular individual who arranges your flights for you, makes specific suggestions about your travel; they become your friend. It's a very powerful model and is enormously successful,' he said.[78]

Of course, FCL is not the only company to have borrowed from evolutionary psychology. Other examples that were previously mentioned have continued to thrive. The federation of businesses under the Semco umbrella in Brazil is famously divided into small, self-organising sub-units of six to eight workers. Under this model, Semco increased its annual revenue between 1994 and 2003 from US$35 million to US$212 million.[79] WL Gore and Associates, the multi-million-dollar US company that makes the water-resistant Gore-Tex fabric, operates on a flat, team-based structure and still keeps all of its businesses under the Dunbar Number of 150 'associates'. As is the case with Flight Centre Limited, when a tribe grows larger than 150, it is split in two. The late founder of the company, Wilbert 'Bill' Gore, told an interviewer he only ever put 150 car parking spaces at each of his businesses. 'When people start parking on the grass, we know it's time to build a new plant.'[80]

Tony Hsieh, chief executive officer of the billion-dollar Las Vegas-based online retailing juggernaut Zappos.com, said the culture intuitively created at his company was codified in the evolutionary psychology theories that support tribal organisation.[81] Speaking at the 2012 Flight Centre Global Conference in Singapore, Hsieh said Zappos' culture of 'delivering happiness' to employees and customers was aided by the sense of community created through the tribal structure of the organisation.

In Australia, other companies have applied elements of the model championed by Flight Centre Limited. Metcash Limited implanted the Family, Village, Tribe culture into its Independent Grocers of Australia (IGA) chain. Each individual grocery store (family) is empowered to act locally. The stores trading in a common region or area combined to form a village and the tribe formed when all the villages within a state came together. IGA has five tribes representing the five states that they trade in. Throughout 2006 and 2007, IGA leveraged the internal Family, Village, Tribe strategy to create a marketing campaign positioning the IGA store as a 'Local Hero', or an integral family, within its community. The combination of new store development, supply chain improvements and the success of the internal Family, Village, Tribe culture and its underpinning of the 'Local Hero' campaign were credited with IGA increasing its market share to 19 per cent in 2007.[82]

In 2010, Metcash acquired 50.1 per cent of hardware retailer Mitre 10. Mitre 10 CEO Mark Laidlaw said the Family, Village, Tribe cultural infrastructure subsequently implanted by Metcash was a driver in the 420-store Mitre 10 tribe's strategy to increase its market share against other hardware retail chains in Australia.[83]

The Flight Centre model has also been applied to Australia's mining boom. In a submission to the Australian Federal Government, it was proposed that planning the accommodation camps for fly-in fly-out and drive-in drive-out workers using Family, Village, Tribe grouping principles could help overcome some of the problems associated with camp life. High on the list of problems under the old organisational model of mass groupings were poor health outcomes, high staff and operational costs, and poor relations with nearby towns. The government was told the Family, Village, Tribe model would mean a significant shift away from existing accommodation camps – which were described as more akin to detention centres – and many of the problems they created.[84]

Craig Scroggie, Pacific Region vice president and managing director for US company Symantec, experienced a similar light bulb moment to the one that struck Turner sixteen years earlier. Like Turner, Scroggie had grabbed a magazine that focused on evolutionary psychology as he prepared to board a business flight. Scroggie, who has since become CEO and executive director of data centre deliverer NextDC, said that after reading the theories about human instinct and how they applied to the workplace, he redesigned Symantec's

Australian and New Zealand structure. He did it to counter problems caused by managers being overburdened by their responsibilities, the existence of too many management layers and staff feeling disengaged. Scroggie established teams in groups of seven or eight and installed a raft of new team leaders. He said that after the program of changes, Australian employees were polled as having the highest engagement levels across Symantec's 20,000-strong global workforce.[85]

Scroggie said the catalyst for his Symantec restructure was the work of Australian management consultant Andrew O'Keeffe, who frequently cites Flight Centre's Family, Village, Tribe structure and has drawn upon the findings of renowned chimpanzee researcher Dr Jane Goodall.[86] During Dr Goodall's 2011 visit to Australia, she joined O'Keeffe to speak to business audiences about behaviour and instinct in both chimpanzees and corporate organisations. Featured in O'Keeffe's presentation was, of course, Flight Centre Limited.

Under Turner, Family, Village, Tribe and its basis in evolutionary psychology has remained an immutable feature of FCL. 'I've read some experts saying the Family, Village, Tribe structure is not proven to work,' Turner said.[87] 'There's no fucking logic in stating it's not proven to work. It can work and it does work.' This does not mean, however, that the Flight Centre Limited model itself has not evolved.

Since instilling the Family, Village, Tribe structure, the company's understanding of how and why it works has developed considerably. The theory that humans inherently prefer to work under a hunter-gatherer system remains the cornerstone of Turner's and the company's adherence to the structure. Their commitment is supported by evidence, discussed in detail in Chapter 8, that for hundreds of thousands of years humans lived within this hunter-gatherer structure and survived, suggesting that Stone Age behaviours are hard-wired into our modern, evolved nature. FCL's commitment is further strengthened by the proof that this physical, emotional and cultural clustering, as it has been adapted to the corporate world, has cultivated and aided the company's successes. Equally, the corruption of the concept and its practices, as occurred during events such as the flightcentre.com call centre debacle and Full Throttle, has been a contributing factor in Flight Centre's more significant mistakes.

According to Turner, the village concept has historically been the least clearly defined throughout the company and was not universally done well. Villages are an integral part of the Family, Village, Tribe formation. In the Stone Age community, the village or camp was the heart of the greater entity. Turner realised that while the essence of the village structure was defined in the FCL philosophies, it was not often leveraged in practice. From 2010, a new focus on the village became his mission. 'The village is a key part of our structure. If we neglect this because of our size, we do that at our own peril,' he said. The basic definition of a village is three to seven businesses or teams, generally within close proximity or in the one location, which support each other. The structure mirrors that of Stone Age villages, which were not formally declared or established, but rather created by the close vicinity and common interest of family groupings. Like an unfunded self-help or support group, the village acts as a bridge between the family unit and the greater area (sub-tribe) or tribe in the Flight Centre structure.

As with everything in the Flight Centre model, working in a smaller structure, with smaller targets and a strong community environment, makes what may seem impossible attainable. The post-2010 village is key to FCL's next growth phase as a working example of 'thinking small to grow big' – a philosophy also subscribed to by such successful business operators as Semco's Ricardo Semler, Virgin's Richard Branson and Microsoft's Paul Allen.[88] According to FCL's blueprint for growth to 2017, in the future of Flight Centre, the village is 'where the rubber hits the road'.

According to Turner, the village worked as long as the core ingredient for a successful village model was present. Having the right village elder or leader was key. Just as they were necessary in hunter-gatherer times to ensure groups of families could work together agreeably and effectively, in a village or a camp, village elders were vital in

---

How do you establish a village?

1. Identify how many villages you require in your area – this will be dependent on the size of your area and the number of potential leaders
2. Set up villages based on geographical location so that there is ease of travel for village meetings and support between shops
3. Identify skills and behaviours required of your village leaders – provide a village leader role description
4. Appoint village leaders by means of application
5. Establish a village name and colour
6. Establish village expectations and guidelines
7. Hold monthly village leader meetings to discuss village issues and roll out village initiatives
8. Drive your business through village incentives, quarterly commitments and Buzz Night activities by village.

---

the business sense to keep the group humming. The village elder was generally an honorary role in FCL, just as it was in the Stone Age, as opposed to a strict hierarchical or leadership appointment. The village elder became a point of contact for day-to-day advice for team leaders and consultants. The village elder helped team leaders to sort out problems, cover staff shortages and generally communicate any business issues or problems arising in the area. The role rewarded the village elder by giving them some leadership experience and greater influence in the direction and decisions of the area. For the company overall, it meant villages bred and trialled elders who could be developed for future area leadership roles.

The focus on the village, village elders and role of area leaders had a profound effect on Turner. It shifted his thinking on one of Flight Centre Limited's previously entrenched philosophies. Incentives have always been an integral part of the company's story and success. 'I have changed a bit on this,' he said. 'I used to think: Get the incentives right and the right people and teams will be successful.' However, he has made a 'correction'. The FCL experience had shown that incentivising behaviour was no substitute for the hard work and discipline it took to achieve behavioural change. 'It is a common thing to think incentives can be used to change behaviour. We made that mistake.

Role of the village leader

The village leader is a key leadership role responsible for the day-to-day running of the village. The village leader, together with the area leader, has responsibility for the success of their village growth in sales, profits, customer service and staff retention.

The village leader is also responsible for mentoring team leaders in the area. It is a key development role for all individuals who have a 'Brightness of Future' for being an area leader, creates succession planning in the business and it allows experienced leaders to mentor others and contribute.

Expected outcomes by a village leader:
- People retention – goal is 18 to 28 per cent people turnover in retail
- Increasing profits – 20 per cent is generally considered a good goal
- No leadership vacancies in the village.

Expected behaviours of a village leader
- Leads by example in attitude and figures
- Willingness to contribute to people and the business
- Passionate about the company, creating culture and adding value.

One result of the focus on the village leader is the more strategic role of the area leader. With the support of their own family of as many as five experts, the updated area leader role includes responsibility across the following seven areas:

1. Sales – daily proactive involvement from the area leader to drive sales and a consistent customer experience
2. Operational One Best Way – oversee expert audits and impose discipline to ensure consultants and teams are using travel booking systems in accordance with One Best Way
3. People and team growth – grow team and consultant numbers in line with budget
4. Leadership development – identify and develop suitable leaders
5. Product – develop, communicate and drive product strategy, especially in areas where customers may require different or unique product
6. Marketing – visit shops to assess adherence to 'retail is detail' checklist
7. Financial control – drive adherence to financial minimum standards.

Source: Leader Recipe for Success, August 2012

Sure it can be a lazy way to change behaviour, but rewarding people for producing the right outcomes is a much more important role for incentives.' Incentives would not change behaviour to achieve outcomes FCL needed such as profit growth, he said. That took training, hard work and discipline. 'It was a big lesson, and I think we've still got a fair way to go in correcting that.' FCL's fifth philosophy, Incentives, has been updated to reflect this emphasis on reward rather than motivation. It now reads:

> Incentives are based on measurable and reliable outcome-based KPIs. We believe that 'what gets rewarded, gets done'. If the right outcomes are rewarded, our company and our people will prosper.

FCL's newfound emphasis on the village, village elders and area leaders has caused the village concept to be not only refreshed at its fundamental level, but also embraced in a new global sense. Because Flight Centre Limited had grown so rapidly and diversely across the globe, in 2011 the leaders of some countries formed their own self-help groups, or global villages. By 2012, FCL had three global villages for the ten countries in which it operated: the Northern Lights, made up of the leaders of Canada, the UK, and the USA; the southern hemisphere ANZACS; and the dubiously named Asian Delights.

Members of the original global village, the Northern Lights, described the arrangement as one in which they met regularly to work together and test ideas. It meant that independent country operations didn't have to solve problems alone or with the help – or, in some instances, what they saw as the interference, mismanagement or misunderstanding – of the Australian head office.

The Northern Lights primarily worked because the FCL model was identical internationally, and the problems and opportunities in each of the geographical areas, despite their vast distances apart, were similar. The uniform nature of the model also meant that corporate travel leaders, brand leaders and IT leaders, among others, could form their own global villages in which to apply their combined expertise to problems and opportunities.

The Northern Lights village has contributed to faster and better trialling of new ideas within FCL. Under the global village arrangement, one of the Northern Lights countries could try something, get it to work, systemise it and then roll it out to the other markets. It is the system that Jim Collins in *Great by Choice* described as 'firing bullets, then cannonballs'.[89] According to Collins, a bullet is a low-cost, low-risk and low-distraction experiment, and successful companies fired numerous bullets to test what actually worked. Only when they had empirical evidence did they concentrate their resources and replace the bullet that hit its mark with a cannonball, securing large returns from a weighted bet. FCL admitted it had been guilty in the past of firing off cannonballs when they really should have been bullets – among the more costly impulsive cannonball shots were the RewardPass and flightcentre.com call centre howlers. While adopting Collins' bullet and cannonball concept, FCL has also added an extra metaphoric shot to the armoury courtesy of Google innovator Alberto Savoia. After hearing Savoia speak at Google's San Francisco headquarters in early 2013, the FCL Taskforce added a precursor to the bullet. Savoia introduced the term 'pretotype' or 'pretendotype' to the innovation vocabulary. He convinced the FCL Taskforce that the step before the bullet was actually to pretend to implement an idea before firing a test shot to determine its buy-in or success.

Despite all the light munitions options, Northern Lights member Canada began calibrating a cannonball on behalf of the village in 2012. Headquartered in Vancouver, Flight Centre Canada has 215 shops and businesses throughout British Columbia, Alberta, Ontario and Nova Scotia. After five years trialling the idea, or bullet, the company was preparing to move into Quebec, Canada's second largest and second most populated province. Quebec is predominantly French speaking. To protect its language and unique culture, Quebec's laws require that every facet of business, from a company's name to its interaction with customers and employees, be conducted in both French and English. Signs, posters, brochures, publications, order forms and invoices all have to be produced in French, according to Quebec's Charter of the French Language. For FCL, Quebec would be its first non-English speaking operation in the world, as despite having outposts in countries such as China and India, FCL businesses there predominantly targeted the English speaking corporate and expat markets. This was different and had enormous ramifications. 'It is a bit of a big deal,' said Flight Centre Canada president Greg Dixon. It opens up enormous opportunities for Flight Centre around the globe, including the massive South American market. For the Northern Lighters – especially the UK, with its proximity to non-anglophone Europe – a great deal of interest has been trained on village member Dixon and his Quebec cannonball.

Another bullet that hit its mark was originally fired in London in 2008: the FCL hyperstore. Having trialled and tweaked the prototype in the UK, from 2012 FCL planned to completely open the gunnels, roll out the cannons and rain hyperstore cannonballs on Madison Avenue in New York and Hay Street Mall in Perth, as well as three more locations in the UK.

The hyperstore might not look or sound like the conventional FCL set up, which is traditionally based on small teams. Yet the stores did fit the model, and had the added bonus of being situated in prime locations. The hyperstore was essentially a complete village in one location. It fit with the village model because different FCL businesses, in teams of no more than seven people, operated in the one store, which was overseen by a general manager or village elder who also ran their own team. To cover the hyperstores' extended hours of operation, which in the UK meant 7.30 am to 10 pm seven days a week, teams would also 'hot desk'. This meant even more teams working out of the one location in different businesses and at different times.

The hyperstore stretched some of the fundamental tenets of the Family, Village, Tribe doctrine, but it worked. However, it was not the only variation to put central principles of the model to the test and present a potential new phase in the FCL tribal evolution.

Around lunchtime on 22 February 2011, a magnitude 6.3 earthquake struck Christchurch in New Zealand's south. The quake hit just 10 kilometres south-east of the crowded Christchurch CBD and 2 kilometres west of the suburban town of Lyttelton. Already weakened by a 7.1 magnitude quake five months earlier, Christchurch buckled. Buildings crumbled, cars and buses were squashed by debris, and people were trapped amid ruins and chaos.

A total of 185 people died in the February quake. No FCL people in New Zealand were killed, but one group that had been on a training session in the Holiday Inn Avon hotel in Christchurch narrowly escaped, scrambling out onto the street over the rubble of the ground floor, which had collapsed. Of the 75 FCL staff members in Christchurch, 26 lost their homes. Many lost friends and family. Before the earthquake, FCL had seventeen stores in Christchurch. In the space of ten minutes on 22 February, that number was cut to eight. The shops were razed or so badly damaged that they were 'red-stickered' as being unsafe to enter.

Aftershocks continued to rattle Christchurch, including more than 360 in the week following the February quake. Four months later, two giants hit again. One tremor measuring 5.7 and another an hour later of 6.3 collapsed more buildings, cut power and injured dozens more people. Then another series of large shocks rocked the stricken city just two days before Christmas, injuring at least another 60 people. The city of Christchurch and its people, many of whom anecdotally sleep with their glasses and shoes on in readiness for another tremor strike, have done their best ever since to recover.

Mike Friend started as Flight Centre Limited's New Zealand leader on 1 March 2011 – a week after the second deadliest natural disaster in the country's history. On his arrival in New Zealand, Friend flew straight to Christchurch. He went to area leader Kim Grafton's house. Every staff member was called in and assured they still had a job if they wanted one. They were asked if they wanted to stay or leave. FCL paid the relocation costs of those who departed Christchurch for jobs elsewhere in the network. People went to Auckland, Wanaka, Wellington and Nelson in New Zealand, as well as Brisbane, Melbourne, Sydney and Perth in Australia. Most stayed. They stayed to pick up their lives and look to a future in Christchurch.

Friend determined it was important to open new shops as quickly as possible. FCL opened a number of shops, including one in the eastern Christchurch suburb of Ferrymead in April 2011. It was open ten days before another tremor shut it down. It has been closed ever since. Other shops sustained damage as new tremors stuck. One of the city's most profitable shops, in Papanui's Northlands Centre, had three new ceilings in sixteen months.

With just nine shops and limited prospects of opening more, Friend was forced to make a decision under the uniquely trying circumstances of running a growth business in the wreckage of a natural disaster. And so he challenged the growth and family-size basics of the Flight Centre model. The result has been the first real test of Flight Centre's unbending Rule of Seven. Each of the shops in Christchurch took on eight or nine people. 'I guaranteed I would find them a job. Those that wanted to stay in Christchurch, I had to put them somewhere,' Friend said.

It has proved a conundrum for FCL. In the latter half of the 2011/12 financial year, the nine shops operating in Christchurch recorded higher turnover per month than the seventeen stores in the city combined before the quake. The nine Christchurch shops, plus Nelson, Blenheim, Ashburton and the South Island's West Coast, made $1 million front-end profit. 'There's never been an area making one million in front-end profit in New Zealand's history,' said Friend. 'And they've done it. It's absolutely extraordinary.'

The challenge to the model was not only in the results produced with the rule-breaking number of people in each family. With a similar number of people as before the quake working in half the number of shops, the Christchurch success story was in utter contrast to FCL's mandated requirement of growth by opening new stores. With extended trading hours and lower costs due to fewer shops and less rental outgoings all contributing to better results, the structure fundamentally challenged the company status quo.

Still, the Christchurch experience has not been a conclusive blow to the model. Friend said the challenge remained to determine whether the Christchurch variation would work elsewhere in New Zealand, or if the results were an anomaly thrown up in the most extraordinary of circumstances. 'But it's not that they had the earthquake happen, lost so much money, then got back to normal. It's that they've had the highest front-end profit ever in New Zealand,' he said.

However, New Zealand failed to reach the sales volume targets for the year that earn FCL the higher return in its agreements with its suppliers. Because the eight months following the quake recorded such sluggish sales, FCL NZ was shy of the turnover growth the big back-end commission results ride on. The result begged the question whether carving out the extra shops from Christchurch was the reason FCL NZ did not hit the targets, or whether it was the slump in sales due to the earthquake disaster. Still, the turnover with just nine stores in 2012/13 was on track to significantly exceed that of the pre-earthquake seventeen Christchurch stores, meaning there could well be merit to the tweak of the model in Christchurch. One ingredient in the Christchurch story, however, has not been in dispute: the value of the village and area leaders. 'It has been Kim Grafton's leadership that has been remarkable,' said Friend.

Chapter 19

THE FUTURE, FOR THOSE WHO PLAN FOR IT TODAY

In 1988 we were trying to get into shopping centres. We produced an eight-page shitty colour brochure saying how big we were to be in 1995. We then had fifty shops and said by 1995 we would have one hundred. Outrageous. We didn't really believe it. I am sure shopping centres didn't either. But it still got us shops. By 1995 we had two hundred.

Extract from the 'Global FCL Story 2012–2017', outlining why the company believes it will achieve its next-phase expansion plans

Flight Centre, and in particular Turner, likes to tell stories of its past and where it is going. Just like its history, the story of the company's future – what it will look like, what it will sell, how big it will be and how much profit it will make over the next five years – is not your typical corporate plan. Challenges that were unthinkable in the travel agency industry when Flight Centre started – many of them inconceivable just a few years ago – are central to Flight Centre Limited's push to the future. While the company's brand and geographical diversity may have buffered it from impacts in any one sector or country, it has also made FCL vulnerable to shocks or crises anywhere in the world.

In every modern industry, incidents in any part of the world can have potentially far-reaching effects. A volcano in Iceland, the mysterious murder of a Russian spy, a military coup in Fiji, swine flu outbreaks in Mexico, a nuclear crisis in Japan – all have drastic and potentially costly financial and personal ramifications within the global marketplace. Perhaps few commercial concerns feel the impacts of such incidents more sharply than the global travel industry.

New York has always been a particular passion for Turner. Everyone knows that if you can make it there, you can make it anywhere. Liberty, having prevailed over all the impediments to its revitalisation from 2008, was making real headway by 2012. The US was FCL's second largest market, with a turnover of $1.7 billion and $9.9 million annual profit. In October that year, the company celebrated the 'triumph of Times Square' with the opening of its flagship hyperstore, the New York Travel Centre, on Madison Avenue. Then Sandy struck. On Monday 29 October 2012, Hurricane Sandy savaged the Atlantic Seaboard, flattening entire neighbourhoods in New York and New Jersey. As the superstorm swept through the city, FCL's Liberty operation was among the thousands of businesses smashed. Stores were closed and people were devastated by personal and property loss. The wreckage wrought by Sandy was brutal and unforgiving, with the damage bill estimated at more than US$42 billion.[90]

The morning after the storm, only 27 of Liberty's 170 businesses were operating with staff on location. But by midday, as damage was assessed and power could be fed to stores, that number had more than doubled to 64. By 4 pm, 100 businesses were back operating – including the new Manhattan hyperstore. Due to the small, local team strategy, just 20 per cent of the GoGo operation was impacted by the storm. In a remarkable recovery from yet another disaster for the business, Liberty's October commission figures were only a few thousand dollars short of the same month the previous year. Of course, the storm not only impacted US operations: it struck the entire global company. Thousands of corporate and leisure customers flying to or from the US required extra assistance from FCL as Sandy drove her devastation towards the US coast. In the UK, consultants worked frantically to alter the plans of thousands of customers travelling to their second largest market.

This increased international interconnectedness has forced changes to the company in regards to its crisis preparedness, its 24-hour helpline capabilities and its engagement in communities affected by disaster. Since the September 11 terrorist attacks in 2001,

Flight Centre business has been struck by devastating events including the 2002 and 2005 Bali bombings, the 2004 Boxing Day tsunami, the 2005 London bombings, the 2006 coups in Fiji and Thailand, the 2008 and 2011 Mumbai attacks, the 2010 volcanic eruption in Iceland, the 2010/11 Queensland floods, the 2011 Christchurch earthquake, the 2011 Japanese earthquake and tsunami, and Hurricane Sandy in 2012.

It was the 2004 Boxing Day tsunami that forced FCL to establish a consistent and efficient system for identifying and managing crises. The disaster, which killed around 200,000 people in countries bordering the Indian Ocean, was an event that grew in magnitude with each new day. It affected FCL people. It affected hundreds of thousands of travelling customers. It crushed suppliers and business. Twelve Flight Centre Australia customers died. It was a wake up call for the company. It showed that as a global operation, more than ever before and wherever a natural disaster, act of terror, airline crash, supplier collapse, financial risk crisis or military action occurred, Flight Centre Limited – its own people and its customers – could become part of the crisis itself.

Beyond natural disasters, the crises affecting the travel industry have become increasingly varied. 'It used to be that when people travelled they were worried about losing their property or getting sick,' said FCL retail product leader Sue Henderson. 'Now we can't even imagine what to worry about.'

FCL customers were even caught up in the mysterious assassination of Alexander Litvinenko, the former Russian spy who defected to Britain. The Kremlin antagonist's death by radiation poisoning in 2006 sparked worldwide coverage for its sinister spy thriller storyline and the mysterious method by which the agent was poisoned. Following Litvinenko's death, traces of a radioactive substance were found on two British Airways planes at Heathrow Airport. FCL had to contact all of its passengers who had been aboard the planes on European flights to ensure they got tested for radiation.

On 15 April 2010, UK airspace was closed because an ash cloud from a volcanic eruption in Iceland had spread at high altitude across northern and central Europe. It triggered the biggest aviation shut down in Europe since World War II and sent the global travel industry into a spin.

When Qantas CEO Alan Joyce grounded the carrier's entire domestic and international fleet due to ongoing industrial disputes on 29 October 2011, it disrupted the travel plans of around 68,000 passengers. A total of 447 Qantas flights were cancelled worldwide during the grounding. Flight Centre's corporate arm, FCm Travel Solutions, alone had to provide assistance to about 10,000 travellers.

The regularity and range of external crises with the potential to affect FCL business has prompted a new policy for the company. Under chairman Peter Morahan, the board determined that cash holdings were needed as a 'war chest' to protect the business from the increasingly frequent disasters that were part and parcel of the new global travel industry. The company's cash reserve level was set at three months trading. In 2012, FCL held cash and investments of $1.1 billion, with $400 million in general cash. Debt was $107 million.

Improbably, one of the biggest challenges to the future of Flight Centre Limited comes from what Turner tagged the 'good parts of the global financial crisis'. Australia's consumer watchdog, the Australian Competition and Consumer Commission (ACCC), which forced FCL to change its 'Lowest Airfares Guaranteed' slogan to 'Price Beat Guarantee' and later 'Fly Free' in 2005, pursued the company again in 2012. Unlike previous run-ins with the regulator, however, this time Flight Centre struggled to play the role of people's champion taking on the establishment. The case has had far uglier implications for the company. This time, the ACCC accused FCL of price-fixing.

The ACCC suit potentially leaves FCL open to significant penalties and a hit to its reputation, but more significantly it is a test case for the entire travel industry. It is a case that could challenge the nature and status of the agency relationship between travel agents and airlines. It could have ramifications for online retailers in other industries, indeed any situation where a wholesaler or supplier chooses to sell directly, through the internet or otherwise, as well as through a distribution network or agent. The ACCC has described its action against FCL as a priority area. ACCC chairman Rod Sims told the 2012 Competition Law Conference on 5 May that the digital and online economy posed the 'biggest regulatory challenge in a generation'. 'Online technology is revolutionising competitive dynamics. We will do all we can to prevent incumbents misusing their market power against the many new competitors that will emerge,' he said.

The ACCC instituted proceedings in the Federal Court against Flight Centre Limited on 9 March 2012, with hearings held over six days in Brisbane in October. The ACCC alleged that on six occasions between 2005 and 2009, Flight Centre attempted to induce Singapore Airlines, Malaysia Airlines and Emirates to stop directly offering and booking their own international airfares over the internet at prices less than Flight Centre was able to offer. It told the court that Flight Centre attempted to maintain the level of its commissions by stopping the airlines selling the tickets more cheaply.

In reply, FCL branded the ACCC action as 'seeking to take the price-fixing provisions of the legislation to absurd lengths because of naive, uncommercial and incorrect assumptions'. According to Flight Centre, all it did was ask the airlines for access to the same fares they were selling directly on the internet, so that FCL could sell them too.

The case has its roots in the global financial crisis. Turner saw an opportunity for FCL during the economic meltdown, when airlines were in increased need of travel agents and 'any business we can give them'. He said Flight Centre's services, such as promoting an airline's fares through FCL's $80-million annual marketing and advertising spend, generating enquiries and selling tickets through thousands of street-front shops around the world, and acting as the point of call for passengers during a travel interruption, was all the more valuable in the depressed market. In short, FCL considered the global financial crisis to have given it increased bargaining might in renegotiating total contract margin.

What FCL wanted – and was prepared to use its muscle to achieve

– was to move away from the increasingly difficult targets that earned it the more lucrative back-end commissions in favour of more guaranteed revenue at point of sale. It also wanted to take a stick to the practice by some airlines of selling flights direct on the internet at cheaper prices than Flight Centre had access to. The economic crisis didn't cause Flight Centre to take action on these festering disputes, rather it provided it with the opportunity to play hardball with the airlines in question. It was this prospect that Turner relished as the 'good part' of the terrible economic times.

When Flight Centre Limited's preferred agreement with Singapore Airlines expired on 31 March 2009, FCL made its move. FCL said it primarily wanted an acceptable total contract earn under the preferred agreement and, in addition, wanted Flight Centre consultants to have access to the same fares Singapore Airlines offered on the internet or elsewhere, so that its consultants could sell them to customers. Getting access to the same fares meant protecting consultants from the awkward scenario of selling a Singapore Airlines fare to a customer, only to have the customer find the same ticket cheaper online. The outcome was not only loss of face: the price beat guarantee at the time meant Flight Centre had to beat the cheaper price by a dollar and give the customer a twenty-dollar voucher. To Flight Centre it was an untenable business structure, whereby a supplier wanted to compete at their wholesale price, but expected the retailer to continue selling.

Turner became involved in the negotiations and on 12 May 2009, six weeks after the agreement expired, emailed Singapore Airlines regional vice-president (South West Pacific Region) Subhas Menon to arrange a lunch 'to either stitch up a mutually [sic] agreed arrangement or to go our separate ways'. Turner wanted a 'commitment' from the airline on its total contract margin. He also didn't want the airline to 'undercut' FCL on the internet. He told the airline there could be 'consequences'.

Over the ensuing lunch in the stylish E'cco Bistro in Brisbane, Menon and Singapore Airlines Australia marketing manager Dale Woodhouse met with Turner, Melanie Waters-Ryan and FCL global air leader Greg Parker. Despite the benign surrounds, discussions at the table turned heated. The following day Turner fired off another email to Menon, which began a chain of correspondence that ultimately resulted in the failure of the parties to reach an agreement for 2009/10.

FCL had threatened consequences, so it delivered. In late May, Flight Centre Limited imposed a 'Turn the Screw on SQ' campaign to stop-sell the airline. (Singapore Airlines' international airline code is SQ.) After six weeks of the stop-sell, FCL said their sales of Singapore Airlines tickets were down about 70 per cent. Even though Singapore Airlines slashed fares and went into overdrive on direct sales, FCL said the airline's market share on flights out of Australia in May 2009 was significantly reduced.

A deal did follow for 2010/11. Effective from 1 April 2010, Singapore returned as a FCL preferred airline and Flight Centre obtained the margin it considered fair for the sale of Singapore Airline fares, as well as access to all of the airline's fares.

The ACCC's radar picked up on the dispute. It claimed Flight Centre tried to persuade Singapore Airlines – and on other occasions Malaysian Airlines and Emirates – to stop selling their international airfares directly to customers, including over the internet, at prices lower than Flight Centre could offer. It said Flight Centre threatened the stop-sell action that it ultimately carried out against Singapore Airlines because the airline wouldn't stop selling the cheaper seats. The ACCC told the court that Flight Centre attempted to induce the airlines to adopt prices that would allow FCL to maintain its commission on the flights. Flight Centre maintained in court that its primary aim was to negotiate an acceptable total contract margin and that it didn't ask the airlines to raise their fares, it just wanted its consultants to have access to the same fares that the airlines were offering so it could sell them to its customers. The Federal Court of Australia judgment is expected in 2013.

Another significant battle also came to a head in late 2012: one in which the Australian Federation of Travel Agents (AFTA), including Flight Centre Limited, scored a legislative win. The Australian Government had been considering abolishing the Travel Compensation Fund (TCF), which has been an irritation to Flight Centre ever since it almost cost FCL its licence in the '80s. Back then, AFTA was right behind licensing and the TCF. But now the worm had turned, with the CEO of AFTA, Jason Westbury, aided and abetted by FC's David Smith, leading the fight for its disintegration. According to AFTA, the TCF was too costly, was no longer relevant, its coverage was selective and it created too much red tape.

The Travel Compensation Fund reimbursed consumers if a licensed travel agent became insolvent or failed to pay for travel after taking consumers' money. But the latest independent review of the scheme found the TCF was 'unduly burdensome'.[91] It found the cost of the travel agents regulatory scheme – including licensing and the TCF – was $25.3 million a year, compared to the average annual payout to consumers of $2.9 million. In other words, it cost almost nine times more to run the scheme than the value of consumer funds lost. The review found there wasn't much risk for consumers anyway, because the industry had changed, making the scheme no longer 'fit for purpose'. Significantly, it said there were few consumer protection issues with travel agencies, but there were numerous issues with the air travel industry. The main problem was airlines going broke, such as Air Australia, Air Paradise and Ansett, but there were also ongoing issues with cancellations, delays and service quality. The review urged the government to look at measures to address these issues instead.

The Travel Compensation Fund had set FCL back more than $600,000 in contributions a year. It had directly cost the company more than $12 million in fees alone since it was introduced. Some might argue that the TCF had actually benefitted FCL, because its fees and compliance requirements may have kept some potential players out of the industry. 'But that never meant we were happy to have it,' Turner said.

The TCF's biggest failure, said Turner, was that the scheme was ineffective when the most significant events occurred. For example, when Air Australia collapsed in 2012, leaving thousands of Australian passengers without a flight in or out of the country, the TCF was unable to assist those affected because it only compensated people when a travel agency folded, not when customers bought direct from an airline or supplier. 'We pay all the costs, then if someone goes broke we still have to take the hit because the customers don't get the service.'

In December 2012, the Australian Government announced that the TCF is to be phased out by 2015.

The potential removal of some niggling burrs under the saddle has helped invigorate FCL's next-phase planning and its story for the five years to 2017.

Sitting by the pool on holiday in Miami in early 2012, Chris Galanty was consumed with future planning. The managing director of Flight Centre UK was tossing up growth targets for the UK operation's next five years. He had a vision to take the UK from its 2012 turnover of £750 million to a £1.5 billion company.

As he added up the different brands, the figure kept coming in under £1.5 billion. 'My initial thought was that I had to bump up some of these figures. But the number it came to was 1492. That's obviously the year Columbus discovered the New World,' said the university history major. It was the story Galanty needed. He set a course and Flight Centre embarked upon '1492 the New World'. In the New World plan, the UK business would turn over £1.492 billion and record a profit of £43 million by 2017.

In 2013, Flight Centre Limited was already sitting at a high-water mark. It recorded the best sales and profit results in the company's history. All ten countries were profitable for the second consecutive year. Australia, the USA, the UK, Singapore, Greater China and Dubai had achieved record results. Global turnover had reached

$13.2 billion – a figure that has more than tripled since 2002 – and the company exceeded the magic $200 million profit benchmark.

The FCL story to 2017 aims for more than $20 billion in sales and to potentially double its profit. It plans to open as many as 900 new businesses, with more than half of them to be located outside Australia. Growth is targeted in all markets, but overseas businesses and non-travel businesses are expected to make larger contributions.

The forward plan		
FCL projected company results 2012 to 2017		
Year	**Turnover**	**Businesses**
2012	$13.2b	2400
2013	$14.52b	2640
2014	$15.972b	2904
2015	$17.569b	3194
2016	$19.326b	3514
2017	$21.259b	3865

Such growth depends on the company's enduring model, culture and philosophies, which have driven its success so far. But to be a major player in the modern global travel industry, the company has recognised it needs to make changes. The first phase of its future story involves making these revisions and improvements – building the ships to take on the challenges ahead and set sail on the journey to far horizons. Areas from the fundamental sales process, the tools equipping consultants to do their jobs, the alignment of the company's multitude of brands, and its plan to overcome the great challenge of the internet are all on the slipway.

At its most basic level, Flight Centre Limited is built on the transaction between the customer and the consultant. The customer experience during the sales process ultimately determines the brand's success. The company updated its second philosophy to reflect that no matter how many shops or businesses it opened, its customers

would always have other options for purchasing travel. It now
reads:

> We recognise that our customers always have a choice. Therefore, a
> superior customer service experience, provided with honesty,
> integrity and a great attitude, is key to our company's success, as is
> the travel experience we provide.

FCL Australia managing director Melanie Waters-Ryan said the
quality of the company's customer service had been compromised due
to lack of discipline and allowing consultants too much discretion.
A shocking 10,000 to 12,000 email enquiries to Flight Centre's retail
brand went unanswered each month in Australian alone. In 2011, the
company began a research project to assess the quality of customer
service by recording live calls between consultants and customers. 'We
were a bit horrified listening to them,' Waters-Ryan said. It led to
2012 being named 'Year of the Customer'. 'It had become possibly
more about our own people,' said 28-year FCL veteran Aileen
Bratton. 'We do need to acknowledge our people and look after them,
but if we don't have customers we don't have a business.'

   As part of the 'Year of the Customer', Flight Centre established the
Global Sales Academy (GSA) to train consultants and institute
the One Best Way sales process across the business. UK boss Galanty
approached Emma Anderson to come up with a blueprint for the
GSA model and establish it as a business within FCL. She showed him
a customer service grading system using a measure called the Granny
Factor – a score out of 100 based on a seven-step process and evaluation of the ultimate experience if the customer were the consultant's
grandmother. This measurement tool and its accountability process
would ensure a good, consistent customer experience, and was something that Galanty could present to the board and senior management. Skroo, not realising that it was a tool that was driven by the
business leaders, said it was the 'worst idea he'd ever heard', but gave
the UK GSA team three months to prove him wrong. Anderson went
on to gather the evidence and prove that a higher Granny Factor
equalled increased sales. The first area to institute the complete GSA

program, the UK's 'Beautiful South', was the company's Most Improved Retail Area in the UK and among the Most Improved Areas Globally in 2012. The GSA has since been set up in the USA, South Africa, Australia and Canada, and is soon to be introduced in New Zealand.

GSA and the Granny Factor

- The GSA is the expert provider of training, audits and discipline on the One Best Way for the Flight Centre brand sales process
- Area leaders work closely with the GSA to ensure their consultants are following the process
- It is a fully commercialised relationship, whereby the area leader pays the GSA to help drive the consistency of their customer experience
- The GSA records live calls between customers and consultants
- The GSA grades the calls according to a 1–100 measurement called the Granny Factor
- Area leaders and consultants also listen and grade the calls
- The GSA reports on the number of calls, Granny Factor ratings and section reporting
- The GSA monitors daily figures and communicates updates of Granny Factor and sales correlation
- The GSA runs sales skills workshops and coaching visits for all consultants to improve their sales techniques
- Granny Factor KPI is 75 per cent.

Of course, even with improved customer service measures and discipline, not all Flight Centre customers have the perfect experience. Turner is well aware of this. He is renowned for generating new ideas based on one person's feedback, so he thought fielding customer calls was a great way to tap into customer service. Turner's personal email and phone number were intermittently published on the FCL website under Complaints. 'It's a very gutsy move by a CEO. Not many would do that,' said global marketing chief Colin Bowman. Of the direct complaints Turner received daily in late 2012, grievances included everything from refund requests to FCL consultants not following up with customers who had requested more information. Not all complaints turn out to be Flight Centre Limited's fault. Turner wryly detailed the time he spent pursuing a refund for a disgruntled customer who had to cancel his flight because he had a knee operation, only to find the customer didn't book with Flight Centre at all. He'd booked with an airline direct.

Turner said the tools of Flight Centre's retail model had been the 'biggest single point of failure' in the system. 'Our consultants just about have to be brain surgeons,' he said. As well as dealing with numerous systems and processes, which were often slow and cumbersome, Flight Centre consultants were up against increased competition from online bookings and more informed customers. 'It's a much tougher environment now,' said Aileen Bratton. 'When we first started we were trailblazers, because we were the first people who did discount, we were airfare savvy: that was our field of expertise. Now everyone's got all the information at their fingertips.'

It is not only a tougher environment in which to trade on expertise, but also to make the kind of profit that was once available. One of the dominant challenges for Flight Centre Limited has been to make the retail shop more profitable. While costs including wages and rents have gone up, commission has not grown to the same extent. 'We're approaching a crucial point. The only way to make money is to make more sales per individual at the shop level,' said CFO Andrew Flannery.

To address the problem, Flight Centre retail has undergone a reinvention. A project called 'The Big Easy' was introduced in 2012 to provide FCL consultants around the world with new booking systems aimed at making their jobs quicker, easier and more effective. The Big Easy also prepared consultants for a major development in Flight Centre's retail model – one it hopes will be a beacon for future growth of the brand. In the new age of travel shopping, FCL has overhauled its old 'clicks and mortar' strategy to carve out an industry world-first category called 'the Blended Travel Agent'.

As a traditional bricks and mortar agency, FCL backed up its shops and consultants with the company's websites. The FCL websites, including flightcentre.com.au, with its increased transactional capabilities allowing customers to book and pay for international flights, are equally backed up by the shops and their more than 12,000 staff. The interplay between FCL's offline and online service is the key to the blended model. It is also the key to servicing the new shopper profile that has emerged internationally and, more recently, in Australia – the omnichannel shopper.[92] Studies of the phenomenon describe the omnichannel shopper as equally comfortable researching and shopping on the internet as they are in a store. Instead of reading or watching advertisements locally, they will scan the internet to 'comparison shop' and check peer recommendations on social media networks, even while they are in-store. Omnishopper behaviour differs from traditional shopper traits in that they keep their purchase options open right up to point of sale, rather than deciding where to purchase early on. They will browse and purchase whenever is convenient to them, rather than being restricted by the opening hours of a store, and will find the product that best suits their needs globally or locally rather than being confined by what is available in a physical store.

Under Flight Centre's blended travel agency model, customers, including omnishoppers, have instant access to all FCL services, 24 hours a day. Customers have the benefit of a consultant to help them find and book travel, as well as look after them if something goes wrong. Customers are able to blend the way they shop for travel, such as discussing travel plans with a consultant in a shop, over the phone or online, then booking and paying online at home. Waters-Ryan said the model aimed to give customers increased access and convenience without losing any of the Flight Centre service and support, in much the same way that UK department store giant John Lewis has become a pioneer of omnichannel retail without losing the customer service or quality for which it is renowned. The John Lewis example utilised three key strategies to show how a retail business could integrate the online and in-store experience. Primarily, to ensure the online store did not cannibalise bricks and mortar sales, physical stores were rewarded for online sales made in their physical trade area. This tactic ensured that channels were collaborating, not competing. Secondly, the customer was made to feel as though online or in-store was part of the same shopping experience, by being able to order online and pick up at a store of their choice, or order in-store and have the product delivered to their home. Finally, the company brought the online experience in-store, by enabling consultants to help shoppers with their online purchases or research on the company's website. The results show the omnichannel shopper has become John Lewis's most valuable customer, spending 3.5 times more on average than the customer who shops exclusively in-store or online.[93] It is this blended shopping experience that Flight Centre has sought to create. 'There's an opportunity if we can capture it, but more than capture it, if we can systemise it,' said Waters-Ryan. 'The blended travel agency model could fuel the company for the next ten years.'

It's a big step, or perhaps a compromise, for Turner, who has always refused to see the internet as a threat. He remains committed to FCL's strength being its vast number of shops and sprawling geographical footprint. While Turner was written off as a 'Neanderthal' and incapable of change some years ago, when he was a lone voice arguing that the internet would not destroy his shops, he now has tangible proof. He has empirical data to support his case, as well as Flight Centre's new blended direction. For many years, Australian retailers have seen the decision to trade online as an alternative to trading in a physical store. The story has been considerably different overseas, where traditional retailers have embraced online trading as well. In the UK, for example, traditional bricks and mortar operators dominate the list of top online retailers. High street chains Tesco, Next, Debenhams, John Lewis, Currys, Topshop and B+Q all made the February 2012 MRG Experian Hitwise Hot Shops list of top twenty online retailers, with six of them featuring in the top ten. In the USA, traditional bricks and mortar retailers also dominate the list of top online retailers. The Internet Retailers 2012 Top 500 list included Staples, Apple, Wal-Mart, Office Depot, Sears and CDW in its top ten.

Turner is convinced the blended model could create a world-beating travel agency that would surpass all single-platform agencies in the market. 'We've got to make sure that the things that the internet's good at — it's twenty-four seven, it's relatively simple and easy — we've got to be good at as well,' he said. 'But you still only get information from the internet, you don't get advice.'

The Blended Flight Centre

By incorporating the blended travel agency model, the updated technology and booking systems for consultants, and fine-tuning elements such as incentives and villages in the model, the SMaC recipe for the Flight Centre brand from 2013 looks like this:

Hedgehog: Flight Centre has expertise in all types of airfares. We specialise in both simple and complex airfares, as well as creating unique fares that cannot be found online. Our people are available 24/7 through a variety of channels. We blend the convenience of the internet with the passion of our people to create a unique travel shopping experience that consistently yields a front-end margin of more than 10 per cent. Volume growth of at least 10 per cent every year ensures that our suppliers and partners consistently give us the best override returns in the market.

1. Our travel consultants

Airfare experts. We hire for talent, passion for travel and sales potential because our systems make it easy for our consultants to book travel that matches our customers' needs. Our consultants are regularly upskilled to ensure that they are the most knowledgeable travel experts in the industry.

2. Airfare geniuses and land gurus

Ensure our consultants give our customers the best-suited and best value airfares and holidays. Upskill our consultants.

3. Airfare and product databases

A comprehensive and unbeatable airfare database.

4. 24 hours a day, 7 days a week, 365 days a year

Our business is always open. Customers can choose to communicate with a consultant in store or via phone or email at any time.

5. Our blended model

Our offline strengths are fully blended with the latest online capability. Every customer, whether they book offline or online or a mixture of both, is linked to a consultant.

6. Reward and recognition

Consultants are remunerated for producing the right outcome. The results of our people are recognised and celebrated through vehicles of inspiration such as newsletters, Buzz Nights, balls and global gatherings.

7. Structure

The FCB structure is simple, lean, flat and transparent, with accessible leaders. We work in teams of up to seven people in a shop. Four to seven teams work in a village with a village leader and 20 to 25 teams work in an area that is run by an area leader. Area leaders work with experts in sales, finance, recruitment, training, systems, airfares, product and leadership, to ensure that they achieve a minimum growth of 10 per cent every year.

8. FCB iconic captain and guarantee

FCB has our famous captain as our brand icon. Everyone in the brand proudly honours our longstanding 'Lowest Airfare Guarantee'. 'The Airfare Experts' is our slogan.

9. The FCB growth model

Growth is crucial year on year in turnover for front- and back-end profit (minimum 10 per cent in mature markets and 15 to 20 per cent in non-mature markets).

Flight Centre's future is also about diversity. In February 2012 the company was restructured – again – into an alignment of the 36 brands in the FCL stable, rather than a purely geographic structure. Niche brands such as Australia's Escape Travel, Student Flights, Cruiseabout, Intrepid Retail/My Adventure Store and Travel Money Oz, and the premium retail brand Travel Associates – the top FCL retail brand in the world in terms of front-end profit – became its own division, which was separate to 'the beast' of Flight Centre. Aimed at forcing the niche brands to stand on their own two feet, it was also to stop the dilution of the flagship Flight Centre brand. 'Skroo likes to throw chaos into our world,' said Australian niche brand leader Joell Ogilvie. 'But it also makes sense.' Niche brands were not airfare specialists. They demanded their own unique skills and culture. The logistical skills needed to helicopter a global pop star to an alternate five-star hotel at a moment's notice – an example dealt with by sport and entertainment industry travel provider Stage and Screen – were not necessarily the same skills required at Campus Travel to transport academics on a fact-finding tour.

Flight Centre Brands

As at December 2012, Flight Centre had 36 brands across leisure, corporate, wholesale, procurement and other businesses:

Retail:
Flight Centre (including First and Business, and Flight Centre Business Travel)
Flight Shop (India only)
Escape Travel
Student Flights
Travel Associates
Round the World Experts
Cruiseabout
Intrepid Retail/My Adventure Store
Liberty Travel
Gap Year Travel

Corporate:
Corporate Traveller
FCm Travel Solutions
Stage and Screen
Ci Events
Campus Travel

Wholesale and procurement:
Infinity Holidays
Explore Holidays
Escape Holidays
GoGo Vacations
Ticket Centre
Flight Centre Global Product

Online:
Flightcentre.com (USA transactional)
Flightcentre.com (non-Flight Centre retail nations)
Quickbeds.com
Discountcruises.com
Travelthere.com.au

Services:
Employment Office
Moneywise
Healthwise (and Active Travel)
FC Business School
Recruitment Coach

Travel-related:
Back Roads Touring
Travel Money
Gapyear.com

Bikes:
99 Bikes
Advance Traders

In October 2011, FCL carried out an audit on the consultant to customer experience in its niche brands. Just like the Global Sales Academy phone call recordings, which sent shockwaves through upper management levels, the niche brand results were awful. Two days later, Joell Ogilvie went shopping. She found herself in one of celebrity sleepwear retailer Peter Alexander's stores. Behind the counter was a photograph of Alexander with a woman. When Ogilvie enquired who the woman in the photo was, the sales assistant proudly explained that it was Alexander's mother. The pyjama entrepreneur had been given $500 to set up his business by his mother, who also let him start it in her garage. 'And now look what he's done,' the girl said. It made Ogilvie realise that Flight Centre's niche brands either didn't know or had forgotten where they came from. 'I thought, we have a story but we've lost sight of it. We've lost the knack of telling our story around the fire to our people, so we know where we've come from and can feel proud of it. We have to make sure we all know the story about our crackpot vet.'

As a result, the Brand Warriors program was introduced in January 2012. Initially rolled out across niche brands in Australia, Brand Warriors was designed to ensure consultants across all of the company's brands understood Flight Centre Limited's history, their own brand, how their brand fit into the bigger picture, and the specialist market they were servicing. It was a reinvestment in the company's culture.

Long-time FCL leader Sue Garrett, who has worked across a range of Flight Centre businesses and brands, said the model that Turner had created and the ability of each business to write its own chapter of the story was the key to the company's vitality. 'If I think back after sixteen years with the company, its success is that you do feel you belong to something – your team, your village and your tribe – no matter how big or how different the business gets,' Garrett said. Brand Warriors aimed to instil in the niche brands the basics and fun of the FCL business, even though it had grown so monumentally from driving travellers around in old buses to a multi-billion-dollar travel conglomerate. With Brand Warriors, the story of the company became recognised as an essential recruitment and retainment tool. Student Flights brand warrior Jessica Vestin, who was awarded 2012 Global Top Novice from FCL's Youth and Adventure brands, said she felt part of the story and could see a longer-term career for herself across the company as a result of the program. 'All my friends are now asking me how they can get in,' she said.

With a proliferation of businesses operating in a number of different countries, Flight Centre Limited has taken steps to ensure a degree of global consistency and quality within each brand. To achieve this, it has introduced global brand and business planning systems. The systems aim to create a brand model that can be replicated anywhere in the world. They ensure that everyone from the greenest recruit to the longest-serving leader has a clear understanding of the brand, and that rather than each new business trying to reinvent the wheel, their energies are channelled into a proven model. What is has meant in reality is that FCL has become more and more like a franchisor company, with the regional or geographic brand leaders acting as the master franchise holders of each brand.

Within this inviolable operating system, each brand has a standardised planning process at a country, national, area and shop level. These include a five-year strategic plan for the country, an annual country plan, national brand plans, area plans and six-monthly team plans facilitated by the area leader.

The Brand Book

The Brand Book is integral to the global brand management system and contains a detailed map of the seven elements that each brand must deploy and operate.

Main element:	Broad content details:

1. **The global brand's hedgehog and picture of success**	• The three dimensions of the hedgehog:
	  • What can you be best in the world at (and what can't you be best in the world at)?
	  • What drives your economic engine?
	  • What are you most passionate about?
	• Develop a picture in words of what the brand will look like in one year's time and/or in five years time.

Main element:	Broad content details:
2. The global brand's SMaCs and SMaC recipe	• Essentially the core features of the business model • The processes or elements of the business that have to be specific, methodical and consistent • A SMaC recipe is a set of durable operating practices that create a replicable and consistent success formula; it is clear and concrete, giving clear guidance regarding what to do and what not to do.

3. The global brand's overall marketing systems
  a. The marketplace
  b. Product and pricing
  c. Customer proposition
  d. Advertising plan
	This covers:
	The marketplace:
	• Key customer groups and segmentation.
	Product and pricing:
	• Key product categories and offerings
	• Key global supply (purchasing) and distribution systems (functions and platforms) for those products offline and online
	• Pricing strategy, including yield management and fees and charges structure.
	Unique customer value proposition:
	• The basic premise behind the global brand's existence
	• The global brand's well-defined and persuasive marketing statement that details the reasons why a customer would benefit from purchasing it
	• Is it unique and specific?
	• Indicate how the global brand solves a problem or fulfils a need the customer has.
	Advertising plan:
	• The advertising goals and plans
	• The branding features and benefit
	• The global brand's look and feel, taglines, slogans and unique selling propositions (USPs)
	• Brand positioning
	• National advertising plan global guidelines.

Main element:	Broad content details:
4. The global brand's key operating systems	How this brand operates (makes things happen) in the marketplace:
	The brand's:
	• Operating structure and support roles
	• Expertise systems (including air training and air expert support)
	• Sales system
	• Consulting system (including customer documentation)
	• Financial system
	• Business leadership system – team leader and area leader.
5. The global brand's Peopleworks/HR, people, remuneration models and communications systems	• Who do we select as people for the global brand? What are the criteria?
	• How do we identify, select and recruit the people the global brand needs?
	• The Peopleworks processes and systems
	• Leadership: recruitment, selection and development
	• The global remuneration system (retainers, incentives and business ownership schemes [BOS])
	• Global and national systems for brand communication and planning events.
6. The global brand's global key business drivers (KBDs), goals, strategies and action plans	• What are the global KBDs of the brand? A KBD is something that has a major impact on the performance of your specific business
	• The brand's goals and budgets
	• The global major issues and strategies for the brand.
7. The global brand's one-year and five-year stories.	• A narrative linking the above with the picture of success.

Despite the increasing systemisation, some of Flight Centre's brands still manage to do things a little differently. Services brands have emerged from the commercialisation overhaul of 2004, in which former 'support' areas were forced to adopt the structure, systems and philosophies of the retail businesses. Non-travel businesses, including the Flight Centre Business School that started in 2010, internal staff services such as Healthwise and Moneywise, and the Employment Office recruitment service joint venture that was acquired in 2008, all started as Flight Centre internal services but have since moved to the external market.

Moneywise was the first to go external, when telecommunications company Optus engaged it to provide financial planning services for its employees. The Moneywise client list has grown organically, recording a $1 million profit in 2012. Virgin Australia and Westpac Bank are among numerous high-profile clients using Healthwise to provide health and fitness services for their staff, while the Employment Office recruitment business reaped $2 million profit in its fourth year servicing an external client base. The Flight Centre Business School is one of the most successful examples of a non-travel operation expanding FCL's business base, making $7 million in 2012 through providing accredited vocational training courses in travel, tourism and hospitality. FCL sees the Flight Centre Business School as having the potential to be one of the largest tourism training providers in Australia.

The external businesses that have grown out of Flight Centre are predominantly based on the company's strengths in the personal services field. Flight Centre is not only a market leader in the travel industry, it is also one of the largest recruiters in the country, specialising in training, leadership and business management.

The company's newest support service, Grape Therapy (formerly Boozewise), is also based on one of the company's strong suits. Grape Therapy is an internal business that consolidates the procurement, wholesale and distribution of liquid refreshments for the company's myriad Buzz Nights, after-work drinks and lunch meetings, vertically integrating all stages of the process beyond the actual manufacture of the alcoholic beverages. Unsurprisingly, it has turned into a veritable goldmine.

With its plethora of businesses and technical operations across a wide range of industries, Flight Centre has proven that the Family,

Village, Tribe model is replicable and transferable. One of the company's non-travel businesses, however, is a real test of the FCL way. Bike retailer 99 Bikes, which started as Turner's son Matt's endeavour before he entered a joint venture with Flight Centre Limited, aims to transform the bike sales industry just as Flight Centre did the travel industry 30 years earlier.

It was in conversation around the family dinner table one night that Matt, a physiotherapist, said he thought he might like to open a bike business. A keen triathlete, Matt said the experiences he'd had in bike shops had been pretty average and there was no dominant bike retailer in Australia. He said he thought he could do better and wanted a crack at running a business himself. His dad told the 26-year-old it was about time.

Matt immediately underwent Flight Centre team leader training. It affected him in two ways. The first was that he learned the philosophies, structure and model of the Flight Centre machine. 'I didn't really know anything much about Flight Centre. Dad's always been really good about not talking business at home,' he said. Secondly, he learned about his father. 'I got this depth of understanding that I didn't have before. The principles of the company are how he lives his life. None of it was ever shoved down my throat, but I could see it was all about the way I was brought up – take responsibility, look within for solutions, don't externalise, it's all there in the philosophies.'

But the young bike entrepreneur wanted to do things his own way. The first 99 Bikes shop opened in Brisbane in 2007, growing to three shops a year later. But the business struggled to make profit. 'Our first vision was that we wanted to sell ninety-nine bikes a day within our first year. We were really fired up, but were so naive. We thought we'd create a website and people would just flock to it. That didn't happen.' Matt soon realised that wholesale was the key. It was at this point, in 2008, that 99 Bikes entered a joint venture with Flight Centre Limited, acquired the bike wholesaler Advance Traders and together entered the bike retail and wholesale business.

Matt said he was in no doubt that 99 Bikes was a test case for FCL's non-travel business expansion. From a model that was already very similar to the Flight Centre blueprint, 99 Bikes has been converted to a streamlined FCL cannonball being fired at the $1.2 billion Australian cycle sales market. 'It's what you sign up for when you sign a JV with Flight Centre. They won't want to be involved if you're not looking to be successful in the market.'

99 Bikes operates similarly to Flight Centre's model, with teams of seven or so people, incentives, the opportunity to buy into shops, a live sales leaderboard that includes monthly earnings, and communications structures made up of teams, villages and areas, complete with leaders and elders. The company has adopted similar philosophies and is disciplined about its systems, from sales through to the back-end of the business. 'We are completely embracing it. We do have faith it works – the fact that it comes from Flight Centre does give it a certain amount of credibility,' Matt said.

Matt soon discovered that recruiting the right people was fundamental to the success of both the retail and wholesale business. With the right people and the right leaders, he said, he was confident of achieving the company's strategic plan. In 2012, 99 Bikes opened shops in Sydney and Melbourne, taking the total number of retail shops to eleven, and launched an online presence offering bikes, parts and accessories nationwide. Its wholesaler, Advance Traders Australia, also works with a network of independent retailers throughout the country.

Selecting the right people to drive the business at every level has repeatedly been identified as a challenge for Flight Centre Limited. It is a recurring theme through the experience of Full Throttle and the development of travel, niche and non-travel brands. It was vital during acquired and start-up operations overseas. It has surfaced as the way forward with the company's new focus on village elders and area leaders. It is fundamental to the ubiquitous issue of who will succeed Graham 'Skroo' Turner, which is perhaps the biggest question about the future of Flight Centre Limited.

Global corporate executive general manager Rob Flint said he believed many of the challenges the company had experienced, and was facing into the future were due to the lax, 'she'll-be-right' abdication of responsibility in identifying and promoting future leaders. The company's experience of appointing two chief executives after a less than rigorous recruitment and selection process, merely opting for whomever seemed like a good idea at the time Turner was leaving, might well stand as examples of significant failures in its leadership planning. 'I think that's where we might have lost our way. If you grow your business without leaders, you're going to implode at some stage. We have to take it seriously,' he said.

Chapter 20

IF YOU PLAY TO WIN, THE GAME NEVER ENDS

For Skroo, it's the intellectual challenge of making a business work that is really what it's all about. And doing whatever it takes to make it work. It's his life.

Peter Barrow, FCL director (1995–2012)

odyguards surrounded the group clustered at the base of the ladder. It was a huge night on Singapore's Sentosa Island. About 2000 of Flight Centre Limited's top business performers from around the world had been unleashed on the beach at the annual Global Awards welcome party. Renowned DJ Fatboy Slim prepared to take the stage, elevated high above the wildly partying throngs. Graham Turner had just introduced the headline act, corrected just in time by minder Haydn Long from committing the faux pas of calling the superstar DJ 'Slimboy Fat', and had descended from the stage to the sand. A lone girl came pushing through the ropes and ring of bodyguards, closing in on the British dance music legend, his posse and the Australian pair. 'Did you really think you could get through to Fatboy Slim?' Long asked the despondent girl as she was about to be bundled back to the celebrating crowd. 'Oh no,' she responded. 'I wanted my photo taken with Skroo.'

Turner is the icon of Flight Centre Limited. At Flight Centre company events, he is mobbed like a celebrity pin-up by fans seeking photos and autographs. He is described as a visionary and a mastermind by those with whom he works, in appreciation of his insight, strategic thinking and nous. Some colleagues who call him a friend even get misty-eyed when recalling their favourite anecdotes involving their inscrutable mate, Skroo.

Flight Centre Limited may have changed under his guidance from an industry-revolutionising airfare discounter in 1982 to a $14.2-billion-dollar, globally integrated, blended travel network. The way the business operates may have changed from a knockabout bunch of mates flying by the seats of their pants, cutting corners and making a bit of money, to a highly systemised market leader, a trail-blazer among business organisational models, and a high-growth, high-profit machine. But Turner, by all accounts, has changed little.

He has befuddled many over the seeming contradiction between the culture and character of the company he has created and his own persona. Even those who know him best personally and in business describe him as an enigma. 'We are absolutely built on the premise that it's about people, it's about connection, it's about challenging people and rewarding. He understands it so well, but he doesn't know how to, or want to, do warm and friendly. Yet he's considered by our people as God in our company,' said Joell Ogilvie. He may be the figurehead for all that Flight Centre Limited and its people stand for and believe in in business, but that doesn't mean he's the embodi-ment. 'It happens without him engaging in it, but it is for him – a little bit like the Queen,' said Alissa O'Connell. Marg Mulholland, who has been with Flight Centre since 1982 and was appointed to the FCL board from 1995–98 (still the only woman to have served on the FCL board), said people worked hard for Turner and bought wholeheartedly into his vision. 'He challenges everybody to their absolute core. If you fight it you'll die. If you go with it you can have one of the best experiences of your life. He's crazy mad, but beautiful.'

All of which makes it an elusive ambition to establish what makes Graham Turner, the force behind Flight Centre Limited, tick. On the Myers Briggs Type Indicator (MBTI), which lists sixteen different personality types,[94] Turner scores highest in the categories of introver-sion, intuition, thinking and perception, making him an INTP – one of only 1 per cent of the general population. INTP-types are charac-terised as private, intellectual, impersonal, analytical and reflective. They value ideas, principles and abstract thinking above all else and seek to understand the universe, not control it.

This explains why he appears to see business as one big experi-ment. Like a scientist, Skroo is driven by a need to understand things that are not yet understood. He has an ability to break down the most complex issues into very simple terms. This clarity is the subject of frequent comment by his associates. Talk to him on just about any subject and he will have a viewpoint that will seem so blindingly logical and obvious that people can't believe they didn't think of it themselves. It's not surprising then that the two people he admires most in the world, Nelson Mandela and Warren Buffett, are renowned for the lucid way they explain their ideas.

Because Skroo is only concerned with objective truth he has an almost unflappable nature. His daughter Jo says that she's never seen her dad mad or heard him raise his voice. His colleagues agree, save for one notable exception over a 40-year run during the 2007 privatisa-tion drama. His face rarely shows emotion, and this impassiveness can be unnerving to people unfamiliar with him.

But he's also blessed with a Pied Piper-like, charismatic quality. His wife of 36 years, Jude, remarks: 'In some ways he gets other people to do what he wants them to do. He convinces them somehow that there are no limits to their own possibilities.' Perhaps this is a reflec-tion of his self-sufficiency. It would be difficult to find an individual with less need for other people's approval or affirmation. Because of his self-reliance, however, Skroo forgets that others don't share his fortitude. Woe betide anyone who works with him and craves praise. Like moths around a candle, many people have battered themselves to near-extinction in a vain attempt to draw a few words of commen-dation from Graham Turner.

He may be a man of few words when eulogising, but he's positively garrulous when it comes to total information sharing. Want to discuss your salary or future career path with him? No problem, just sit down with him in his office while the rest of the team works away on their computers. Skroo would be bewildered (if bewilderment was part of his profile) as to why you'd prefer a little privacy to discuss these personal issues. Although he has learned that he sometimes needs to indulge people in this odd whim, it doesn't come instinctively.

Similarly, send Skroo Turner an email complaining about somebody and it inevitably results in him forwarding the message on to that person. (As one abashed executive explains, 'You only need this to happen two or three times and you soon learn to deal with the person directly.') Skroo simply has no time for game-playing or secrets. He doesn't forward things on with malicious intent. It's merely commonsense: if you have a problem with someone, sort it out with them, not him. So people do.

Managing director or not, he never tells anyone what to do, and nor does he forbid anything outright. Don't be fooled, however. He is not a consensus leader. People who have worked with him know that if he suggests something more than twice, then they would be wise to action it. Ignore his suggestion and fail, and the consequences will be on your head.

People are often puzzled by this subtle approach. 'But he was in the room when we discussed this!' they protest. 'He didn't stop me.' No, but he probably mentioned that it might not be a great idea to go down that path . . . Because he always lets others make the final call (after all, he doesn't want to do all their thinking for them), people often take this as tacit approval for their ideas. People used to working with Skroo are familiar with this low level of interference and learn to listen closely to his 'suggestions'.

Similarly, people who have battled through tough times with him are often disappointed. You're only as good as your last result. There are no free rides. If you do great once, thanks, but now you have to do it again. And again. And again. Some people perceive this as a lack of loyalty. To Skroo, it's commonsense again. He doesn't believe in diluting the company with sacred cows. And in the event that your job is axed, you won't be told by Turner personally. He would argue that this is because FCL leaders have total autonomy to hire and fire themselves. It does, however, work in very conveniently with his nonconfrontational management style.

The MD is a fervent believer in the right roles for the right people. If you've been an achiever but you've bottomed out, he'll do everything he can to find a role for you. It just might not be the one you aspired to.

Skroo prefers to fly below the radar (or should that be above?). Media interviews, corporate lunches, public speaking – why spend time telling people what you do when you could be doing it? Socially, he is an introvert. An animated speaker in a group of twelve people, he will be the first to leave in a crowd of 100. In spite of this, he is a frequent guest and speaker at in-house Buzz Nights and conferences. He is well received. As one longstanding manager explains, 'He's gotten better at public speaking over time – his passion comes out more than the obscenities.'

Turner is renowned throughout FCL for his opening line, 'What the fuck is going on?', when entering an office or meeting someone for the first or twentieth time. A non-politically correct question, delivered with a glint of mischievousness, it disarms the recipient and opens up an honest dialogue about exactly what the fuck *is* going on.

The fact that Flight Centre Limited is a major corporate player appears to have had little impact on the company's founder. Trappings are of no interest to him. In stark contrast to the dress-to-impress corporate world, his work clothes are the standard FCL uniform with short-sleeve shirt and a sporadic tie. When he was invited to a lunch at the Tattersall's Club in Brisbane, he had to borrow a jacket from someone at the head office. Yet Skroo sees nothing remarkable about this. Commonsense (that word again) dictates that in a tropical climate it would be crazy to wear a suit and long-sleeve shirt. So he doesn't.

He also doesn't drive a flash car or have a plush office with expensive paintings and marbled foyer. He doesn't throw around company money. He travels business class on work-related flights, but pays for the upgrades from economy out of his own pocket. And so does the rest of his executive team. He's not out to make a statement; it's just that he doesn't need any of these things. Give Skroo a good bottle of red wine, a sturdy mountain bike and a reliable pair of running shoes, and he's happy.

Turner's recipe for a good life is 'a close family, good health and constant challenges'. He regularly meditates and is a voracious reader of literary classics, autobiographies, non-fiction texts and, of course, every business book ever written. His preoccupation with abstract ideas makes his surroundings irrelevant to him. It wasn't until 1998 that Jude finally 'convinced' him that it was time to move from their farmhouse in Brookfield, on Brisbane's rural outer, to a river-front home in the inner-city suburb of Chelmer.

Apart from the Brisbane house and a few other residential proper-ties, the Turners' private assets are predominantly their fifteen million-odd FCL shares. The couple's wealth, however, did open up one door that has turned into a labour of love as well as a new business chal-lenge. As part of his interest in preserving some of Australia's natural bush heritage, Turner decided to buy two small cattle stations several years ago. He then convinced Jude to refurbish the homestead on one property and build a lodge on the other. Under Jude, the properties became the founding stations of Spicers Group, an award-winning network of 'intimately unique' Australian lodges, hotels and escapes. Turner has continued to be involved in the preservation of the envi-ronment. In 2012 he challenged the re-opening of a coalmine near the Spicers Hidden Vale property because he said it would threaten the local koala population. He is also a significant financial supporter of the Stable Population Party, registered by the Australian Electoral Commission on 23 September 2010, which campaigns against what it sees as the negative impacts of population growth on the environment and Australians' quality of life.

Leading into the 2012/13 financial year, Turner himself gave Flight Centre area leaders insight into why he controlled the business as he did and the origins of some of the values and interests that underpinned the company. He described the key elements behind the shaping of the company as part of the story that shaped the man. He said growing up on a family-run apple orchard taught him what hard work was about. 'And that hard work was overrated.' As a student at a one-teacher primary school in rural Queensland, he said for years he had very little teacher time, which taught him independence. To get to the school, he said, he had to ride his bike ('I would have preferred a horse') six kilometres there and home each day, navigating the obstacles of six barbed wire fences in each direction. 'As a result, I really like mountain biking.' Turner said the Top Deck experience in the 1970s and almost going broke in 1979 taught him the value of sound business principles. It was a rapid-fire snapshot of the life lessons that had forged his business desires and attitudes.

Jude Turner says her husband has achieved and done more with the company than she ever thought he would or could: 'He's amazing for seeing no end to it. He thinks so big it's ridiculous.' But as she points out, just as an elite athlete needs complete focus and dedication to their pursuit, Turner had been allowed to give 110 per cent of himself to the Flight Centre business. The rest of the Turner family have made that contribution to FCL's success. 'He can give so much to Flight Centre, because he's not required to give anything else,' she says.

It has meant Turner has been able to ride every high and low of the Flight Centre journey. It has meant he has steered the company through innumerable changes and issues, usually by 'gut feel' and borrowing from the best thinkers in business. For the past 30 years he has been able to mould the company to the stage where it now has a considerable voice in the international business conversation. He is also the conductor of its future vision. Turner says that so long as he is still fit and healthy, he is prepared for another ten years at the helm of FCL. Though rather than the athlete, he may prefer the role of super-coach: less hands-on, but more strategic. Laden with modesty, he says as managing director he continues to offer the company 'a bit of thinking, a bit of creativeness'. He says his ongoing strength is 'listening to senior leadership and trying to identify the things we should be focused on, rather than telling the people who are more knowledgeable what to do.'

FCL's great highlight, in Turner's eyes, remains the 1995 float – even though he tried to take it back into private hands – because it put the company on a business footing by having to get results and report to people outside itself. Since then, expanding FCL into a truly global business and having all ten countries return profit is an achievement he rates as a particular milestone of success. The most personally gratifying accomplishment of the past ten to twelve years, however, is FCL's enduring success. 'We've got a reasonably successful business in an industry where people have for years been predicting its demise,' he says. Despite the internet, despite suppliers encouraging customers to go to them direct, despite the setbacks that travel agents have had to navigate, the travel agency industry – and Flight Centre Limited within it – has survived and prospered. And he predicts an equally strong future. The internet was moving away from being a threat towards being a facilitator of a new modus operandi in the retail sphere, he says. FCL's wait-and-see approach on the internet, which is seeing it break through with the blended travel agency model, is a strategy that is forging the future path for the company. Turner feels he has been proven right about not jumping aboard the online agency craze. 'I'm sure we're right on this. It's whether we can get it right for our customers.'

Flight Centre Limited has had its share of down times. Turner rates the moment the partners had to cough up the TCF guarantee just before the Gulf War among FCL's lowest points. His list of other 'FCL fuck-ups' includes the Vietnam operation; taking too long to change one standard commission to cost of seat and one level of commission on profit of seat in corporate and leisure businesses; the way the company handled the Infinity wholesale operation after buying it from Skinny Forsyth; an Invercargill-to-Brisbane airline venture they started ('God knows why!') that lasted only two months; the Papua New Guinea operation; the initial development of the FCL website and the set-up of dotcom; and the start-up of the US venture and the timing of the American Liberty/GoGo acquisition right on the cusp of the global financial crisis. He also rates letting black-hole funding of commercialised businesses get out of control among the low points. And, of course, Full Throttle. 'If our business model is right, external factors play only a minor part,' he says. 'The most impactful issues are the internal ones, such as not recruiting the right people or support costs getting out of control. That's been our history.' A history it has, to date, been destined to repeat, though Turner says he hopes the impact of Full Throttle means it can finally be chalked up as lesson learned.

A constant for Flight Centre Limited is that it has proudly worn its anti-establishment and trailblazing tags, which have arisen largely out of its Family, Village, Tribe structure and culture. The company, however, acknowledges that the FCL model was not necessarily a panacea for other businesses. 'We like to think differently about things. It works for us,' Turner says. There was no one culture that was right for companies across the globe. While successful companies shared some similarities, every organisation needed to develop, grow and hone its own culture and philosophies, he says. 'We have some issues and some changes to make. But our philosophies and our culture do work. They are totally relevant to the way we have been successful.'

The company and the FCL way have indeed won many accolades and admirers. So has Turner, despite, or perhaps due to, his enigmatic, no-holds-barred style. In 2010 he was inducted into the Queensland Business Leaders Hall of Fame – a Queensland Government-supported award for businesses and leaders who have enhanced the state's reputation and economy. FCL co-founder Geoff Harris says Turner has not only created a successful global company from its humble Queensland roots, he has become an international business success story in the process. 'I have personally seen Skroo grow from a rough-and-ready, average-type business person in those days to someone I would consider in the top half-dozen business people in Australia,' he says.

More importantly, says Harris, Turner has created a company that will have ongoing success, regardless of when the MD chooses to leave. For new Flight Centre Limited non-executive director John Eales, appointed in October 2012, his drafting meant the opportunity to join a successful and intriguing corporate star, seemingly at the top of its game. The international rugby champion and Wallabies captain, who led Australia to World Cup victory in 1999, says he's never experienced another business like it. Eales has served in executive or advisory positions with a number of companies since retiring from rugby. He co-founded corporate consultancy the Mettle Group in 2003, which was acquired by Chandler Macleod in 2007. As well as rugby and business, he has a background in psychology. FCL's outstanding success over a sustained period of time attracted him, he says, but it was the unique culture he found most fascinating. 'The best description I can give is that it feels like a sporting club, like my own Brothers Rugby Club – whether you're an international or fifth grade strapper, as soon as you walk in the door, you're all equal.'

The egalitarian nature of Flight Centre is unlikely to change, underpinning as it does the purpose and philosophies of the company. Nor will Turner's love affair with the business or his desire to take it to the next level. 'There are a lot of challenges still to happen,' he says. 'With our growth we probably double in size every seven or eight years. Every few years we're a totally different organisation, in a sense. It's pretty interesting to be a part of that.'

NOTES

1 Unless specified otherwise, all dollar amounts given in this book are in Australian dollars.
2 Unfortunately it is difficult to pinpoint which article this was as Skroo lent the magazine to finance director Jim Goldburg, who then accidentally threw it into a wastepaper bin at Launceston Airport. Neither man can remember the name of the magazine, and Nicholson himself is not sure which of his articles it might have been. Although published some time afterwards, Nigel Nicholson's 'How hardwired is human behavior?' (*Harvard Business Review*, July–August 1998) contains many of the arguments that so influenced the FCL board of directors.
3 John Rawls, *A Theory of Justice*, Oxford University Press, Oxford, UK, 1999.
4 Jim Collins, *Good to Great*, Random House, London, 2001, p 165.
5 Bill James, *Top Deck Daze*, Halbooks Publishing, Avalon, NSW, 1999, p 11.
6 Bill James has written extensively about the hilarious events of the first tour in his book *Top Deck Daze*.
7 James, *Top Deck Daze*, p 42.
8 James, *Top Deck Daze*, p 59.
9 James, *Top Deck Daze*, p 85.
10 Top Deck's owners had little use for formal titles in their day-to-day dealings. The more informal 'partners' has been used to describe the owners and key decision-makers of the business until the time of the Flight Centre Limited float, at which stage the more correct 'directors' is used.
11 James, *Top Deck Daze*, p 327.
12 Anthony J. Cordato, *Australian Travel and Tourism Law* (3rd edn), Reed International/Butterworths, Sydney, 1999, p 322.
13 Quoted in the Trade Practices Commission document *Application A3485 for Authorisation under Section 88 (1) of the Trade Practices Act 1974 of IATA Arrangements Other Than Accreditation of Travel Agents and Related Matters*, 31 July 1984, p 45.

14   In an article dated 11 January 1982.

15   In an article dated 8 November 1983.

16   In an article dated 30 January 1984.

17   Trade Practices Commission, *Application A3485*, pp 36, 101–2.

18   Michael E. Gerber, *The E-Myth*, Harper Business, New York, 1986.

19   Michael E. Gerber, *The E-Myth Revisited*, Harper Business, New York, 1995, p 100.

20   The letter 's' was also dropped in 1994, much to Bill James's dissatisfaction. As an ex school teacher, he always felt that 'Flight Centre' was grammatically incorrect when used as a company name, describing a number of outlets.

21   As explained in the Introduction, 'Flight Centre' is used throughout the book to describe the company until the 1995 float.

22   Quoted in Gerber, *The E-Myth Revisited*, pp 69–70.

23   It is now estimated that the Ticket Centre had made a $100,000 loss in that first year of operation.

24   FCL's full 'Company Vision, Purpose and Philosophies' mission statement is provided in Appendix 1 of this book.

25   Cordato, *Australian Travel and Tourism Law*, pp 352–53.

26   Turner believes that this was one of the unheralded factors that contributed to Ansett's eventual demise in September 2001.

27   Michael Le Boeuf, *How to Motivate People: Reward, the Greatest Management Principle in the World*, Schwartz & Wilkinson, Melbourne, 1985.

28   Le Boeuf, *How to Motivate People*, p 95.

29   Le Boeuf, *How to Motivate People*, p 100.

30   Le Boeuf, *How to Motivate People*, p 96.

31   Robert Gottliebsen, *10 Best and 10 Worst Decisions of Australian CEOs 1992–2002*, Penguin, Camberwell, Vic, 2003, p 256.

32   At first all the new overseas areas had difficulties recruiting people of the same calibre as in Flight Centre's Australian operation because they were unknown employers and had few shops. In the UK, Boxer and I were lucky that, due to the huge population, we were inundated with job applications; in South Africa, however, the start-up team had to lower the recruitment criteria for the first twelve months until they had enough shops and testimonials to attract a higher standard of recruits. In this way, Flight Centre's overseas expansion was not so dissimilar to the company's early days in Australia.

33   In an article dated 2 March 2003.

34   As explained in note 2 above, the title of this article is something of a mystery. It's not conceivable, in fact, that the piece was authored by someone else who was commenting on Nicholson's findings, which in turn led Turner to search out the professor's work.

35   Nigel Nicholson, *Executive Instinct*, Crown, New York, 2000. (The book was also published under the title *Managing the Human Animal*.)

36 Nicholson, *Executive Instinct*, p 24.

37 Nicholson, 'How hardwired is human behavior?', p 135.

38 Robert L. Kelly, *The Foraging Spectrum: Diversity in Hunter-Gatherer Lifeways*, Smithsonian Institution Press, Washington, DC, 1995, p 297.

39 A number of critics have branded him 'Neanderthal' in the sense of primitive or archaic. One was William Baker, in a letter headed '"Neanderthal" Turner out of touch with modern thinking', which appeared in *Travelweek* magazine on 30 September 1989. Indeed, Bill James felt the need to move to the defence of his friend and fellow partner in the 7 October issue by highlighting Skroo's homo sapiens qualities: 'Only a blind man, as well as being deaf and dumb, could possibly mistake that brow and deep-set eyes as anything other than Cro-Magnon.'

40 Nicholson, *Executive Instinct*, p 227.

41 Richard B. Lee & Irven De Vore (eds), *Kalahari Hunter-Gatherers – Studies of the !Kung San and their Neighbors*, Harvard University Press, Cambridge, MA, 1976, p 21.

42 Nicholson, 'How hardwired is human behavior?', p 147.

43 Sam Walton, *Sam Walton: Made in America*, Doubleday Dell, New York, 1992.

44 In 2003, all three founding partners of FCL made *BRW*'s Top 200 Rich List.

45 Collins, *Good to Great*, p 121.

46 The total possible Baldridge score is 1000, although the majority of reasonably successful companies score about 200 points.

47 Matthew Hart, 'High-flyer Flight scores again,' *The Courier-Mail*, 30 August 2002, p 33.

48 American Airlines Annual Report 2003, p 4.

49 According to global online publisher Eyefortravel in its article 'Online travel segment soars to increasingly impressive heights' (www.eyefortravel.com), 10 March 2005.

50 Corporate Research Foundation, *The Most Promising Companies in Australia*, Harper Business, Sydney, 2003; Emily Ross & Angus Holland, *100 Great Businesses and the Minds Behind Them*, Random House, Sydney, 2004.

51 Extract from Brisbane newspaper *The Courier-Mail*, Opinion & Letters page, 3 February 2005.

52 'Leaders of the pack', *Sunday Times*, 2 March 2003, p 15.

53 Seth Godin, *Purple Cow: Transform Your Business by Being Remarkable*, Portfolio, New York, 2003.

54 Clive Humby, Terry Hunt and Tim Phillips, *Scoring Points: How Tesco is Winning Customer Loyalty*, Kogan Page, London, 2004.

55 Steve Worthington and Josh Fear, *Retail Therapy: The Hidden Side of Loyalty Card Programs*, Australian Centre for Retail Studies, Monash University, Melbourne, 2009.

56 Melissa Maugeri, 'Flight Centre shares soar', *The Courier-Mail*, 26 October 2006.

57 Flight Centre Information Memorandum, 2006.

58 Lachlan Colquhoun, 'Flight Centre is Target of A$1.6bn Buy Out', *Financial Times*, 26 October 2006.

59 Colin Kruger, 'Travel group joins privateers', *Sydney Morning Herald*, 26 October 2006.

60 'Asia's Top Private Equity Deals and their Legal Advisers', *Asialaw*, August 2007.

61 'Proposal to offer minority shareholders $17.20 per share to be recommended by independent directors', Flight Centre Limited, 26 October 2006.

62 'Xmas Company News by Skroo', Flight Centre Limited, December 2006.

63 'Company News by Skroo', Flight Centre Limited, August 2007.

64 Tan Weiyun, 'Feng Shui Forecast for Dragon Year', *Shanghai Daily*, 19 January 2012.

65 'Company Law Board Member held taking bribe', *Times of India*, 25 November 2009.

66 Details of the Apple Store and similarities between the Apple and FCL flagship retail store approaches can be seen in Carmine Gallo, *The Apple Experience: Secrets to Building Insanely Great Customer Loyalty*, McGraw-Hill, Columbus, 2012, p xviii.

67 London Directory (www.alondondir.com), 2012.

68 Warwick J McKibbin and Andrew Stoeckel, 'The Global Financial Crisis: Causes and Consequences', Working Papers in International Economics, No.2.09, Lowy Institute for International Policy, November 2009.

69 FLT Statement to ASX, 12 November 2007.

70 'Company News by Skroo', November 2007.

71 'Final News from Skroo for a While', 18 August 2008.

72 'Australia's New International Airline Takes Off', Virgin Australia media release, Sydney, 27 February 2009.

73 AAP, *The Australian*, 16 March 2009.

74 'Cheap Flights and Soaring Dollar Means Early Christmas Present', FCL media release, 16 October 2009.

75 News.com, 27 February 2009.

76 The Canadian Press, 'Canada to stop counting swine flu cases', *Toronto Star* (thestar.com), 17 July 2009.

77 As noted in the 'Tourism Sector Monitor' section of Canadian Government publication *BC Stats*, April 2009.

78 Roisin Robothan-Jones, *AlumniNews*, Issue 110, London Business School, January–March 2007.

79 Ricardo Semler, *The Seven-Day Weekend*, Portfolio, New York, 2004.

80 Malcolm Gladwell, *The Tipping Point: How little things can make a big difference*, Little, Brown, London, 2000.

81   Introduction to Dave Logan, John King and Halee Fischer-Wright's *Tribal Leadership: Leveraging Natural Groups to Build a Thriving Organization*, Harper-Collins, New York, 2008.

82   From Metcash Limited's 2007 Annual Report.

83   Mark Laidlaw, '2012 Mitre 10 National Conference and Expo', *Australian Hardware Journal*, November 2011.

84   Michael Makeham, 'Submission to the House Standing Committee on Regional Australia: Use of FIFO/DIDO Workforce Practices', October 2011.

85   Fiona Smith, 'Balance of nature helps nurture group dynamics', *Australian Financial Review*, 13 March 2012.

86   O'Keeffe's most recent work on the subject is *Hardwired Humans: Successful Leadership Using Human Instincts*, Roundtable Press, New York, 2011.

87   An example is Tom Skotnicki's article 'Tribal Wisdom' in *Management Today*, June 2012.

88   Joseph H Boyett and Jimmie T Boyett, *The Guru Guide to Entrepreneurship: A Concise Guide to the Best Ideas from the World's Top Entrepreneurs*, Wiley, New Jersey, 2000, p 233.

89   Jim Collins and Morten T Hansen, *Great By Choice: Uncertainty, Chaos and Luck—Why Some Thrive Despite Them All*, HarperBusiness, New York, 2011, Chapter 4.

90   Thomas Kaplan and Raymond Hernandez, 'Cuomo, in Aid Appeal, Cites Broad Reach of Storm', *New York Times*, 26 November 2012.

91   PricewaterhouseCoopers' 'Review of consumer protection in the travel and travel related services market' was prepared for the Australian Government's Department of Treasury on behalf of the Standing Committee of Officials of Consumer Affairs and released in November 2010.

92   Released in August 2012, Telstra's white paper 'How You Can Join the Omnichannel Shopper in Transforming Australian Retail' surveyed 813 shoppers in March 2012 to identify the Australian omnichannel shopper and the omnichannel shopping experience. The paper included international research as well as this first Australia-based study.

93   Telstra's August 2012 white paper 'How You Can Join the Omnichannel Shopper in Transforming Australian Retail' presents a John Lewis case study based on figures from John Lewis annual reports (2002–2012) and IDC Retail Insights' 'John Lewis: The Path to Omnichannel', May 2012.

94   The Myers Briggs Type Indicator is regarded as the most accurate and scientifically researched personality inventory available. The major purpose of the MBTI is to gain more understanding of different personality types.

FLIGHT CENTRE LIMITED'S PHILOSOPHIES

Flight Centre Limited's philosophies began evolving after the Bangkok conference of November 1987. With the introduction of Michael Gerber's concept of a standard business model, the FCL directors began writing down and fine-tuning some of the ideas that were important to them. A 1988 company profile documents 'Our People Assets' and 'The Flight Centre Specialisation'; the 1995 prospectus groups the company's fledgling ideas together under the heading 'The Flight Centre Philosophy' (and includes such gems as 'There is to be minimal bureaucracy and head office expenses resulting in lower airfares to customers').

By 2002, the philosophies had become detailed and highly sophisticated, and were updated to include the new 'Brightness of Future' philosophy as well as the company's purpose. As of 2013, FCL's values, as defined under the heading 'Company Vision, Purpose and Philosophies', remain unchanged from 2002:

For our company to survive, grow and prosper for the next 100 years and beyond, we must clearly define and live by our purpose. We must protect and further develop our company culture and philosophies. Our culture must be robust and independent, able to outlive our current and future leaders.

Our Vision

'To be the world's most exciting travel company, delivering an amazing experience to our people, customers and partners.'

Our Purpose

'To open up the world for those who want to see.'

For our people this means our purpose is to open up their world by helping them develop professionally and personally. For our customers this means opening up their world through the exciting medium of well-organised, targeted and great value travel experiences. For our shareholders it is giving them a magnificent return on their investment.

Our Philosophies

1. Our People
Our company is our people. We care for our colleagues' health and wellbeing, their personal and professional development, and their financial security. We believe that work should be challenging and fun for everyone and that through work we contribute to our community.

2. Our Customer
We recognise that our customers always have a choice. Therefore a superior customer service experience, provided with honesty, integrity and a great attitude, is key to our company's success, as is the travel experience we provide.

3. Profit
A fair margin resulting in a business profit is the key measure of whether we are providing our customers with a product and service they value.

4. Ownership

We believe that each individual in our company should have the opportunity to share in the company's success through outcome-based incentives, profit-share, Business Ownership Schemes (BOSs or franchises) and employee share schemes. It is important that team leaders and team members see the business they run as their own.

5. Incentives

Incentives are based on measurable and reliable outcome-based KPIs. We believe that 'what gets rewarded gets done'. If the right outcomes are rewarded, our company and our people will prosper.

6. Brightness of Future

We believe our people have the right to belong to a Team (family), a Village, an Area (tribe) and a Nation (hierarchy) that will provide them with an exciting future and a supportive working community. They also have the right to see a clear pathway to achieving their career goals. Promotion and transfers from within will always be our first choice.

7. Our Standard Systems – 'One Best Way'

In our business there is always 'one best way' to operate. These are standard systems employed universally until a better way is shown. This improved way then becomes the 'one best way' system. We value common sense over conventional wisdom.

8. Family, Village, Tribe

Our structure is simple, lean, flat and transparent, with accessible leaders. There is a maximum of 4/5 layers. The Village is an unfunded, self-help support group that forms an integral part of our structure.

1. Teams/Family (minimum 3, maximum 7 members) and Villages (minimum 3, maximum 7 Teams)
2. Areas/Tribe (minimum 10, maximum 20 Teams)
3. Nations (minimum 8, maximum 15 Areas)
4. Regions/States/Countries (minimum 4, maximum 8 Nations)
5. Global Executive Team/Board.

9. Taking Responsibility

We take full responsibility for our own success or failure. We do not externalise. We accept that we have total ownership and responsibility, but not always control. As a company we recognise and celebrate our individual and collective successes.

10. Egalitarianism and Unity

In our company, we believe that each individual should have equal privileges and rights. In Leisure and Corporate, in Australia and overseas, and in organically grown and acquired businesses, there should be no 'them and us'.

BIBLIOGRAPHY

Boyett, Joseph H. & Boyett, Jimmie T., *The Guru Guide to Entrepreneurship: A Concise Guide to the Best Ideas from the World's Top Entrepreneurs*, Wiley, New Jersey, 2000

Collins, Jim, *Good to Great*, Random House, London, 2001

Collins, Jim & Hansen, Morten T., *Great By Choice: Uncertainty, Chaos and Luck—Why Some Thrive Despite Them All*, HarperBusiness, New York, 2011

Cordato, Anthony J., *Australian Travel and Tourism Law* (3rd edn), Reed International/Butterworths, Sydney, 1999

Gallo, Carmine, *The Apple Experience: Secrets to Building Insanely Great Customer Loyalty*, McGraw-Hill, Columbus, OH, 2012

Gerber, Michael E., *The E-Myth*, Harper Business, New York, 1986

Gerber, Michael E., *The E-Myth Revisited*, Harper Business, New York, 1995

Gladwell, Malcolm, *The Tipping Point: How little things can make a big difference*, Little, Brown, London, 2000

Godin, Seth, *Purple Cow: Transform Your Business by Being Remarkable*, Portfolio, New York, 2003

Gottliebsen, Robert, *10 Best and 10 Worst Decisions of Australian CEOs 1992–2002*, Penguin, Camberwell, Vic, 2003

Humby, Clive, Hunt, Terry & Phillips, Tim, *Scoring Points: How Tesco is Winning Customer Loyalty*, Kogan Page, London, 2004

James, Bill, *Top Deck Daze*, Halbooks Publishing, Avalon, NSW, 1999

Kelly, Robert L., *The Foraging Spectrum: Diversity in Hunter-Gatherer Lifeways*, Smithsonian Institution Press, Washington, DC, 1995

Le Boeuf, Michael, *How to Motivate People: Reward, the Greatest Management Principle in the World*, Schwartz & Wilkinson, Melbourne, 1985

Lee, Richard B. & De Vore, Irven (eds), *Kalahari Hunter-Gatherers – Studies of the !Kung San and their Neighbors*, Harvard University Press, Cambridge, MA, 1976

Logan, Dave, King, John & Fischer-Wright, Halee, *Tribal Leadership: Leveraging Natural Groups to Build a Thriving Organization*, HarperCollins, New York, 2008

McKibbin, Warwick J. & Stoeckel, Andrew, 'The Global Financial Crisis: Causes and Consequences', Working Papers in International Economics, No.2.09, Lowy Institute for International Policy, November 2009

Nicholson, Nigel, *Executive Instinct*, Crown, New York, 2000

Nicholson, Nigel, 'How hardwired is human behavior?', *Harvard Business Review*, July–August 1998

O'Keeffe, Andrew, *Hardwired Humans: Successful Leadership Using Human Instincts*, Roundtable Press, New York, 2011

Peck, M. Scott, *The Road Less Travelled*, Arrow, London, 1990

Rawls, John, *A Theory of Justice*, Oxford University Press, Oxford, 1999

Semler, Ricardo, *The Seven-Day Weekend*, Portfolio, New York, 2004

Trade Practices Commission, *Application A3485 for Authorisation under Section 88 (1) of the Trade Practices Act 1974 of IATA Arrangements Other Than Accreditation of Travel Agents and Related Matters*, 31 July 1984

Walton, Sam, *Sam Walton: Made in America*, Doubleday Dell, New York, 1992

Worthington, Steve & Fear, Josh, *Retail Therapy: The Hidden Side of Loyalty Card Programs*, Australian Centre for Retail Studies, Monash University, Melbourne, 2009

ACKNOWLEDGMENTS

One of the challenges of researching a book on a company like Flight Centre Limited is that because everyone is 'incentivised' on outcomes, people have little time to spare on such unproductive activities as interviews. Hence Katrina and I are very grateful to those who took their valuable time to share their knowledge with us. For some it involved a small amount of bribery such as a guaranteed place in the acknowledgments section (an enticement we used liberally). Others were simply keen to ensure the authenticity of the record. We are deeply grateful to all those who were involved – without them this book could never have been completed:

Jenna Abell, Phillip Abood, Wayne Ackerfeld, Kerin Acton, Tony Agnew, John Ahern, Nancy Ahern, Atay Akbiyik, Emma Anderson, Mark Aponas, Greg Ashmore, Vicki Astley, Cynthia Baker, Joanne Barber, Tanya Ballard, Peter Barrow, Steve Becker, Tracey Binnie, Robyn Blacklock, Daryl Blake, James Blankley, Sharyn Bleakley, John Boagey, Steve Bowden, Valerie Bowden, Colin Bowman, Andrew Boxall, John Boyd, Katie Boyle, Moira Brady, Aileen Bratton, Bruce Brown, Peter Browne, Norbert Byrne, Pat Caffrey, Danny Cahalan, Adrian Campbell, Niqui Campbell, Simon Canning, Michael Carroll, Libby Carroll, Paul Carroll, Trevor Carroll, Susie Cassells-Brown, Peter Cathie-White, Andrew Challinor, Angela Christie, David Churchman,

David Clarke, Ian Clarke, Jo Cole, Libby Collins, Vivienne Collins, Simon Conquest, Garry Court, Adrian Cridland, Miranda Crisci, Tim Crommelin, Andrew Crook, Victoria Courtney, Nicky Dance, Nathan Dare, Mark Davies, Ivana De Colle, Rachael Deede, Margje de Groot, Murray Dempsey, Zac De Silva, Greg Dixon, Brendan Drover, Gavin Durbin, Robin Durham, Tony Duthie, John Eales, Brian Egan, Anita Emilio, Charles Esposito, Chela Evans, Jude Evans, Ken Evans, Brendan Fallon, Matthew Fealy, Edith Feher, Grania Fingleton, Andrew Flannery, Rob Flint, Shane Flynn, Anne Ford, Peter Forsyth, Dave Fraser, Pru Freemantle, Ross Freemantle, Tony Friedman, Mike Friend, Norm Fussell, Chris Galanty, Fiona Gallagher, Sue Garrett, Mary Gava, Chris Gavras-Moffatt, Heather Gilbert, Jo Gilbert, Richard Glew, Jenny Goldburg, Jim Goldburg, Chris Greive, Howard Greive, Liz Greive, Sue Grigg, Anthony Grigson, Debbie Hamilton, Rick Hamilton, Wayne Hamilton, Tracey Hamilton-Dowd, Ray Hands, Geoff Harris, Len Harris, Sue Harris, Sue Henderson, Tricia Henderson, Brian Hickey, Lin Hilditch, Andrew Hill, Katrina Hinds, Rachel Hirst, Gary Hogan, Lisa Hogan, Christie Hopp, Margaret Horne, Todd Horton, Danny Hovey, Grahame Hubbard, Paul Hughes, Tony Illingworth, Bob Irving, Bill James, Nicole Johnson, Mary-Anne Josefski, Brad Jukes, Emma Jupp, Christina Katic, Michael Keating, Jane Kennedy, Stephen Kennedy, Tom Kenny, Anthony Kirk, Ian Knights, Andrew Knox, Scott Kyle-Little, Kate Laird, David Lanning, Gerrie Larsen, Suyin Lee, Anne Leggett, Kerri Lester, Warren Livingstone, Greg Lloyd, Geoff Lomas, Haydn Long, Tina Los, Jenny Lourey, David Lovelock, Nick Lucock, Pam Macdonald, Mark MacKerras, Lindy Mahon, Ron Malek, Kelly Marshall, Peter Markey, Howard Martin, Jenny Martin, Scott Martin, Sue Matson, Dione Mauric, Michael Maude, Paula Maxwell, Michelle McCallum, Catherine McCasker, Tessa McCormick, Billy McDonough, Rod McEwin, Di McEwin, Carrie McFarlane, Michelle McGuffog, Heather McKay, Kelly McMaster, Rhonda McSweeney, Rebecca Miskin, Chris Gavras Moffatt, Lynaire Monnery, Barry Moore, David Moore, Graeme Moore, Sophie Moore, Peter Morahan, Therese Moss, Marg Mulholland, Jody Mulvey, Terry Mulvey, Michael Murphy, Candice Nash, James Nathan, Naren Nautiyal, Lex Noller, Natalie Nucifora, Robyn Nuttall, Daniel O'Brien, Rachel O'Brien, Shannon O'Brien, Geoff O'Callaghan, Alissa O'Connell, Simone O'Connor, Darcy O'Donnell, Julie O'Reilly, Trevor O'Rourke, Maureen Oakhill, Joell Ogilvie, Tim Oliver, John Olsen, George Patrikios, Terry Patterson, Maree Peel, Marco Peters, Paula Phillips, Allisa Pollock, Dominique Pomario, Simon Poole, Joe Ponte, Greg Pringle, Raelene Prosser, Lew Pullbrook, Gina Raccanello, Catherine Rankin, Dot Raymond, Dave Reed, Sue Rennick, Clare Ritchie, Danny Roche, Renos Rologas, Malcolm Ross, Eileen Ross, Vanessa Roud, Michael Rudny, Kerryn Rundell, Tina Saunders, Wendy Scott, Glad Shepherd, Andrea Slingsby, Peter Sharry, David Smith, Dean Smith, Gary Smith, Jackie Sommers, James Sommers, Alan Spence, Howard Stack, Keith Stanley, Bob Steele, Stan Steinhardt, Jim Sturgess, Jarrad Sutherland, Leandra Thomas, Max Thomas, John Thompson, Kim Tomlinson, Aileen Tonkin, Dave Tonkin, Max Tonkin, Bonnie Tsui, Frank Turner, Graham Turner, Iris Turner, Joanna Turner, Jude Turner, Matthew Turner, Geoff Tyerman, Lynn Ure, Marie Van Gend, John Van Rouden, Jessica Vestin, Mary Vincent, Richard Waddington, Kerry-Anne Walker, Alison Walsh, Helen Ware, David Warner, Melanie Waters-Ryan, Kate Watkins, Peter Watson, John Wells, John Whateley, Dale White, Jenny Wilder, Andrea Williams, Ailsa Wilson, Steve Wilson, Leticia Wood, David Worland, Kate Ziebarth.

My humble apologies to anyone we may have inadvertently missed. It is not through lack of gratitude.

Some people, however, deserve a special mention because of the time and energy they invested in the original draft. A number of the events in this book happened nearly 30 years ago, so I was reliant on many people's oral testimony. My thanks go to the Flight Centre founders – Bill James for his honesty; Geoff Harris for fielding my non-stop questions; Mick Carroll for his hilarious anecdotes and photos; and Geoff 'Spy' Lomas for his patience whilst I dug around in his memories.

I am also grateful to managing director Graham 'Skroo' Turner, who gave me carte blanche to scrutinise every aspect of Flight Centre Limited and facilitated my access to the appropriate people, both within the company and outside it. Skroo's wife Jude has been FCL's unofficial record keeper for many years and I was thankful for her many photos, newsletters and documents. She was also kind enough to open her house for several Flight Centre Limited 'old-timer' gatherings; and along with Skroo's parents, Frank and Iris, and his children Joanna and Matthew, gave me insight into Skroo's personality and influences.

My thanks also go to the company's first chairman Norm Fussell, former director Chris Greive, former CEO Shane 'Flynnie' Flynn, and company secretary Greg Pringle, who were all kind enough to read my original manuscript and offer useful comments.

Evolutionary psychologist Nigel Nicholson gave unstintingly of his time and wisdom for the 'Family, Village, Tribe' chapter. Meredith Curnow from Random House offered me many insightful comments that led to significant improvements in each draft. My parents, Rodney and Esther Johnson; my mother-in-law, Nancy Ahern; and my fellow writers Christina Katic, Robyn Singer Rose and Margaret Arthur also helped in this capacity. I am also grateful to editors Jon Gibbs and Clare Marshall, who pulled out all the stops to make both editions of this book better than I could ever have hoped.

And finally my husband John, who put up with my virtual disappearance into the halls of Flight Centre Limited for several years with good humour and encouragement; who read and critiqued every draft with patience; who put in hours of labour acting as my agent on the final manuscript without receiving a cent of commission; and whose inside knowledge of the company made this book far better than it would otherwise have been. He deserves the biggest thanks of all.